The Form of
American Romance

The Form of American Romance

Edgar A. Dryden

The Johns Hopkins
University Press
BALTIMORE/LONDON

813.09
D79f

The Johns Hopkins University Press
701 West 40th Street
Baltimore, Maryland 21211
The Johns Hopkins Press Ltd., London

The paper used in this publication meets the minimum requirements
of American National Standard for Information Sciences—
Permanence of Paper for Printed Library Materials, ANSI Z39.48-1984.

Library of Congress Cataloging-in-Publication Data

Dryden, Edgar A.
  The form of American romance / Edgar A. Dryden. p.   cm.
  Bibliography: p.
  Includes index.
  ISBN 0-8018-3675-1 (alk. paper)
    1. American fiction—History and criticism.   2. Romanticism—
United States.   3. Literary form.   I. Title.
PS374.R6D79 1988
813'.009—dc19   88-6490
                                                       CIP

For
Jonathan,
Stephanie,
and Nathan

CONTENTS

PREFACE

Before going about putting a certain example to the test, I shall attempt to formulate, in a manner as elliptical, economical, and formal as possible, what I shall call the law of the law of genre. It is precisely a principle of contamination, a law of impurity, a parasitical economy. In the code of set theories, if I may use it as least figuratively, I would speak of a sort of participation without belonging—a taking part in without being part of, without having membership in a set.

—Jacques Derrida,
"The Law of Genre"

The idea of romance has long been an important one to writers and readers seeking to establish the borderlines that will circumscribe the field of American fiction by setting it apart from other national literatures. Such demarcations of a literary corpus, however, are accompanied by theoretical and practical difficulties. Recent questionings of American romance as a formal and generic category have disturbed the serene methodological self-assurance that characterized earlier studies of the American novel by reminding us of the extent to which, in Fredric Jameson's words, "categories, such as those of genre ... are implicated in the literary history and formal production that they were traditionally supposed to clarify and neutrally to describe."[1] Nevertheless, while we may question the taxonomic certainty of generic categories we must also recognize that, as Derrida has shown, "there is no genreless text."[2] And indeed American romance illustrates in a remarkable way the principle of contamination that for Derrida marks the idea of genre. For even the individual texts generically identified as such by a sub-titled designation, as in *The Scarlet Letter: A Romance,* seem at the same time to resist confining generic categories and to violate their formal purity by the blurring and crossing of border-lines. Such texts suggest that we must consider the category of genre theoretically rather than to take it for granted as a transparent concept whose meaning we can know unequivocably and can use as an unexamined starting point for interpretation. So while my study, for the most part, works with texts from the established canon of the American novel arranged in traditional canonical ways, it does so in a fashion designed to question and unsettle traditional categories. It attempts at once a theoretical and reflexive approach to the concept of American romance by focusing on the question of form, taking "form" as a term for the enabling principles of a work rather than for its external shape. My guide here is Ortega y Gasset's discussion of literary genre in his admirable *Meditations on Quixote.* Seen from his perspective American romance becomes not merely the name of a fictional form but of a fictional content which "reaches fulfill-ment in the process of its expansion or manifestation."[3] It becomes at one and the same time "a certain thing to be said and the only way to say it fully" (113). But for the writers that I discuss there is an incompatibility between the shaping power and that which is shaped, and this problem of form enters into their works as an essential theme, with the result that they stage the process of their own self-engendering.[4] My first chapter attempts a description of the manifestation and temporal unfold-ing of the basic tendencies or directions that constitute that process by placing them within the larger context of some of the fundamental aspects that mark the novel as a form. I am not, in short, claiming that American fiction has a history exclusively its own. It is not my intention to strengthen what one critic has called the "myth of American exceptionalism."[5] But I shall argue that for the writers that I discuss the author's place or situation as an American becomes a metaphor for his artistic concerns, and the dark, magical, and dreamlike narratives that he produces bring to the foreground the problem of fictional form in an especially interesting way. However, the concept of literary form as I understand it is one that resists a purely theoretical description, one that must emerge narratively from the process of rigorously interpreting individual texts. Hence I follow the initial chapter with careful readings of five American novels. This focus on individual texts, while it may seem at times to lead away from the main line of the argument, is intended, rather, to suggest new ways of conceiving it, of allowing a sense of the form of American romance to arise out of the process of reading itself.

Now, as Northrop Frye has shown, romance is the paradigm of all storytelling, and, for that reason, perhaps, since the Renaissance it has been defined in terms of its problematic relation to a reader.[6] Indeed A. C. Hamilton argues that "of all the genres only romance enchants or 'takes'" the readers by drawing them into the text in order to absorb and possess them. Hence the experience of reading becomes the essential theme of romance, a fact that leads Hamilton to suggest that reader response criticism offers the most useful approach to the form.[7]

Since I shall argue that the act of reading generates the enabling energy of American romance and take advantage of the insights of a number of critics whose works are associated with the recent refocus of criticism on the reader, I want to emphasize here that I am not primarily concerned with developing or using a theoretical model of reading. My main interest is not with readers reading but rather with the implications of the ways reading is represented in certain American texts. More specifically, I am concerned with exploring the curious and troubling moment where the act of reading appears to mark and disturb the American novelist's passage from life to writing and to entangle experience with an intertextual system of relationships. By describing the unique and special problem that that moment generates in five American texts, I want to sketch a "history" of American romance that will complicate the question of its uniqueness by illustrating ways in which it is exemplary.

As Joseph Riddel has noted, the historical moment that the American critical fable identifies as marking the beginning of a distinctive native voice coincides with the one the French see announcing the advent of modernism.[8] And, perhaps for similar reasons, the "history" of the American novel echoes in a remarkable way the preoccupations of both domestic and European critics of the novel. This relationship forms the subtext that I try to articulate in the notes to the first chapter while I focus directly on the problem of elaborating a genealogy of American romance, but one that is understood to be constructed rather than natural, or, to use Edward Said's formulation, one that emphasizes a relationship of affiliation rather than one of filiation or natural descent.[9]

A word about the novels that form the line of relationships that I chart. The ones that I discuss may seem somewhat arbitrarily chosen, but no choice of examples is an entirely innocent one, and my selection privileges the novels in several senses. They are, first of all, texts that focus on the formal implications of the problems of writing and reading in a way that has a long genealogy in the history of the novel as well as a specific importance in the configuration of its development in America. Each has been chosen with the others in mind with the hope that the interplay of my examples will suggest the nuances of my argument. For instance, in all the novels that I discuss echoing is a figure of representation which carries with it a set of associated themes including broken or substitute genealogical relations, problems of originality and repetition, fragmented voices, and misdirected, delayed, or torn letters, and these issues become the enabling impulses that seek their fulfillment in the form of the individual novels. Moreover each of my novels occupies an exemplary position in a particular authorial career and hence illustrates its author's struggle with his chosen form in especially revealing ways. Finally, taken together, the five novels chart a line of development that provides representative examples of what literary history calls romanticism, realism, modernism, and postmodernism and hence suggest a certain story about the continuity of the

American novel. But this is a story whose plot must emerge from the readings of the individual texts, readings that I have tried to organize in such a way that they will echo one another and thereby convey my sense of the enabling themes that each text shares with the others and will make possible a concluding description of the form of their relationship.

In preparing this study I have incurred a number of debts and take pleasure in acknowledging them here. First I want to thank my colleagues at Arizona who read and commented on portions of the manuscript: Patrick O'Donnell, Suresh Raval, and Charles Sherry. More than ever I am grateful for the continuing support of my old friends Homer Brown, John Rowe, and Joseph Riddel. Their enduring friendship and the example of their scholarship have provided a large part of the enabling energy for my study. A major portion of the book was written during my tenure of a fellowhip from the John Simon Guggenheim Memorial Foundation, and I am deeply grateful for the free time it provided.

Early versions of parts of this book have already been published. Chapter 1 was published as such in *Genre* 17 (Winter 1985): 335–61. A few paragraphs of the Hawthorne chapter first appeared in *Individual and Community: Variations on a Theme in American Fiction,* ed. Kenneth H. Baldwin and David K. Kirby (Durham: Duke University Press, 1975) and are reprinted here with the permission of Duke University Press; part of the Melville chapter was published as "From the Piazza to the Enchanted Isles: Melville's Textual Rovings," in *After Strange Texts: The Role of Theory in the Study of Literature,* ed. Gregory S. Jay and David L. Miller (University: University of Alabama Press, 1985), 46–68 and is reprinted here with the permission of the University of Alabama Press; another part of the Melville chapter has been published as "The Entangled Text: Melville's *Pierre* and the Problem of Reading," *Boundary 2* 7 (Spring 1979): 145–73; an early version, since extensively revised, of the James chapter appeared as "The Image in the Mirror: The Double Economy of James's *Portrait,*" *Genre* 13 (Spring 1980): 31–49.

ABBREVIATIONS
USED IN
THE TEXT

AA   William Faulkner, *Absalom, Absalom!* New York: Random House, Vintage Books Edition, 1972.

BR   Nathaniel Hawthorne, *The Blithedale Romance*. Edited by William Charvat, Roy Harvey Pearce, and Claude M. Simpson. Columbus: Ohio State University Press, 1964.

C   John Barth, *Chimera*. New York: Random House, 1972.

FIN   Nathaniel Hawthorne, *The French and Italian Notebooks*. Edited by Thomas Woodson. Columbus: Ohio State University Press, 1980.

FR   William Faulkner, *The Faulkner Reader*. New York: Random House, 1961.

HHM   Herman Melville, "Hawthorne and His Mosses." In *Moby-Dick*. Edited by Harrison Hayford and Hershel Parker. New York: W. W. Norton, 1967.

HSG   Nathaniel Hawthorne, *The House of The Seven Gables*. Edited by William Charvat, Roy Harvey Pearce, and Claude M. Simpson. Columbus: Ohio State University Press, 1965.

L   John Barth, LETTERS. New York: G. P. Putnam's Sons, 1979.

LIF   John Barth, *Lost in the Funhouse*. New York: Doubleday & Co., 1968.

M-D   Herman Melville, *Moby-Dick*. Edited by Harrison Hayford and Hershel Parker. New York: W. W. Norton, 1967.

MF   Nathaniel Hawthorne, *The Marble Faun*. Edited by William Charvat, Roy Harvey Pearce, and Claude M. Simpson. Columbus: Ohio State University Press, 1968.

MOM   Nathaniel Hawthorne, *Mosses from an Old Manse*. Edited by William Charvat, Roy Harvey Pearce, and Claude M. Simpson. Columbus: Ohio State University Press, 1974.

P   Herman Melville, *Pierre*. Edited by Harrison Hayford, Hershel Parker, and G. Thomas Tanselle. Evanston: Northwestern University Press, 1971.

P   Herman Melville, "The Piazza." in *Piazza Tales*, edited by Egbert S. Oliver. New York: Hendricks House, 1962.

PL   Henry James, *The Portrait of a Lady*. Edited by Leon Edel. Boston: Houghton Mifflin, 1963.

SL   Nathaniel Hawthorne, *The Scarlet Letter*. Edited by William Charvat, Roy Harvey Pearce, and Claude M. Simpson. Columbus: Ohio State University Press, 1974.

TT   Nathaniel Hawthorne, *Twice-Told Tales*. Edited by William Charvat, Roy Harvey Pearce, and Claude M. Simpson. Columbus: Ohio State University Press, 1974.

UC   Nathaniel Hawthorne, *The Snow Image and Uncollected Tales*. Edited by William Charvat, Roy Harvey Pearce, and Claude M. Simpson. Columbus: Ohio State University Press, 1974.

W   Sir Walter Scott, *Waverley*. Dutton, 1906.

The Form of
American Romance

ONE

The Thematics of a Form: Waverley *and American Romance*

In the summer the sun pours down torrents of fire on La Mancha, and frequently the burning earth produces the effect of a mirage. The water which we see is not real water, but there is something real in it: its source. This bitter source, which produces the water of the mirage, is the desperate dryness of the land. We can experience a similar phenomenon in two directions: one simple and straight, seeing the water which the sun depicts as actual; another, ironic, oblique, seeing it as a mirage, that is to say, seeing through the coolness of the water the dryness of the earth in disguise. The ingenuous manner of experiencing imaginary and significant things is found in the novel of adventure, the tale, the epic; the oblique manner in the realistic novel. The latter needs the mirage to make us see it as such. So it is not only that *Quixote* was written against the books of chivalry, and as a result bears them within it, but that the novel as a literary genre consists essentially of such an absorption.

—Ortega, *Meditations on Quixote*

For Ortega literary genres are at once historic and thematic categories, "certain basic themes, mutually exclusive," a particular literary genre being "at one and the same time a certain thing to be said and the only way to say it fully."[1] Because each epoch is a "basic interpretation of man . . . each epoch prefers a particular genre" (113). The novel, genre of the modern epoch, is born of the Renaissance's discovery of the "*me ipsum,* the consciousness, the subjective" (138) and names a "basic poetic content" (113) that can best be described in terms of a thematics of perception and interpretation. *Don Quixote* focuses on the shifting play between hallucinated and oblique modes of reading, and all subsequent novels, which "bear *Quixote* within [them] like an inner filigree" (162), echo that troubling relationship.

The law of the modern and the law of the novel, then, is a mode of reading or understanding that results in the "criticism," "destruction," and "absorption" (139) of one book by another. From this point of view the history of the novel may be seen as a history of reading that takes the form of putting into question a process that seems at first to possess the force and dignity of a natural arrangement.[2] As Frank Kermode perceptively observes, the novel seems "somehow a *substitute* for critical thought about the interpretation of earlier narrative."[3] In that sense it is a manner of reading that is a writing, an oblique, ironic "seeing" that at once reveals the innocence of naive narratives and naive readers and uses that innocence as a mode of self creation. "By itself, seen in a direct way," Ortega writes, "reality, the actual . . . would never be poetic" (139). But when we consider it "obliquely," through the lenses of the "mirage," we perform the reading that is at once destructive and creative.

This is the logic that allows us to see *Don Quixote* as establishing the basic pattern and enabling theme for the genre: two kinds of text, the romance and the novel, the old and the new, with the new directed against the old, which is regarded as naive, mystified, and potentially dangerous, but at the same time tied to it and dependent on it as a point of departure; and two kinds of reader, the one naive and innocent, enchanted by

2

the magic of story and doomed by his or her very involvement to disillusionment, and the other, serious, critical, and interpretive, suspicious of story as leading away from productive, active involvement with the text and the world of which it is a part, but, at the same time, aware of the undeniable pleasures associated with its magic.[4]

A particularly interesting version of this pattern exists in the eighteenth-century English fiction, in those texts that have been said to mark the "rise of the novel." Both the novelists and their critics were vitally interested in the possibly subversive effects that fiction could have on readers, especially the naive and innocent ones. For these readers, novels and romances might serve as instruments of debauchery capable of perverting the imagination, turning the head, and making young ladies unfit for marriage.[5] According to one reviewer, "wild scenes" in novels "excite, tend to debauch the mind, and throw an insipid kind of uniformity over the moderate and rational prospects of life, consequently adventures are sought for and created, when duties are neglected, and content despised."[6] This remarkable and frightening power presumably derives from the novel's ability to excite the curiosity and thereby to divert the attention from the real world to a world of make-believe that is found so absorbing that one becomes apathetic to real life.[7] Apologists for the novel as well as its detractors acknowledge fiction's magical powers, but its defenders, following the example of earlier apologists for poetry and drama, point to the way that magic may be used for moral and pedagogical ends. Through the careful use of novels and romances the "Rigour of Precepts" may be mollified by the "Allurements of Example."[8] Because they entertain, novels may also instruct, but it is important that the entertainment function remain subordinate to the principle of instruction.[9]

To the readers of Richardson and Defoe, of course, this is a familiar theme, one of the most interesting versions of which appears in the preface to *Moll Flanders*.

But as this Work is chiefly recommended to those who know how to Read it, and how to make the good Uses of it, which the Story all along recommends to them; so it is to be hop'd that such Readers will be much more pleas'd with the Moral, than the Fable; with the Application, than with the Relation, and with the End of the Writer, than with the Life of the Person written of.[10]

Defoe distinguishes here between two kinds of readers, one naively fascinated by adventure who focuses on the "Fable," the other, more serious, primarily interested in the "end of the Writer" and the productive "Application" of the text. It is the second, one supposes, who knows how properly to read the text and make the "good Uses of it, which the Story all along recommends," though the passage is ambiguous enough to raise questions. But one point is clear: Defoe sees that the magic of "Fable" is capable of charming even the serious, productive reader. "The Moral 'tis hop'd will keep the Reader serious, even where the Story might incline him to be otherwise" (4). So powerful are the attractions of the private pleasures that story offers, pleasures that may be both erotic and perverse, that they threaten to overwhelm those associated with communal and interpretive activities. Defoe seems to be suggesting here that reading is only superficially related to interpretation, the latter being an activity that is at once more serious and less interesting. This is an attitude that Frank Kermode describes as a "cultural myth" that is "attached specifically to the reading of fictional narrative,"[11] and one, I would add, that is born from the "absorption" that marks the novel as genre. For the "modern" text always contains within itself the earlier narrative and the unfounded assumptions that give it the transparency of a simple tale. And, as Kermode observes, the "mere existence of a story-line, and the more or less traditional devices by which a text can pretend to establish the authenticity of its account of the world, can insure the abandonment of strenuous analytic activity."[12] Even the serious reader may be overwhelmed by the unreality of the story and give in to his desire to see the narrative knot unraveled, the secret of the text revealed. And since this possibility is inscribed within the text itself, it poses a disturbing problem for the author as well as the reader. The author must not only contend with the spell of story, find a way to work with illusions without being deluded, but also establish a contract with the reader that will insure that their relation is grounded on the important rather than the trivial. In short, the author must find a way to establish and maintain authority as an author in the face of a deviant energy that threatens to subvert the dignity and importance of writing.

The emphasis on moral and religious instruction in Richardson's and Defoe's prefaces and the critical commentaries by their contemporaries represents one attempt to control—one might say rationalize—the magic of story. A different but related effort occurs in the fiction and criticism of Sir Walter Scott with results that influence at least a generation of English and American novelists.[13] Early in *Waverley* the narrator interrupts his brief sketch of Waverley Honour to offer an apology to the reader.

I beg pardon, once and for all, of those readers who take up novels merely for amusement, for plaguing them so long with old-fashioned politics, and Whig and Tory, and Hanoverians and Jacobites. The truth is, I cannot promise them that this story shall be intelligible, not to say probable, without it. My plan requires that I should explain the motives on which its action proceeded; and these motives necessarily arose from the feelings, prejudices, and parties, of the times. I do not invite my fair readers, whose sex and impatience give them the greatest right to complain of these circumstances, into a flying chariot drawn by hippogriffs, or moved by enchantment. Mine is a humble English post-chaise, drawn upon four wheels, and keeping his majesty's highway. Such as dislike the vehicle may leave it at the next halt, and wait for the conveyance of Prince Hussein's tapestry, or Malek the Weaver's flying sentry-box. Those who are contented to remain with me will be occasionally exposed to the dulness inseparable from heavy roads, steep hills, sloughs, and other terrestrial retardations; but, with tolerable horses and a civil driver, (as the advertisements have it,) I engage to get as soon as possible into a more picturesque and romantic country, if my passengers incline to have some patience with me during my first stages. (*W,* 89–90)

Here the narrator seeks to establish the rules that will govern the relation between writer and reader, rules that will impose restraints on both the I that writes and the you that reads. Following the example of Fielding in *Tom Jones,* he figures the writer and reader as "Fellow-Travellers in a Stage-Coach"[14] and offers the novel as a mode of travel that will take the reader—albeit slowly—away from the familiar surroundings of the English countryside to the more romantic landscape of the Scottish Lowlands and Highlands. And in so doing he distinguishes his work from those which are "written and read merely on account of the exercise which they afford to the imagination of those who, like the poet Collins, love to riot in the luxuriance of Oriental fiction, to rove through the meanders of enchantment, to gaze on the magnificence of golden palaces, and to repose by the water-falls of Elysian gardens."[15] These are the readers who, "too idle to read, save for the purpose of amusement" and addicted to the "fairy-land of fiction,"[16] prefer to travel in purely imaginative worlds. They have no patience with ordinary modes of transportation and no interest in local people and places. But if the narrator differentiates his work from those that are written to appeal to such readers by emphasizing his commitment to the ordinary and familiar, he does not suggest that he intends completely to replace the "splendid scenes of an imaginary world" with a "correct and striking representation of that which is daily taking place around him."[17] That is the way of Jane Austen.

Upon the whole, the turn of this author's novels bears the same relation to that of the sentimental and romantic cast,

that cornfields and cottages and meadows bear to the highly
adorned grounds of a show mansion, or the rugged sublimi-
ties of a mountain landscape. It is neither so captivating as the
one, nor so grand as the other, but it affords to those who fre-
quent it a pleasure nearly allied with the experience of their
own social habits; and what is of some importance, the youthful wanderer may return from his promenade to the ordinary
business of life, without any chance of having his head turned
by the recollection of the scene through which he has been
wandering.[18]

The pleasure of the Austen text is that of an encounter with
familiar people and places, of a recognition of known land-
marks and shared cultural assumptions. And one can return
from her familiar lanes to the "paths of common life"[19] free of
any fear of having been permanently marked by the magic of
story. The narrator of *Waverley*, however, is committed to moving beyond the local and provincial although that will be his
starting point. And while his reader need not be content with a
simple "promenade" around a familiar neighborhood, he or she
must be willing to face both the dullness of the journey's beginnings and the dangers and difficulties that come with wandering
far from home. For the fellow travelers will undertake a journey
that parallels in an obvious way the one taken by the novel's
hero and one that carries, as Alexander Welsh has shown, important symbolic suggestions. The movement from South to
North, from England to Scotland, from the Lowlands to the
Highlands, from a "verdant, populous, and highly cultivated
country" to "scenes of waste and desolation . . . of solitary and
melancholy" (*W*, 463) represents the dualisms of law and nature,
civilized and primitive, reason and passion, history and romance.[20] However, the narrator seems as interested in the process of moving from one to the other as he is in the point of
departure and the ultimate destination. The implication of this
emphasis becomes clear in the novel's postscript, where the journey metaphor reappears.

7

Our journey is now finished, gentle reader; and if your patience has accompanied me through these sheets, the contract is, on your part, strictly fulfilled. Yet, like the driver who has received his full hire, I still linger near you, and make, with becoming diffidence, a trifling additional claim upon your bounty and good nature. You are as free, however, to shut the volume of the one petitioner, as to close your door in the face of the other.

This should have been a prefatory chapter, but for two reasons: First, that most novel readers, as my own conscience reminds me, are apt to be guilty of the sin of omission respecting that same matter of prefaces; Secondly, that it is a general custom with that class of students, to begin with the last chapter of a work; so that, after all, these remarks, being introduced last in order, have still the best chance to be read in their proper place. (475–76)

The narrator's primary concern in this passage is with the way his readers will relate to the text. He acknowledges that the writer/reader affiliation is a contract relationship, that of producer to consumer.[21] Readers invest their time and money and in return are transported into picturesque and romantic country. But the author seeks an alliance that extends beyond the simple exchange that formally fulfills the contract, and so he turns in his postscript to a discussion of the "purpose" (476) that energizes the writing of the text. Still, he recognizes that his interest in process (writing) may not be shared by the impatient reader who, seeking amusement and driven by a curiosity to know the end of the tale, the solution to the riddle of the text, is willing to skim or to skip whole passages, indeed to read the last chapter first. The reader is not concerned with the integrity of the text. The "interest of eager curiosity" (117) sends him or her rushing ahead looking toward the end of the journey and ignoring the structure of the carriage as well as the details of the passing landscape.[22] Indeed, since the "truly . . . gentle reader" is precisely one who "throws his mind into the attitude best adapted to humour the deceit which is presented for his entertainment, and grants, for the time of perusal, the premises on which the fable depends,"[23] he is unlikely to be motivated on first reading by the "rational pleasure, which admires the author's art."[24]

This is a fact of reading, however, that the author good-humoredly accepts and cheerfully works within its limitations. His final chapter will not contain the answer to the riddle of the story but will present instead an explanation of the writing of the text that takes the form of a demystification of the journey that has so fascinated the reader. Those parts of the narrative that have seemed so marvelous and romantic, those parts that have generated the most excitement and haste will be shown to be those that have a "foundation in fact" (477) so that the text will exist, finally, as history rather than romance. The experience of the reader of *Waverley*, in short, will echo that of its young hero, whose journey is an exploration of the enchantments created by his reading and one which ends with his awakening from the illusions of romantic dreams to the realities of history. Because as a youth he is permitted to read "only for the gratification of his amusement," making himself "master of the style so far as to understand the story" but ignoring "critical distinctions of philology . . . the difference of idiom, the beauty of filicitous expression, [and] the artificial combinations of syntax" (74), he loses the "opportunity of acquiring habits of firm and assiduous application, of gaining the art of controlling, directing, and concentrating the powers of his mind for earnest investigation . . ." (74-75). He seeks "instruction only according to the bent of his own mind" (75); "like the epicure who only deigned to take a single morsel from the sunny side of a peach, [he] read no volume a moment after it ceased to excite his curiosity or interest" (76); and gradually he becomes indifferent to the world around him. His "idle reading," in short, not only renders him "unfit for serious and sober study," but by encouraging "habits of abstraction and love of solitude" (78) prevents him from acquiring the ability to live in society "with ease and comfort" (79) and leads him to give to reality a "tincture" of "romantic tone and colouring" (82).

9

Waverley's adventures, then, suggest those of Don Quixote, but the enabling energy of his story does not derive from "the romance of Cervantes" (82). That text is absorbed by an account of "old-fashioned politics . . . feelings, prejudices, and parties" (89) of "Sixty Years since" (66). As the narrator repeatedly insists, the "action" of his story derives from "motives" that are the products of the "times" (89). And the time is one marked by genealogical disturbances, confusions of issues of paternity, authority, and legitimacy. As is not the case with those of Don Quixote, Waverley's habits of reading are the direct result of the collapse of paternal authority. "The occasional attention of [Waverley's] parents," the narrator writes, "might have been of service to prevent the dissipation of mind incidental to such a desultory course of reading" (77). But Waverly's mother is dead, and neither his father nor his uncle assumes the responsibility for his education. This absence of "paternal authority" (85) is the result of a political conflict between Waverley's father and his uncle, a conflict that itself is implicated in the issues of authority, paternity, and legitimacy that haunt the novel. The historical situation of the 1745 Jacobite Rebellion, which provides the context for Waverley's adventures, is dominated by a quarrel over two forms of authority, one represented by the Stuart claim to the throne based on Charles Edward's direct descent and hereditary right from the last Stuart king, James II, and the other supported by the Bill of Rights and the Acts of Settlement, which established the supremacy of parliament over the king as well as a Protestant line of succession from the House of Hanover.[25] Waverley finds himself in a situation where he must choose between the "hereditary faith of [his uncle] in Highchurch and in the house of Stewart" (67) and the more practical commitment of his father, "an avowed whig, and friend of the Hanover succession" (67).

But since his "habits" have not "led him to investigate the politics in which he lived" (211), he finds himself unable to cope with his own times and feels himself always "at the disposal of others, without the power of directing his own motions" (283).

Consequently, he seeks authority and direction in the "oft repeated tale of narrative old age," of "family tradition and genealogical history" (79) that dominates his uncle's discourse until, like Faulkner's Hightower, "he would exercise for hours that internal sorcery, by which past or imaginary events are presented in action, as it were, to the eye of the muser" (81). This love of the past continues to color his vision even when he enters a "new World" (97) by taking up the "profession of arms" (90) and joining Colonel Gardner's regiment in Scotland, for he feels out of place in the military. Hence he requests a leave of absence and begins a journey that will be a backward-looking enactment of a series of authoritative models from the past. There is the pedantic Baron of Bradwardine whose character is shaped by "prejudices of ancient birth and Jacobite politics, greatly strengthened by habits of solitary and secluded authority, which ... was ... indisputable and undisputed" (111) and for whom "rank and ancestry" are the "last words in the mouths of us of unblemished race" (113). Like Waverley's uncle, the Baron (who acts "*in loco parentis*" [121] to Waverley) is fascinated with heraldry and the tracing of genealogies, objects of study with no application to other aspects of life and involving no real knowledge of history.[26] There is Fergus Mac-Ivor, another model for Waverley, whose "countenance" indicates "something of the habit of peremptory command and decisive authority" (171), who possesses a "patronymic title" (173), is motivated by ideas of "patriarchal power" (216), and dreams of extending his "patriarchal sway" (185). And supporting the claims of these proponents of age, tradition, and hierarchy is the "Young Pretender" who is single-mindedly devoted to the restoration of the Stuart line to the throne of England.

All of these figures suggest the attitudes of an earlier generation, and all to some extent have outlived their times. Hence they appear now as an anacronistic residue in the new order of things. To Waverley's ingenuous eyes they and their doomed enterprise possess at first the interest of pure adventure, but, as he later comes to see, their quest is "strange, horrible and unnatural"

(331) because as a form of usurption it leads to active rebellion and parricide. Fergus will later appear to the young hero as a "second Lucifer of ambition and wrath" (385), an association that is validated by the narrator's description of the Highlanders as resting on a hillside "thick as leaves in Valumbrosa" (333).

Set against these figures associated with failed rebellion and worn-out hereditary authority is Colonel Talbot, a man "devoted to the service of his king and country" (360) who is free of Bradwardine's pedantry and Fergus's personal ambitions and who suggests lines of authority and bonds of relationship based on principles other than that of direct genealogical descent. His devotion to Waverley is an expression of an indebtedness to Waverley's uncle "for benefits greater than those which a son owes a father" (346), for Sir Everard withdraws his "claim to the hand of Lady Emily" (71) and persuades her father to allow her to marry the young Talbot. The result is that Sir Everard remains a celebate bachelor and Waverley becomes his heir. And this process of substitution is repeated when Talbot, "induced" by his "friendship for Sir E" (375) leaves his frail and pregnant wife to seek young Waverley in the Scottish highlands. The result of his actions is the death of the "future heir, so long hoped for in vain" (375) and his replacement by Waverley. Even before the death of Waverley's father Talbot is selected to "take charge of [Waverley's] interests" (412), and he is the one who secures a pardon for the young man by offering the king the fatherly promise that Waverley "will be a good boy in the future" (443).[27]

The relationship between the Waverley and Talbot families suggests a set of social bonds between men and women that substitute for lines of relationship connecting members of the same family from one generation to the next. Within the new system the "path of gratitude and honour" (377) is determined not by "irreprochable lineage" (113) but by obligations and duties based on values that are communal rather than strictly familial. And yet the effect of this order is to restore and maintain a version of the authority associated with the past and with patriarchal power. For it is through the "means" (475) of Colonel Talbot that Bradwardine's "patrimonial property" (467–68), "the mansion of [his] fathers" (469), is recovered and restored and the "Houses of Waverley-Honour and Bradwardine" are united through the marriage of Waverley and Rose. Everything is "as much as possible restored to the state in which [Bradwardine] had left it when he assumed arms some months before," with the "strictest attention to maintain the original character" (469) of the estate. But the restored estate is a represented estate in the sense of being an imitation or copy of a now-vanished original and as such appears as an aesthetic rather than historical category. For example, when the large dining parlor has been renewed and restored "as much as possible according to the old arrangement" (473), there is one "addition" made to this "fine old apartment" (473).

It was a large and spirited painting representing Fergus Mac-Ivor and Waverley in their Highland dress, the scene a wild, rocky, and mountainous pass, down which the clan were descending in the background. It was taken from a spirited sketch, drawn while they were in Edinburgh by a young man of high genius, and had been painted on a full-length scale by an eminent London artist. Raeburn himself, (whose Highland Chiefs do all but walk out of the canvass,) could not have done more justice to the subject; and the ardent, fiery, and impetuous character of the unfortunate Chief of Glennaquoich was finely contrasted with the contemplative, fanciful, and enthusiastic expression of his happier friend. Beside this painting hung the arms which Waverley had borne in the unfortunate civil war. The whole piece was beheld with admiration, and deeper feelings. (473–74)

This painting, like the "renewed or repaired" (469) estate, is the expression of an ironic but gentle nostalgia, for it gives the appearance of presence to that which can only be imagined.[28] Fergus Mac-Ivor, the cunning, self-serving politican, is dead, but he is represented here in a way that not only gives the illusion of presence but portrays him in an idealized and glorified form.

And Waverley himself appears once again in a dream world that is restored to view with the intensity, richness, and size of reality. But this is a realm that vanished with the skirmish at Clifton and one that was challenged even at the moment it was lived.

It was at that instant, that, looking around him, he saw the wild dress and appearance of his Highland associates, heard their whispers in an uncouth and unknown language, looked upon his own dress, so unlike that which he had worn from his infancy, and wished to awake from what seemed at the moment a dream, strange, horrible, and unnatural. (331)

The relationship of the painting to the experience that it [mis] represents points to a central theme of *Waverley* and to a crucial aspect of romance as a form. In "An Essay on Romance" Scott argues that Romance and history have a "common origin" in the account of the "father of an isolated family, destined one day to rise into a tribe, and in farther progress of time to expand into a nation," who narrates to "his descendants the circumstances which detached him from the society of his brethren, and drove him to form a solitary settlement in the wilderness."[29] This original account does not deviate from the facts but when the "tale of the patriarch" (135) is repeated by his descendants, the love of the marvelous, the "vanity of the tribe," and the "interests of the King and the priest" (135) contaminate the purity of the narrative which is now "exaggerated by prejudices and partialities" and "deeply marked by . . . idolatry and superstition" (139). "So that Romance, though certainly deriving its first original from the pure font of History, is supplied, during the course of a very few generations, with so many tributes from the Imagination, that at length the very name comes to be used to distinguish works of pure fiction" (153–54). Hence "Tradition . . . is an alchymy, which converts gold into lead" (177), history into fiction, and, as the years pass, the romancer gradually becomes the "companion and soother only of idle and convivial hours," and his "art is accounted at best an amusing but useless luxury" (164).

Nevertheless the "appetite" for fiction remains "ardent" (178) and the progress of romance continues. For, like the painting of Fergus and Waverley, it excites "admiration and deeper feelings," but because the past that it represents is contaminated by fiction it is unable to maintain the illusion of authority in the face of the stronger realities of the present. "Men must . . . eat, in spite both of sentiment and virtu" and so those who have viewed with pleasure the enchanted realm of the painting turn easily back to the more substantial satisfactions of an "excellent" (*W*, 474) dinner. The painting, then, represents the past, but the past colored by the imagination and robbed of its authority. Indeed the very process of representation seems one in which voice becomes fiction as the original utterance of the patriarch is defiled by substitutions and repetitions. Although the "eminent London artist" seeks to restore, preserve, and celebrate the past, his efforts necessarily involve him in a genetic movement of corruption and contamination.

However, the authority that is at once represented and discredited by the painting is restored in a more compelling aspect in the voice of the narrator of *Waverley*, a "painter of antique or of fashionable manners . . . of the last generation" (65) and in the form of his relation both to his hero and to the reader. For to write and to read novels is to engage in activities that replicate Waverley's own misguided adventures. Not only does the narrator present himself as someone who caters to the questionable tastes of those, who, like his young hero, read only for amusement, but he also reveals himself to be an inveterate reader. One has only to note the literary allusions, quotations, and footnotes that burden the text to see that the narrator is as fascinated by the literary tradition that establishes the genealogy and authority of his text as Waverley and the Baron of Bradwardine are by family history. Indeed, the question of narrative authority is the dominant issue of the introductory chapter of *Waverley* where the narrator seeks to show that he is "profoundly versed in the different branches of his art" (64). However, the "example of [his] predecessors" will dictate neither the "title of [his work]" nor the "name of [his] hero" (63), for to take a name and title from "English history or topography" would suggest "pages of inanity, similar to those which have been so christened for half a century past" (63). "WAVERLEY" the narrator insists is a name "uncontaminated" by tradition, one "bearing" only the meaning which "the reader shall hereafter be pleased to affix to it" (63). And the "second or supplemental title" (63) distinguishes the author's work from that of his predecessors by indicating that it is "neither a romance of chivalry, nor a tale of modern manners," and that its "object . . . is more a description of men than of manners" (64). Names and titles are of course examples of one of the simplest forms of representation and at once mark both individual and generic traits. They are not unique and neutral, for they are subject to the interpretive activity of others. A London newspaper punningly sneers at the *"Wavering Honour of W-v-r-l-y H-n-r"* (213), and the narrator repeatedly calls attention to his hero's "wavering and unsettled habit of mind" (98). Moreover, the narrator himself seems burdened by an inherited authority, for the controlling metaphors of the introductory chapter derive from the "language of heraldry" (65). He begins "like a maiden knight with his white shield" (63) but quickly finds it marked with both "bearings" (66) and tincture. His "narrative," in short, like the painting of Fergus and Waverley, at once asserts and discredits an authoritative model from the past.

The author was destined, of course, to become himself a dominating authority and the establisher of a tradition. As "the Author of Waverley" (15), he becomes the father of the historical romance and a seminal figure for a generation of British, European, and American novelists. Nevertheless, as Edward Said has noted, novelistic authority is not absolute, since the fathered text is always subject to a comparison with reality, a process that reveals it to be the result of a conceptual rather than an organic relationship.[30] When the author of Waverley, that great unknown, at last identitifies himself in the general preface to the Waverley Novels, he "acknowledges the paternity of these novels" (18) and argues that the "disclosure of the Author's name" restores "to him a sort of parental control over these Works" (3), but he also portrays himself not as Scott the father and author but as Scott the "spoiled child" (20) and reader. As he traces his development as a writer, preserving the "traces" of his "advance toward romantic composition" (11) and explaining the reasons for his curious desire "to remain concealed, in the character of the Author of these Novels" (15), he appears as Waverley himself making it ironically appropriate that all the novels bear the name of that first childish hero. He begins with a description of the "concealed pleasure" (6) of tale-telling with boyhood chums and moves on to an account of a youthful illness that throws him "back on the kingdom of fiction, as it were by a species of fatality" (6).

I was plunged into this great ocean of reading without compass or pilot; and unless when some one had the charity to
play at chess with me, I was allowed to do nothing save read,
from morning to night. I was, in kindness and pity, which
was perhaps erroneous, however natural, permitted to select
my subjects of study at my own pleasure, upon the same principle that the humours of children are indulged to keep them
out of mischief. As my taste and appetite were gratified in
nothing else, I indemnified myself by becoming a glutton of
books. . . .
   The vague and wild use which I made of this advantage I
cannot describe better than by referring my reader to the desultory studies of Waverley in a similar situation; the passages
concerning whose course of reading were imitated from recollections of my own. . . . (6–7)

It is the consumption of these texts that marks the first step in Scott's "advance toward romantic composition" (11) and the subsequent steps in his journey are equally bookish. He men-tions in particular a desire to imitate *The Castle of Otranto* and a curious inclination to complete Strutt's unfinished romance, *Queen Ho Hall.* In short the "unravelling" (14) of the mystery of "the Author of these Novels" takes the form of an account of

Scott's reading habits. But these are habits that associate him with his hero and imply a parallel between the success story recorded in the preface and the famous account of Waverley's awakening contained in the novel. "He felt himself entitled to say firmly, though perhaps with a sigh, that the romance of his life was ended, and that its real history had now commenced" (401). At issue here is a distinction between things as they are and things as they appear when colored by an "intense curiosity and exalted imagination" (281), between real life and adventure. But the true "Adventurer" (335) in *Waverley* is a historical character, the romantic, Byronic, Bonnie Prince Charles, transformed by Jacobite story and legend into a figure of romance. This "royal Adventurer" (296), this "Italian knight-errant" (354) is demythologized by the narrative which points to the Quixotic and self-interested aspects of his enterprise. Waverley's reaction to the pretender and his legend is that of a reader to a narrative of adventure, and Charles takes advantage of his simplicity as such fictions do of naive and youthful readers. Hence the history that Waverley reluctantly awakes to when he becomes disenchanted in the service of Charles is simply everyday life.

Of course the "real" history of Waverley's life is the narrative of adventure that the reader responds to as Waverley does to Charles and the Highlands, and the author's assurances in the postscript that the romantic parts of the narrative are precisely those that have a foundation in fact do not change the nature of the first-reading response. As Scott is well aware, his emphasis on the historical is an attempt to keep the "universal charm of Narrative" in control so that it does not completely "generate an indisposition to real history and useful literature."[31]

Indeed *Waverley* is haunted by the charm of story and by the ghost of a naive reader, a spectre that troubles the "conscience" (475) of the writer. For while at times he seems secure in his role as the father of these novels, "profoundly versed in the different branches of his art" (64) capable of tyrannizing over his reader (64, 200) by the exercise of his "arbitrary power" (199), at others he represents himself as a "spoiled child," an "idle truant boy" (465) engaged merely in a "game of bo-peep" (17) with the public. It is his reader, in short, who reminds him that reading is the origin of writing, the child the father of the man, and forces him into a confessional mode. Scott is, he admits, attracted to the poet Gray's notion that it is "no bad emblem of Paradise to lie all day on a couch and read new novels,"[32] but he is deeply troubled by the figure of an idling reader, indolently giving himself up to the charm of narrative and pleasures of curiosity and allowing himself to be played by the story.

This is a problem that Scott (anticipating some recent attempts) at times tries to solve by developing a notion of a "second reading"[33] performed by a competent reader. Naive reading he associates with the "young and indolent," with the "joys of infancy" that lose their charm for our "riper judgement" and with works that "require little attention in the perusal."[34] The more mature reader demands "a plan of narrative, happily complicated and ingeniously resolved" which "continues to please after many readings; for, although the interest of eager curiosity is no more, it is supplied by the rational pleasure, which admires the author's art, and traces a thousand minute passages, which render the catastrophe probable, yet escape notice in the eagerness of a first perusal."[35] Nevertheless one needs to note that the desire that motivates a second reading is still a form of curiosity even though it may be legitimate and reasonable, and this reader may be thought of as a "child to whom a watch is shown" who after becoming "satiated with looking at the outside," will "acquire a new interest in the object when it is opened, and the internal machinery displayed" (19).

This ambivalence regarding the acts of writing and reading that is inscribed in Scott's theory and practice is less the expression of his biography or psychology than it is the manifestation of a certain thematics of form that receives its clearest and most influential expression in his writings. And it is an ambivalence that persists in the English novel through the nineteenth and into the twentieth centuries. As George Levine observes, "*Waverley's* formula—its resolved and unresolved tensions—is the formula upon which almost every major English writer of the nineteenth century plays variations."[36] But the formula is displaced as novelists become more concerned with maintaining the artistic and social dignity of their fiction and the problems of reading and story are absorbed and completely thematized. From Austen through Dickens, George Eliot, and Conrad they exist primarily in the form of characters whose devotion to one sort of dream or another results in their taking romantic views of experience that lead them away from the duties of ordinary life but whose mistakes provide the mirage that illuminates the nature of the real. The Quixotic preoccupations of such characters as Emma, Dorothea, Pip, and Lord Jim suggestively echo the problems of writers and readers at the same time that they measure the distance that separates imagination from perception.

In the nineteenth-century American novel, however, the twin problems of reading and writing are not so easily displaced. As Geoffrey Hartman has noticed, the psychological drama of reading and an "'explicit reader' enters certain American authors . . . in the fictional guise of a narrator who has barely escaped a visionary merger, or else as a too palpable authorial presence."[37] Hawthorne and Melville, in particular, feel the necessity to examine directly the formal and personal problems of story telling that they inherit from Scott. Neither writer, of course, is in any sense an uninhibited story teller.[38] Hawthorne's preoccupation with the themes of sin and guilt as well as his concern with social reform is evidence enough of a serious side; and Melville's concern with truth telling burdens his fiction in obvious ways. Nevertheless both of these writers face the contradictions between such serious intentions and the nature of story in such a way as to suggest a different, more oblique reading of Scott than that which resulted in the realistic fiction of Victorian England.

Washington Irving, for example, finds in Scott an ironic uncertainty that strongly suggests the self-questionings of Hawthorne and Melville.

Whenever Scott touched, in this way, upon local antiquities, and in all his familiar conversations about local traditions and superstitions, there was always a sly and quiet humour running at the bottom of his discourse, and playing about his countenance, as if he sported with the subject. It seemed to me as if he distrusted his own enthusiasm and was disposed to droll upon his own humours and peculiarities, yet at the same time a poetic gleam in his eye, would shew that he really took a strong interest and relish in the theme.[39]

Irving's analysis, focusing as it does on Scott's self-reading, emphasizes what George Levine has called Scott's "peculiar, almost modern, sort of self consciousness,"[40] but it also insists on his commitment to a kind of naiveté that belongs to poetic and imaginative vision. And this unresolved tension, which Irving sees between the poetic gleam in Scott's eye and the sly and ironic play in his discourse and countenance, between oblique and ingenuous modes of experiencing, finds its formal expression in the eccentricities of the American novel, for it has the effect of bringing to the surface a set of problems normally hidden by the conventions that govern the relationship between writer and reader.

Missing in the works of Hawthorne and Melville is the naturalness of a movement toward resolution and closure as well as the happy conventional relation between a revered author and honored reader that one associates with the great eighteenth- and nineteenth-century English novel. Even Sterne, who seriously questions the conventions that govern reader/writer relations, is willing to respect the "reader's understanding ... to halve this matter amicably, and leave him something to imagine, in his turn, as well as yourself."[41] Such easy solutions seem unavailable to Hawthorne and Melville perhaps because their struggle to create a new, original literature forces them to a deeper, more subversive questioning of inherited conventions and leads them to focus with a special sense of urgency on Scott's image of the reader as a sort of ghostly double who may either validate or subvert the work of writing. Both American writers begin with a conventional conception of a certain ideal reader, but they soon develop a troubled sense of the distance that separates that ideal from their actual audiences and the work of reading and writing. The result is a tortured re-examination of the now highly suspect relations between author and reader.

This investigation generates in each case not only a particular narrative strategy but an enabling theme as well. The theme of reading appears obsessively in the works of Hawthorne and Melville. Hawthorne's starting point as a writer is most often an "Old Time Legend," some object or scrap of gossip from the past, pregnant with an undisclosed meaning that he sets out to uncover for his reader. The most explicit treatment of this theme, of course, appears in his account of his discovery of the source of *The Scarlet Letter.* The story he tells us derives from his reading of a faded scarlet A, which represented itself as "most worthy of interpretation," and "several foolscap sheets, containing many particulars respecting the life and conversation of one Hester Prynne" (*SL,* 32). In both cases Hawthorne's reading is the last of a series of interpretations. As Charles Feidelson notes in his seminal discussion of this episode, everyone in the novel reenacts the scene in which Hawthorne attempts to read the meaning of the letter,[42] and the letter is interpreted in a variety of ways by Hester and her contemporaries as well as by Hawthorne and the reader. Moreover, Hester herself is the "text of the discourse[s]" (85) not only of Puritan clergymen but also of the "aged persons, alive in the time of Mr. Surveyor Pue . . . from whose oral testimony he had made up the narrative," and his narrative, in turn, forms the basis of *The Scarlet Letter.* Hawthorne seeks to uncover the "dark meaning" (31) in the faded scarlet A as well as the "traces of Mr. Pue's mental part, and the internal operations of his head" contained in the "half a dozen sheets of foolscap" (33). And as Hawthorne is Pue's commentator, so the reader is his, seeking in Hawthorne's text the elusive meaning of the mysterious A as well as the features of its current interpreter. But no matter how interpretations proliferate something will always remain hidden, for the wonderful A "gives evidence of a now forgotten art, not to be rediscovered even by the process of picking out the threads" (31).

It is this "forgotten art" that haunts Hawthorne's career as a writer. *The Marble Faun* and the unfinished romances are a record of his discovery that both creative and interpretive acts are finally nonproductive. The threads of the fabric of *The Marble Faun* are "Fragmentary Sentences," signs of a meaning scattered, dispersed, and lost forever. Because the novelist is unable to begin with an unequivocal core of meaning but must be content with something that already is an interpretation, the act of writing becomes a task "resembling, in its perplexity, that of gathering up and piecing together the fragments of a letter, which has been torn and scattered to the winds" (*MF*, 92–93). And the text that the writer produces demands not the gentle and sympathetic reader who accepts the work "at its worth, without tearing the web apart, with the idle purpose of discovering how its threads have been knit together" (455), but rather a questioning, probing reader who must violate that which he seeks to understand. Both writer and reader become like Hilda little more than disillusioned copyists.

For Melville even more than Hawthorne the writer is at first a reader. His creative powers depend on the scope of his reading, "spontaneous creative thought" being a process whereby "all existing great works are federated in the fancy; and so regarded as a miscellaneous and Pantheistic whole" (*P,* 284). The text of *Moby-Dick*, for example, is woven more from the threads of the texts that fill Ishmael's library than it is from the lines and ropes of the whaling world. Indeed, Ishmael's relation to that world is that of a reader to a text, and he tries to organize and arrange it as he has previously done his library by establishing a bibliographical system. Reading, however, is no easy or passive activity. In "Hawthorne and His Mosses" Melville distinguishes between that reader who sees Shakespeare as a "mere man of Richard-the-Third humps, and Macbeth daggers," who responds to the "popularizing noise and show of broad farce, and blood-besmeared tragedy," and the more discriminating reader who is "content with the still, rich utterances of a great intellect in repose" (HHM, 541, 542). In the place of "blind, unbridled" (542) reading, Melville proposes a deep, careful one which is capable of discerning those truths that the writer "craftly says" or "insinuates" (541) in his texts. As Ishmael demonstrates when he tells "The Town-Ho's Story" by "interweaving in its proper place the darker thread [the secret part of the tale] with the story as publicly narrated on the ship" (*M-D*, 208), story telling is the process of conveying a dark truth that will only be available to the reader whose response is in the form of a deep and probing examination.

Melville soon finds, however, that both writer and reader are themselves woven into the fabric of the story. *Pierre* and *The Confidence Man* are records of his discovery of the extent to which writer and reader are entangled in the web of fictions that surround them. In *Pierre* he attempts to distinguish between the "countless tribes of common novels" that "laboriously spin vails of mystery, only to complacently clear them up at last"; and those "profounder emanations of the human mind" that never "unravel their own intricacies, and have no proper endings" (141); but he then goes on to demonstrate the way in which the "infinite entanglements of all social things, which forbid that one thread should fly the general fabric, on some new line of duty, without tearing itself and tearing others," (191) make it impossible either for a writer to produce an original text or for a reader to respond to it in any but a mystified way. "Like knavish cards, the leaves of all great books are covertly packed," and any new author but packs "one set the more" (329). As *The Confidence Man* makes clear, all stories are at least twice told and are designed, primarily, to divert and charm. Here the writer is portrayed as the confidence man, a contradictorily derivative but original character who has no fixed identity, and readers—both naive and suspicious—are represented by his many victims. Writing is a sham and reading the activity of fools.

Similar doubts trouble even a novelist as confident in his craft as Henry James. A character in his novels will attempt to read the secret intentions of lives, the hidden subjectivities of others only to discover that the act of reading itself violently changes those lives and creates the results of the reading. And James himself will reenact that drama in the prefaces to the New York edition of his works as he attempts to comprehend the hidden elements and motives of the characters that he has created and to communicate those qualities to a reader who is primarily interested in being entertained. For James the acts of reading and writing appear to be mutually dependent but incompatible activities. The object of the novel is to represent life but the effect is to entertain, and the effect seem to contaminate the object.

The unpublished fragments of Hawthorne's last years and Melville's long period of silence following the publication of *The Confidence Man* are indications of the extent to which both writers were overwhelmed by the exhaustion of the possibilities of writing and dismayed by their realization that their relation to their readers is based on deception and bad faith. And in a quite different way the work of rereading that produces the prefaces for the New York edition underscores James's preoccupations with these same problems. However through their willingness fully to investigate the nature of story and the problems of reading these writers suggest the possibility of a fiction where the real is absorbed by the mirage, the "moral" by the "fable," history by romance. One thinks here of Faulkner's preoccupation with the "rag-tag and bob ends of old tales and talking" (*AA,* 303) and John Barth's undisguised fascination with the "element of story—just sheer extraordinary marvelous story," that is to say "yarns—elaborate lies." "Scheherazade's my avant-gardiste," he says after commenting that the "nouveau roman isn't . . . my cup of tea."[43]

This emphasis does not, however, mark an unexamined return to the simplicity of an ingenuous manner of reading and writing. No one is likely to accuse John Barth of practicing a naive and innocent art that appeals primarily to readers of "restricted competence."[44] He is as aware as any student of *la nouvelle critique* of the problematic nature of such categories of the classic text as selfhood, origin, and end. A sense of the fictive status of these concepts lies behind his impulse to "imagine alternatives to the world," to "re-invent philosophy and the rest—make up your own whole history of the world,"[45] His books, he says, are "novels which imitate the form of the Novel by an author who imitates the role of Author," and no one is more aware of the subversive effects of imitation than he.

If this sort of thing sounds unpleasantly decadent, nevertheless it's about where the genre begins, with *Quixote* imitating *Amadis of Gaul,* Cervantes pretending to be the Cid Hamete Benengeli (and Alonso Quijano pretending to be Don Quixote), or Fielding parodying Richardson. "History repeats itself as farce"—meaning, of course, in the form or mode of farce, not that history is farcical. . . . The first attempts . . . to imitate actions more or less directly, and its conventional devices—cause and effect, linear anecdote characterization, authorial selection, arrangement, and interpretation—can be and have long since been objected to as obsolete notions, or metaphors for obsolete notions: Robbe-Grillet's essays *For a New Novel* come to mind. There are replies to these objections, not to the point here, but one can see that in any case they're obviated by imitations of novels which attempt to represent not life directly but a representation of life. In fact such works are no more removed from life than Richardson's or Goethe's epistolary novels are: both imitate "real" documents, and the subject of both, ultimately, is life, not documents. A novel is as much a piece of the real world as a letter, and the letters in *The Sorrows of Young Werther* are, after all, fictitious.[46]

For Barth the generic formal situation of the novel is to duplicate or repeat not life itself but an imitation of life. And as an order of duplication it offers a realm of counterfeit imitation, one that is the product of a desire rather than the expression of a natural arrangement. Indeed, as he suggests, the art of story-telling originates from an impulse that seems both impractical and unnatural, a fact that may explain why traditionally it has been regarded suspiciously. The words "once upon a time" can at once comfort and unsettle, for while they conserve, transmit, and confirm a past, a history, an entire system of values, they also initiate a process that breaks from the past by repeating it in a farcical mode thereby expressing a dissatisfaction with its expectations and metaphors. For Barth and his characters this contradictory quality is the aspect of story that most fascinates. Consider, for example, the enthusiasm of Harvey Russeck in *The Sot-Weed Factor.*

"No pleasure pleasures me as doth a well-spun tale, be't sad or merry, shallow or deep! If the subject's privy business, or unpleasant, who cares a fib? The road to Heaven's beset with thistles, and methinks there's many a cow-pat on't as well. And what matter if your folk are drawn from life? 'Tis not likely I'll ha'met 'em, or know 'em from your telling if e'er I should! Call 'em what names ye will: in a tale they're less than themselves, and more. Besides which, if ye have the art to make 'em live— 'sheart!—thou'rt nowise liable for what the rascals do, no more than God Almighty for the lot of us. As for length, fie on't!" He raised his horny finger. "A bad tale's long though it want but a single eyeblink for the telling, and a good tale short though it takes from St. Swithin's to Michaelmas to have done with't. Ha! And the plot is tangled, d'ye say? Is't more knotful or bewildered than the skein of life itself, that a good tale tangles the better to unsnarl? Nay, out with your story, now, and yours as well, sir, and shame on the both o' ye thou'rt not commenced already! Spin and tangle till the Dog-star set i' the Bay—nor fear I'll count ye idle gossips: a tale well wrought is the gossip o' the gods, that see the heart and hidden point o' life on earth; the seamless web o' the world; the Warp and Woof . . . I'Christ, I do love a story, sirs! Tell away!"[47]

Like Barth himself, who in writing *The Sot-Weed Factor* set out to "make up a plot fancier than *Tom Jones*,"[48] Harvey delights in the spinning and tangling of tale-telling. Of primary importance is not a truth or a moral but an uninhibited joy in the performance of the virtuoso who "with the aid of *very special gifts*" and with the knowledge that all possibilities are exhausted manages to speak "eloquently to our still human hearts and conditions."[49] Harvey is, we recall, a character in a novel which imitates the eighteenth-century novel, the creation of an author who imitates Fielding and other authors, and as he expresses his enthusiasm, he dismisses as irrelevant many of the questions traditionally raised about the art of fiction. The problem of subject matter, the questions of source, of ethical and moral responsibilities, of productive, committed actions: all these are quickly but not naively dismissed. Indeed, Harvey's response suggests that the naive reading associated with the novel from its beginnings may not be innocent at all since the form itself may be seen as socially and ontologically subversive. The special delight that novel readers experience when they give themselves to the magic of story may not represent a passive unquestioning acceptance of the codes and conventions of their society. The very act of turning away from what is to feign belief in what is not violates the natural attitude and puts it into question. The story that so delights Harvey Russecks reveals "an itch for all we lose as proper citizens— something in us pines for Chaos, for the black and lawless Pit" (628).

For Barth a good story is at once evidence that "human work can be magnificent" (305) and a revelation of that "black cosmos whence we sprung and through which we fall." (364) His "favorite teller" is Scheherazade because, among other reasons, her "situation" is "apocalyptic." Faced with death, she is forced night after night to satisfy an "old cynic" whose "epical despair" is bringing ruin to his kingdom, and the "pleasure" generated by her tales "fertilizes as well as spares her, and . . . finally rewards her." And she, "yarning tirelessly through the dark hours to save her neck," at the same time cures the king's despair and saves the kingdom as well as herself. As Barth never tires of suggesting, this scene of reading and writing figures the "estate of the fictioner in general"[50] and suggests a point of view that manages to dignify both naive and enlightened attitudes.

We tell stories and listen to them because we live stories and live in them. Narrative equals language equals life: To cease to narrate, as the capital example of Scheherazade reminds us, is to die—literally for her, figuratively for the rest of us. One might add that if this is true, then not only is all fiction fiction about fiction, but all fiction about fiction is in fact fiction about life. Some of us understood that all along.[51]

For Barth, as for his American precursors, not only do "Romance and real history have the same common origin,"[52] but the one needs the other to make us see it as such. That is the perception that energizes and troubles American romance. American writers tell stories that form family histories and at the same time problematize the idea of a family history or "romance." For them it is unclear whether the notion of narrative derives from human history or whether the very idea or "fiction" of history is the product of an impulse to understand human events as narrative. The result is an entangling of the problems of telling, reading, and living, problems that dominate the novels that I interpret in the following chapters.

TWO

The Limits of Romance: A Reading of The Marble Faun

It was the coming true that was the proof of the enchantment, which, moreover, was naturally never so great as when such coming was, to such a degree and by the most romantic stroke of all, the fruit of one's own wizardry. I was positively—so had the wheel revolved—proud of my work. I had thought it all out, and to have thought it was, wonderfully, to have brought it. Yet I recall how I even then knew on the spot that there was something supreme I should have failed to bring unless I had happened suddenly to become aware of the very presence of the haunting principle, as it were, of my thought.

—Henry James, *The Sacred Fount*

For Hawthorne the shaping impulse of romance is a profound experience of loss and absence. His prefaces are pervaded by a sense of nostalgia, a longing of the heart for some other kind of fulfillment, and that nostalgia most often appears as a lament for a lost, autonomous form, one that brought together poetic, metaphysical, and intersubjective realms and made possible a happy, undisturbed relation between fiction and reality, imagination and perception, and writer and reader. But that form now belongs to an inaccessible yesterday and appears only in the guise of worn fragments and ghostly shadows. Hester's worn and faded A that "gives evidence of a now forgotten art, not to be recovered even by the process of picking out the threads" is "imparted" to Hawthorne by the "ghostly hand" of Surveyor Pue, and his "ghostly voice" exhorts him "to bring his mouldy and moth-eaten lucubrations before the public" (*SL*, 31, 33). For Hawthorne, the writer begins alone in a "dilapidated" world filled with structures "cobwebbed, and dingy with old paint" (7) and haunted by ghosts from the past. Like the attic of the Custom House, with its "heaped-up rubbish" or "the field near the Old Manse" with its Indian arrowheads, the world seems a "corpse of dead activity," "dry bones" from which he must "raise up . . . an image" (29) of life, impart the "glow of passion" and the "tenderness of sentiment" to forms which retain the "rigidity of dead corpses" (34). His is a magic that seeks to give life to the dead by bathing the real in the light of the imaginary thereby producing a "new life" but one that feeds on "time-worn materials, like a tuft of green moss on a crumbling wall" (58). Such an art is one that dematerializes and vaporizes. The real is not desired or valued for its own sake but is placed in the service of the imagination that seeks to relieve it of the weight of gravity and to transform it into a "tribe of unrealities" (34).

But the product is the "semblance of a world" (37), best thought of as a soap bubble or a castle in the air whose continued existence depends upon the operation of literary conventions without which its "paint and pasteboard . . . composition" would be "painfully discernible" (*BR*, 2) and its originating

impulse seen as the result of a "false and unnatural relation with
. . . decay" (*SL,* 75). Hawthorne, therefore, insists on the importance of "a certain propriety, of a kind always recognized in literature" and uses it both to validate the status of his fictive
world and to justify his "assuming a personal relation with the
public" (4). For while he understands that romance feeds on
ruin and cohabits with death, he nevertheless hopes that it will
provide him with a way of opening "an intercourse with the
world" (*TT,* 6). By the use of the conventions of a Faery Land,
an "Honored Reader," and a "prim old author" (*MF,* 1), he will establish and maintain relations with others. However, as an
American writer Hawthorne's relation to literary conventions is
an uneasy one in the sense that he can neither take them for
granted nor do without them. As a romancer he needs the "atmosphere of strange enchantment" (*BR,* 2) that conventions generate but he worries about its effects on writer and reader. His
"magic circle" at the Old Manse, for example, seems to generate
a spell that offers "rest" to "weary and world worn spirits"
(*MOM,* 29), but it is not a spell that can be celebrated unambiguously. "In one respect," Hawthorne writes, "our precincts were
like the Enchanted Ground, through which the pilgrim trav-
elled on his way to the Celestial City. The guests, each and all,
felt a slumberous influence upon them; they fell asleep in
chairs, or took a more deliberate siesta on the sofa, or were seen
stretched out among the shadows of the orchard, looking up
dreamily through the boughs" (28). Hawthorne refers here to
the place in *The Pilgrim's Progress* that comes just before the
Land of Beulah and that is "one of the last refuges that the
enemy to pilgrims has," for the "air there [tends] to make one
drowsy . . . and if a man sleeps, tis a question, some say,
whether ever they shall rise or wake again in this world."[1] The
dark aspects of enchantment that Hawthorne points to with
this reference suggest the ways in which the authority of convention maintains the authority of representation. The narrator of
"The Custom House" cannot be present in his own person but
appears as the "representative" (*SL,* 10) of others who are absent:

his ancestors, his "ancient predecessor, Mr. Surveyor Pue" (43), even an earlier version of himself, a "scribbler of bygone days" (45).[2] Substituting for self presence, according to the "law of literary propriety" (27) is the figure of a "literary man" (43), a "romance-writer" (35). And the magic of his art is one that maintains the illusion of presence. But, as the reference to Bunyan suggests, that conventional magic may be a fatal charm that draws the reader into the realm of the dead. This possibility is present as a troubling suggestion in all of Hawthorne's romances, but in *The Marble Faun*, the last and darkest of his works, it becomes a dominating concern as the "spell of a tranquil spirit" (*MOM*, 29) turns into the "spell of ruin" (*MF*, 409) and death becomes the companion of the author.

The Marble Faun is a book of precipices and chasms, perspectives and distances, fragments and gaps; one haunted by enigmas, unanswered riddles, and impending catastrophes; a book whose characters are all "forlorn and wretched, under . . . [the] burthen of dusty death" (194). Separated from each other by a "voiceless gulf" (113) each finds himself or herself an "alien in the world" with "wholly unsympathetic medium betwixt himself and those whom he yearns to meet" (92). Other people are "within . . view" and yet "beyond . . . reach" (66), isolated by a "strange distance and unapproachableness" (89). And they are also separated from the narrator who is distanced from them as they are from each other and who, in order to "interest" the reader in their "fortunes" (5) must weave a narrative from "Fragmentary Sentences." Indeed, the entire novel is dominated by the difficulties of representing and interpreting the problems of writing and reading, and behind these issues two riddles of origins: "Was Donatello really a faun?" (459) and "What were Miriam's real name and rank. . . ? (466) These are the questions that both generate representations and insure that they, like Kenyon's bust of Donatello, must always remain fragmented and incomplete.

Most spectators mistake it for an unsuccessful attempt towards
copying the features of the Faun of Praxiteles. One observer
in a thousand is conscious of something more, and lingers
long over this mysterious face, departing from it, reluctantly,
and with many a glance thrown backward. What perplexes
him is the riddle that he sees propounded there. . . . It was the
contemplation of this imperfect portrait of Donatello that
originally interested us in his history, and impelled us to
elicit from Kenyon what he knew of his friend's adventures.
(381)

Entangled in this passage are most of the problems of the
novel: the question of the relation between creative and copying
acts, the nature and difficulties of the interpretive process, and
the issue of the ontological status of the characters and their
world and its relation to that of the narrator and reader. One effect of the passage is to complicate the meaning of the title, *The
Marble Faun*.[3] Does it refer to the Praxiteles faun or to Kenyon's
bust of Donatello, which resembles the Praxiteles statue, and
what relationship as a form of literary representation does it
have to these other works of art? How are we to understand the
narrator's "Man of Marble" who is "entirely imginary" (4) and
yet who seems to enjoy an existence that extends beyond the
borders of the fiction, to show himself "in the same category as
actually living mortals" (*BR,* 2)? These are some of the questions woven into the texture of *The Marble Faun,* questions of
the status of fictional truths and the nature of their ground.

The novel begins with a problem of "resemblance," that of
the "vivid likeness" between a "well-known master-piece of Gre-
cian sculpture, and a young Italian" which makes the man seem
the "very Faun of Praxiteles" (*MF,* 7). This recognition of resemblance produces two responses: the first from the narrator, who
is moved to an "effort to express [the statue's] magic peculiarity
in words" (8), a magic that seems to mingle and knead together
the natural and human and invoke a time when "man's affinity
with Nature was more strict, and his fellowship with every living thing more intimate and dear" (11), only to find that the

"idea grows coarse, as [he] handle[s] it, and hardens in [his] grasp," (10); and the second from the characters, who are carried by their perception of the "resemblance between the Marble Faun and their living companion . . . into a certain airy region, lifting up . . . their heavy, earthly feet from the actual soil of life. The world had been set afloat, as it were, for a moment, and relieved them, for just so long, of all customary responsibility for what they thought and said" (16). But this sense of enchantment is only momentary, and as "their play of fancy subside[s] into a much more sombre mood" (18), the "beautiful statue" becomes a "corroded and discoloured stone" (17). With this change in mood comes a shift in setting as the action moves from the "sculpture gallery" to the "vast tomb" (24), the Catacomb of Saint Calixtus. And these introductory movements from rising to falling, enchantment to disenchantment, from the admiration of the "eternal repose of marble" (16) to an encounter with the "white ashes, into which the entire mortality of a man or woman had resolved itself" (24) will dominate the entire novel, for its "key-note" is the "wonderful resemblance" (22) that initiates them.

This "nameless charm" (16) of likeness that energizes the novel, the "spell of the Eternal City" (213) of art, is the natural magic of representation with its illusion of a direct and original relation between the sign and its object. But *The Marble Faun* questions and disturbs this charm of resemblance, for its world is one of pure representations, a world of re-creations, of pictures, sketches, statues, and words that "phantomize"[4] presence by pointing to the absence of the persons and objects that they signify. Here there are no "genuine original[s]" (263), only, at best, things that are "something like the life" (121). The result is that the novel and its characters like Rome are "haunted" (176) by "ugly phantoms" (45). Of course the central phantom in the book, as a living model, is a figure for the process of representation itself.[5] Known only as Miriam's model, he appears first as "the Spectre of the Catacomb" (28), a "dusky, death-scented apparition" (36) who seems to "have stept out of a picture" (19); and it is his "spectral figure" (432) that haunts the world of the novel, blurring distinctions between life and death, object and image, and undermining any notion of meaning as presence and plentitude. But it is this figure, too, that generates narrative, for it is his "death" that is the enabling energy of "the Romance of Monte Beni" (434), the parallel stories of the transformation of Donatello and Hilda.

First there is the story of Donatello, the account of the corruption of natural man, a "beautiful creature, standing betwixt man and animal, sympathizing with each, comprehending the speech of either race, and interpreting the whole existence of one to the other" (13). Because he is able to speak in the "original voice and utterance of the natural man" (248) which has since been "laid aside and forgotten . . . now that words have been feebly substituted in the place of signs and symbols" (77-78), this creature is free of the burden of interpretation. "Before the sophistication of the human intellect formed what we now call language" (248), the world interpreted itself "without the aid of words" (258). In the place of language which seeks through endless analogies to mediate the distance that now exists between man and nature there once existed a power of sympathy that brought all parts of existence together and allowed them to communicate instantly and completely: "he was believed to possess gifts by which he could associate himself with the wild things of the forests, and with the fowls of the air, and could feel a sympathy even with the trees, among which it was his joy to dwell" (235).

As Donatello's adventures make clear, that instinctive sympathy that once united man to his natural milieu no longer exists. When the young primitive loses that "power of sympathy" (320) that binds him to the natural world he finds it impossible to live the life of his forefathers. "He could not live their healthy life of animal spirits, in sympathy with Nature, and brotherhood with all that breathed around them. Nature, in beast, fowl, and tree, and earth, flood, and sky, is what it was of old; but sin, care, and self-consciousness have set the human portion of the world askew; and thus the simplest character is ever the surest to go astray" (239–40).

Nor is it possible to discover the source or origin of that lost unity. "It would have been as difficult . . . to follow up the stream of Donatello's ancestry to its dim source, as travellers have found it, to reach the mysterious fountains of the Nile" (231). Heralds trace the family to the "early morn of Christendom" but at that "venerable distance" give up "in despair." Nevertheless, where written record leaves the genealogy of Monte Beni, tradition takes it up and carries it back to the "sylvan life of Etruria" where it was "supposed to have had its origin" (232). A "romancer" might go "beyond the region of definite and demonstrable fact" but he "must needs follow his own guidance and probably arrive nowhither at last" (231). Moreover, even to him the "original founder of the race" (234) remains hidden, and he must base his speculations on the imperfect copies of the inaccessible original that occasionally appear along the family line. Donatello appears to his butler and to the "peasantry of the estate and neighboring village" as a "Monte Beni of the original type" (236), and this fact seems to Kenyon to afford a "shadowy and whimsical semblance of an explanation for the likeness, which he, with Miriam and Hilda, had seen, or fancied between Donatello and the Faun of Praxiteles" (232–33). But this association complicates further the question of Donatello's origin and status, for it knots together genealogical and representational issues. Donatello seems to resemble not a faun but the representation of one, and that representation is the expression of, rather than the solution to, a mystery. "Praxiteles has subtly diffused, throughout his work, that mute mystery which so hopelessly perplexes us, whenever we attempt to gain an intellectual or sympathetic knowledge of the lower forms of creation" (10). The meaning of the statue, like the source of Donatello's family line, is in the form of a riddle, an unanswered question that is the sign of a primeval origin lost forever and available only in the form of a "poet's reminiscence of a period when man's affinity with Nature was more strict, and his fellowship with every living thing more intimate and dear" (11).

However, this is not to suggest that art can provide a cure for the alienation that results from man's separation from his source. Hawthorne dramatizes the loss at the level of culture as well as of nature. Hilda's initial innocence is not the Arcadian unselfconsciousness of the Old World pagan and does not manifest itself in the form of a special enjoyment of the "warm, sensuous, earthy side of Nature" (13). As a "daughter of the Puritans" (54), she is "perplex[ed]" (13) by Donatello's apparent affinity with nature. Her innocence is the result of a special relationship to divinity; she looks at "humanity with angel's eyes" (53). She is a "poor, lonely girl, whom God has set here in an evil world, and given her only a white robe, and bid her wear it back to Him, as white as when she put it on" (208). Her innocence, therefore, takes the form of a "silent sympathy" not with nature but with the religious paintings of the Old Masters, those products that are at once the expression of man's highest accomplishments and the "true symbol of the glories of the better world, where a celestial radiance will be inherent in all things and persons, and render each continually transparent to the sight of all" (304). By the use of a "guiding light of sympathy, she went straight to the central point, in which the Master had conceived his work. Thus she viewed it, as it were, with his own eyes, and hence her comprehension of any picture that interested her was perfect" (57).

For the unfallen Hilda, as for Donatello, interpretation poses no problem. Her sympathetic insight allows her to penetrate to the "spirit and essence" (58) of the picture and to represent it on her canvas. While other copyists must work "entirely from the outside" and are able "only to reproduce the surface" (60), thereby representing the painting's superficial qualities but missing the inner core of meaning, Hilda is able to "interpret what the feeling is, that gives [the] picture such a mysterious force" (65). And she is able to use this same insight to open the eyes of others: her "silent sympathy was so powerful that it drew your own along with it, endowing you with a second-sight and enabled you to see the excellences with almost the depth and delicacy of her own perceptions" (62).

Because her interpretive powers derive from her special relationship to God—"I had only God to take care of me, and be my closest friend" (359)—these powers vanish when the crime that she witnesses disrupts the relationship: "the terrible, terrible crime, which I have revealed to you, thrust itself between Him and me; so I groped for Him in the darkness, as it were, and found him not—found nothing but a dreadful solitude, and this crime in the midst of it" (359). The result is a "dimness of an insight," a loss of her power of "self-surrender . . . and sympathy" (335), and in the place of that lost sympathy is a "keen intellectual perception" that produces "irreverent" rather than sympathetic criticism as Hilda grows "sadly critical." "Heretofore, her sympathy went deeply—into a picture, yet seemed to leave a depth which it was inadequate to sound; now, on the contrary, her perceptive faculty penetrated the canvas like a steel probe, and found but a crust of paint over an emptiness" (341). The point here is not simply that the process of interpretation is now a violent act but also that the violation reveals not a core of hidden meaning but an absence which implies that the "pictorial act" might be "altogether a delusion" (336), and her earlier response to the pictures therefore the result of a mystification.

Hilda approaches at this point a vision of culture similar to the one voiced by the more pessimistic Miriam. "The chasm was merely one of the orifices of that pit of blackness that lies beneath us, everywhere. The firmest substance of human happiness is but a thin crust spread over it, with just reality enough to bear up the illusive stage-scenery amid which we tread. It needs no earthquake to open the chasm. A footstep, a little heavier than ordinary, will serve; and we must step very daintily, not to break through the crust, at any moment" (161-62). From Miriam's Conradian perspective, human life seems permeated by an artificiality that robs it of durability and significance. Surrounded by the ruins of Rome, she becomes aware of the "transitoriness of all things" (150) and comes to believe that her own culture is doomed to go the way of the cultures of the past, for in Rome one looks "through a vista of century beyond century—through much shadow, and a little sunshine—through barbarism and civilization, alternating with one another, like actors that have prearranged their parts. . . . Your own life is nothing, when compared with that immeasurable distance" (410).

The ruins of Rome, then, point to the same emptiness that the disenchanted Hilda finds beneath the paint-covered canvas of the Old Masters and which the more bitter Miriam senses beneath everything. The ruins are not symbols of human accomplishment and survival but rather ominous reminders of man's mortality. For Hawthorne, material ruins always imply—often contain—decayed human ruins; hence Rome is a "sepulchral store-house of the past" (436), a "vast tomb"(24) containing a "long decaying corpse, retaining a trace of the noble shape it was, but with accumulated dust and a fungous growth overspreading all to more admirable features" (325). The forms of culture, in short, are as fragile as man himself, his memorials symbols of oblivion rather than a protection from it. The tombs of the Appian Way, for example, built by men "ambitious of everlasting remembrance" (420), have lost their human meaning and now retain nothing "except their massiveness" and hence are "alien from human sympathies" (419). Monuments originally designed as memorials perpetuating memories have become instead signs of a lost significance, an abandoned cult, a vanished god, a forgotten family.[6] Even worse, with their suggestions of putrefaction, they stand as reminders of the grossness and horror of man's imprisonment in an envelope of flesh. In a remarkable passage in *The French and Italian Notebooks* Hawthorne observes that "there seems to be something . . . in the monuments of every kind that they [the Romans] have raised that puts people in mind of their earthly necessities, and incites them to defile therewith whatever temple, column, ruined palace, or triumphal arch may be nearest at hand" (*FIN*, 481). It is the odors of rotten flesh and human excrement that poison the atmosphere of Rome, making it "unwholesome" (*MF*, 36) and "corrupt" (54) and create a "contagious element, rising foglike . . . and brooding over the dead and half-rotten city" (*FIN,* 412). Surrounded by the "smell of ruin" and "decaying generations" (*MF,* 74) the resident of Rome seems unable to find comfort and safety anywhere.

But if the atmosphere of Rome can poison, it also seems capable of engendering. To artists it seems so "congenial" that they are "loath" to leave "after once breathing the enchanted air" (132). Here they enjoy a "social warmth from each other's presence" that is missing in the "unsympathizing cities of their native land." However, this "warmth" does not generate "mutual affection" or reduce the "jealousies and animosities" which "knaw into [their] hearts"; nor does it inspire their imaginations, for while "they linger year after year in Italy . . . their originality dies out of them, or is polished away as a barbarism" (132). Perhaps that is why most of the artists in *The Marble Faun* are copyists, reproducing the representations of others rather than creating "original" works of their own. A strong sense of artistic weariness permeates the novel, a sense that art has "wrought itself out, and come fairly to an end" (124). As the Eternal City, Rome has put the artists "at odds with Nature" and made it impossible for them to imitate her directly. Here art itself becomes a "second and stronger Nature . . . a stepmother, whose crafty tenderness has taught us to despise the bountiful and wholesome ministration of our true parent" (*MOM,* 247). Here "whenever man has hewn a stone, Nature forthwith relinquishes her right to it, and never lays her finger on it again. Age after age finds it bare and naked, in the barren sunshine, and leaves it so" (*MF,* 165). The result is works of art that "make us miserably desperate," "pathetic relics," and "dim ghosts," signs of the death of the body rather than "symbols of the living spirit" (303).

Seen from the perspective of Rome's ruins, culture no longer represents the noble dream of the reconciliation of spirit and world but stands as an example of the distance that separates man from his lost origins. *The Marble Faun* sets out to reveal the enchantments in which we live by exposing the spell of ruin that generates them all. Consider, for example, the grounds of the Villa Borghese which offer to "all who breathe the Roman air" an opportunity "to taste the languid enjoyment of the day-dream that they call life" (70). Here man has arranged the land-scape so artfully that his transforming powers seem to bring him closer to nature rather than to separate him from it. Here there is "enough of human care . . . bestowed long ago, and still bestowed, to prevent wildness from growing into deformity; and the result is an ideal landscape, a woodland scene, that seems to have been projected out of a poet's mind" (72). Here the "soft turf of a beautiful seclusion" (70) offers welcomed re-lief from the "stony-hearted streets" (75) of Rome. Here the "ancient dust, the mouldiness of Rome . . . the hard pavements, the smell of ruin, and decaying generations; the chill palaces, the convent-bells, the heavy incense of altars . . . [rise] from . . . consciousness like a cloud" (74). Consequently people of all social ranks and nationalities may meet and celebrate their shared freedom. No longer separated by artificial distinctions, they are able to participate in a "sylvan dance" which celebrates a new transparency and total reciprocity. "Here, as it seemed, had the Golden Age come back again, within the precincts of this sunny glade; thawing mankind out of their cold formali-ties; releasing them from irksome restraint; mingling them to-gether in such childlike gaiety, that new flowers . . . sprang up beneath their footsteps" (88).

Unfortunately, however, such visions of harmony are the re-sult of a mystification produced by the hallucinating air of a present freed from its ties to past and future. "Tomorrow will be time enough to come back to my reality," Miriam decides. "Is the past so indestructible?–the future so immitigable" (82)? And as she gives herself up to the "magic" (87) of the moment, reality seems transformed into fantasy. But this experience is no more than a delusion. The grounds of the "Suburban Villa" cannot duplicate the landscape of the unfallen world because they are the products of artifice and decay. "Scattered here and there, with

43

careless artifice, stand old alters, bearing Roman inscriptions.
... What a strange idea ... to construct artificial ruins in
Rome, the native soil of ruin! But even these sportive imitations, wrought by man in emulation of what Time has done to
temples and palaces, are perhaps centuries old" (72–73). As a result of this artifice, the grounds are "pensive, lovely, dreamlike,
enjoyable, and sad" (73). And adding to the "dreamlike melancholy that haunts the spot" (73) is malaria, a curse which insures
that it will never be the "home-scenery of any human being"
(73) for it can be safely visited only in winter and early spring.

Initially, then, the grounds were the product of a vision that
sought a partial reconciliation of man and nature through the
employment of a mild irony. They were designed not as a Quixotic attempt to recover a moment of lost plenitude but in an attempt to come to terms with that loss by reflecting on it. The
result is the creation of a place where man seeks partially to al-
leviate his alienation by indulging in a gentle nostalgia for the
lost unity. His "sportive imitations" of the effects of time, he
hopes, will place him outside those effects and protect him from
them. But this is a possibility that is put into question by the
narrator's description of the final moments of the sylvan dance.

> Or it [the dance] was like the sculptured scene on the front
> and sides of a sarcophagus, where, as often as any other de-
> vice, a festive procession mocks the ashes and white bones
> that are treasured up, within. You might take it for a
> marriage-pageant; but, after a while, if you look attentively at
> those merry-makers, following them from end to end of the
> marble coffin, you doubt whether their gay movement is lead-
> ing them to a happy close. ... Always, some tragic incident is
> shadowed forth, or thrust sidelong into the spectacle; and
> when once it has caught your eye, you can look no more at
> the festal portions of the scene, except with reference to this
> one slightly suggested doom and sorrow. (88–89).

Here art functions as a mystified defensive strategy that seeks to
offer an escape from the destructive effects of time. Like the

succession of discontinuous movements of the sylvan dance each of which "had a grace which might have been worth putting into marble, for the long delight of days to come" (85), the figures on the sarcophagus seem to imply the supremacy of art over nature through the transcendance of the effects of temporal duration. The "unweariable steps" (88) of the dancers mock the "Demon of Weariness" (336) who haunts the streets of Rome in the same way that the figures on the sarcophagus mock the "ashes and white bones" that it contains. However, at the very moment that man is celebrating his powers of renewal, the destructive forces of time are secretly at work. Death appears as a haunting shadow, as a disturbing echo or suggestion, and its presence disenchants, since from the point of view of death all human activity has the "character of fantasy" (90). "The spell being broken, it was now only that old tract of pleasure-ground, close by the people's gate of Rome; a tract where crimes and calamities of ages, the many battles, blood recklessly poured out, and deaths of myriads, have corrupted all the soil, creating an influence that makes the air deadly to human lungs" (90).

The "suburban Gardens," then, can offer no real escape from the threatening atmosphere of Rome. The "enchanted ground" (75) at best can provide no more than a moment's mystification, and the disenchantment that inevitably follows it invalidates the mildly ironic vision that produced the grounds in the first place. And once the spell is broken the pain of human relations overwhelms the effects of "careless artifice" (72).

A moment afterwards [after the appearance of Miriam's model], Donatello was aware that she had retired from the dance. He hastened towards her and flung himself on the grass, beside the stone-bench on which Miriam was sitting. But a strange distance and unapproachableness had all at once enveloped her; and, though he saw her within reach of his arm, yet the light of her eyes seemed as far off as that of a star; nor was there any warmth in the melancholy smile with which she regarded him. (89)

Donatello and Miriam have not been able to use the artificial gardens to bridge the "great chasm" (207) that separates them. He, it is true, is the representation of a happier time when a closer relationship with nature was possible and seems able even now to identify with the nonself, but that sense of identification can never lead him toward another person. Indeed it is his commitment to another self that destroys his identification with nature. However, an awareness of the distance between nature and self does not insure that interpersonal contacts will be easier to establish, although this is Donatello's and Miriam's initial assumption. Their shared glance that condemns the model, seems at first to establish a "new sympathy" that "annihilated all other ties" and "knits" their "heart-strings together" (175).

"I feel it Miriam," said Donatello. "We draw one breath; we live one life."

"Only yesterday," continued Miriam; "nay, only a short half-hour ago, I shivered in icy solitude. No friendship, no sisterhood, could come near enough to keep the warmth within my heart. In an instant, all is changed. There can be no more loneliness." (175)

As with their experience at the "Suburban Villa," however, this sense of wholeness is a delusion, the result of a "moment of rapture" that ends with the appearance of the corpse of their victim. At this point Miriam can no longer "bring his mind into sympathy with hers" (197), and her words of love and devotion are met with a "heavy silence" (198).

But if human separateness cannot be overcome either by distancing oneself through art from the destructive forces of life or by violating civilization's laws of restraint, perhaps the forms and usages of culture can themselves be used to mediate between isolated selves. Miriam and Donatello explore this possibility when they participate in the "scenic and ceremonial" (436) carnival near the end of the novel. Having failed in their earlier attempts in the suburban villa to transform themselves into faun and nymph, they now adorn themselves with masks and costumes and become "the Peasant and the Contadina" (439). Perhaps the "sympathetic mirth" (438) of others, the "sympathetic exhiliaration of so many people's cheerfulness" (324) will enable them to bridge the distance that separates them. In contrast to the magic of the sylvan dance which thaws the participants out of their cold formalities and mingles them together in a "childlike gaiety" (88), the spell of the carnival seeks to unite people by recognizing and exaggerating the distance that separates them from nature and each other. Here one finds "orangoutangs; bear-headed, bull-headed, and dog-headed individuals; faces that would have been human, but for their enormous noses . . . and all other imaginable kinds of monstrosity and exaggeration"(446). These disguises hardly represent nostalgic attempts to recover the lost resemblance between man and nature. Rather they imply a comic recognition of the differences between the two realms and are an implicit affirmation of the superiority of the human. People are brought closer together when any assertion of a resemblance between the human and natural is made to seem untenable. In a similar way, the other costumes and masks, which from the point of view of unclothed nature imply human separateness and civilized restraint, in the context of the carnival suggest relief from the burdens of class and profession and protection from the dangers of the threatening gaze of others, for they allow individuals to form a "mad, merry stream of human life" (439).

However, the carnival, too, is the product of a deceitful magic that covers a "stern and black reality" with "fanciful thoughts" (428) and the "sympathetic mirth" (438) that it generates is "like our self-deceptive pretense of jollity at a threadbare joke" (437). The sugar-plums that the participants throw at one another "were concocted mostly of lime, with a grain of oat or some other worthless kernal in the midst" (439), and the carnival flowers, which have been "gathered and tied up by sordid hands," are "wilted," "muddy," and "defiled . . . with the wicked filth of Rome" (440). The carnival, in short, is the "emptiest of mockeries" (437) composed of a host of absurd figures who in "pretending to sympathize" (446) with one another only make more obvious the absence of any real sympathy. Miriam, a participant in the "sad frolic" (446), hides a "tear-stained face" beneath her mask and speaks with a "profound sadness in her tone" (448). Appropriately, she and Donatello are arrested by the authorities at the height of the revelry, and their arrest is misinterpreted as "some frolic of the Carnival, carried a little too far" (451).

A deceiving magic is present too in the activities of the Catholic Church. Like the carnival, it is "traditionary not actual" (436) and is "alive, this present year, only because it has existed through centuries gone by" (436). It stands, therefore, as another example of absence, for it has lost the "dignity and holiness of its origins" (345). In the place of "genuine medicants" (345) for the sick soul, it can offer only "cordials" (344) and "sedatives" (345). St. Peter's Cathedral contains no "cure . . . for a sick soul, but it would make an admirable atmospheric hospital for sick bodies" (369). And the deceitful magic that seeks to substitute the physical for the spiritual also attempts to transform a theocentric relationship into an interpersonal one.

Hilda saw peasants, citizens, soldiers, nobles, women with bare heads, ladies in their silks, entering the churches, individually, kneeling for moments, or for hours, and directing their inaudible devotions to the shrine of some Saint of their own choice. In his hallowed person, they felt themselves possessed of an own friend in Heaven. They were too humble to approach the Deity directly. Conscious of their unworthiness, they asked the mediation of their sympathizing patron, who, on the score of his ancient martyrdom, and after many ages of celestial life, might venture to talk with the Divine Presence almost as friend with friend. (346–47)

The sympathy generated by such a relationship is as much a mystification as that produced by the sylvan dance and the carnival.

Donatello kneeling in the public square of Perugia in front of the statue of Pope Julius the Third receives the "bronze Pontiff's benediction" (315) as he seems by his "look and gesture" (324) to approve the young Italian's union with Miriam, only to be separated from her and imprisoned by the "priestly rulers" (465) of Rome. Similarly, Hilda, seeking relief from her troubled conscience, receives the benediction of the old priest who hears her confession and later becomes a "prisoner" (466) in the convent of the Sacre-Couer watched over by that same priest. The forms of the church, in other words, no longer derive authority from a higher power; its "mighty machinery" (345) is managed by human engineers, and it operates in a world where things have lost their analogical senses. High and low no longer indicate the directions of salvation and damnation; the Palazzo del Torre does not "sink into the earth" (400) when the lamp of the virgin is extinguished, as a priest had insisted that it would. Hilda's tower is no more symbolic than Donatello's. One is a "dove-cote" (54), the other an "owl-tower" (252), one a shrine to the virgin, the other a "strong-hold of times long past" (215), and both are "square," "lofty," and "massive" (51, 214), and Kenyon, standing in one tower, is reminded of the other "turret that ascended into the sky of the summer afternoon" (264). The point, of course, is that neither Hilda's tower with the shrine and doves nor Donatello's with the crucifix and death's head allows them to avoid sin or to deal with its consequences. Both structures mock man's "feeble efforts to soar upward" (256), for they imply the absence of any sort of hierarchy. Donatello finds relief only when he leaves his ancestral tower for the crowded marketplace of Perugia and Hilda comes "down from her old tower, to be herself enshrined and worshipped as a household Saint, in the light of her husband's fireside" (461).

The actions of the fallen innocents, then, seem to suggest that the problem of distance can be solved if it is at first secularized. Perhaps the other attempts to overcome it fail because it is seen as a lack, an emptiness, the result of a loss rather than an indication of "human promise" (461). Perhaps what people must do is to renounce the towers, the ceremonies, and representations of the old world, which in seeking to overcome absence only succeed in signifying it, and turn with Hilda and Kenyon toward the new world. To make that turn, however, is to abandon the interpretive enterprise altogether. Near the end of the novel, Kenyon, whose interest in Donatello is the source of the narrator's, offers an interpretation of the meaning of his friend's adventures.

It seems the moral of his story, that human beings, of Donatello's character, compounded especially for happiness, have no longer any business on earth, or elsewhere. Life has grown so sadly serious, that such men must change their nature, or else perish, like the antediluvian creatures that required, as the condition of their existence, a more summer-like atmosphere than ours. (459–60)

Hilda, however, who is "hopeful and happy-natured" (460), rejects his interpretation as too dark, and Kenyon, who loves her, willingly abandons it and offers instead a reading based on Miriam's interpretation of Donatello.

"Then, here is another; take your choice!" said the sculptor, remembering what Miriam had recently suggested, in reference to the same point. "He perpetrated a great crime; and his remorse, gnawing into his soul, had awakened it; developing a thousand high capabilities, moral and intellectual, which we never should have dreamed of asking for, within the scanty compass of the Donatello whom we knew."
. . . .
"Here comes my perplexity," continued Kenyon. "Sin has educated Donatello, and elevated him. Is sin, then . . . like Sorrow, merely an element of human education, through which we struggle to a higher and purer state than we could otherwise have attained? Did Adam fall, that we might ultimately rise to a far loftier Paradise than his?" (460)

But Hilda, "shocked . . . beyond words," by a theory which makes a "mockery . . . not only of all religious sentiment, but of moral law" (460) rejects this interpretation more emphatically than she had the first. At this point Kenyon abandons his interpretive quest altogether, faces the meaninglessness of his exiled condition, and looks to Hilda to provide a ground for his existence.

I never did believe it [his interpretation]! But the mind wanders wild and wide; and, so lonely as I live and work, I have neither pole-star above, nor light of cottage-windows here below, to bring me home. Were you my guide, my counsellor, my inmost friend, with that white wisdom which clothes you as with a celestial garment, all would go well. Oh, Hilda, guide me home. (460–61)

Here, as at the end of the *The House of the Seven Gables,* the enchantment of love is offered in the place of an unequivocal interpretation of the novel's meaning. Hilda does not solve Kenyon's problems, but she smoothes them away, leading him to project on the rest of the world the light of his own happiness. To him the world now seems full of human promise, and he plans to turn his back on the problem of the meaning of Donatello's adventures and return to his "own land" (461). The narrator, however, puts the dream of the lovers' happiness into question by pointing to the possibility that at their return they may discover that their "native air has lost its invigorating quality, and that life has shifted its reality to the spot where we have deemed ourselves only temporary residents" (461). He recognizes, in other words, that the idea of a home, a "house and moderate garden-spot of one's own" (*HSG,* 156) is as much an ideal out of reach, as much "beyond the scope of man's actual possessions" (*MF,* 73) as is the possibility of an unequivocal interpretation.

The ending of *The Marble Faun,* then, seems to validate Kenyon's earlier assertion that the "seven-branched golden candlestick, the holy candlestick of the Jews," which is capable of providing the "whole world . . . the illumination which it needs" (370–71), is lost forever. Nor can the flickering light of the domestic fireside serve as an adequate substitute, for it is not capable of illuminating the "sevenfold sepulchral gloom" (462) cast by the Etruscan bracelet that Miriam sends Hilda as a bridal gift.

Still there is the possibility that the narrator may be able to provide the answers that his characters seek unsuccessfully. Although his position is not the privileged one of the "disembodied listener" (*HSG*, 30) of *The House of the Seven Gables* since he is at times seen as well as seeing, he is nevertheless able to cross the distance that separates Miriam, Hilda, Kenyon, and Donatello one from the other, to view the conduct of each "from his own point of view, or from any side-point" (*MF,* 385). Perhaps this ability will allow him to offer a final and complete interpretation of Donatello's adventures. Unfortunately, however, the narrator knows little more about his characters than they know of each other. For example, he overhears part of a private conversation between Miriam and her mysterious Model that takes place in the solitude of the Borghese Grove, but the fragments of speech that he hears makes their relationship not less but more inscrutable.

Owning, it may be, to this moral estrangement—this chill remoteness of their position—there have come to us but a few vague whisperings of what passed in Miriam's interview, that afternoon, with the sinister personage who had dogged her footsteps ever since the visit to the catacomb. In weaving these mystic utterances into a continuous scene, we undertake a task resembling, in its perplexity, that of gathering up and piecing together the fragments of a letter, which has been torn and scattered to the winds. Many words of deep significance—many entire sentences, and these possibly the most important ones—have flown too far on the winged breeze, to be recovered. If we insert our own conjectural amendments, we perhaps give a purport utterly at variance with the true one. Yet, unless we attempt something in this way, there must remain

an unsightly gap, and a lack of continuousness and dependence in our narrative; so that it would arrive at certain inevitable catastrophes without due warning of their imminence.
(92–93)

The problem of writing is a problem of revealing significant
connections and relations, of unraveling and reweaving the myriad threads of human lives. The "life line[s]" of the characters
whose fates are to form the figure in the tapestry of *The Marble
Faun* are, like those of Miriam and her Model, knotted and
"twisted" (259) together: "Our fates cross and are entangled. The
threads are twisted into a strong cord, which is dragging us to an
evil doom. Could the knots be severed, we might escape. But
neither can your slender fingers untie those knots, nor my masculine force break them" (95) Like the air of Rome which is "full
of kindred melodies that encountered one another, and twined
themselves into a broad, vague music, out of which no single
strain could be disentangled" (163), the "miserable entangled"
(332) lives of the characters do not offer an intelligible pattern.
The connections between them are tangled rather than significant ones, and the narrator must unravel and reweave the
threads of relationship so that random lines of action are made
to form a single structure. And this is as much a process of reading and interpretation as a process of writing, for it is also the
one that is used to discover the significance of both natural symbols and allegorical structures. An "old grape-vine . . . clinging
fast around its supporting tree" has a "moral" that "you might
twist . . . to more than one grave purpose, as you saw how the
knotted, serpentine growth imprisoned within its strong embrace the friend that had supported its tender infancy" (291),
and the "series of frescoes" on the walls of the Monti Beni house
are "bound together" by the "links of an allegory . . . which it
would be impossible, or, at least, very wearisome to unravel"
(227).

However, as the above passage implies, to unravel or untangle
may be to tear or break, and hence in the novel the themes of

tangling and fragmenting are joined. As a romance of Rome, it is a narrative pieced together from "Fragmentary Sentences," for that city is a place of "strewn fragments of antique statues, headless and legless torsos, and busts that have invariably lost . . . the nose" (37), a "confusion of pillars, arches, pavements, and shattered blocks and shafts—the crumbs of various ruin, dropt from the devouring maw of Time" (164), a place where the forms of Western culture "fall asunder" into a "heap of worthless fragments" (424), "pathetic relics" (303) that are no more than "broken rubbish" (110). The writer, therefore, through the magic of his art must try to convert a "heap of forlorn fragments into a whole" (423) so that the fragmentation will be replaced by a formal and thematic continuity, unconnected pieces joined together in a carefully structured narrative. Needless to say the pattern produced by such novelistic weaving is likely to be both fragile and unconvincing.

The Gentle Reader, we trust, would not thank us for one of those minute elucidations, which are so tedious, and, after all, so unsatisfactory, in clearing up the romantic mysteries of a story. He is too wise to insist upon looking closely at the wrong side of the tapestry, after the right one has been sufficiently displayed to him, woven with the best of the artist's skill, and cunningly arranged with a view to the harmonious exhibition of its colours. If any brilliant, or beautiful, or even tolerable, effect have been produced, this pattern of kindly Readers will accept it at its worth, without tearing its web apart, with the idle purpose of discovering how its threads have been knit together; for the sagacity, by which he is distinguished, will long ago have taught him that any narrative of human action and adventure—whether we call it history or romance—is certain to be a fragile handiwork, more easily rent than mended. (455)

To seek the meaning of his story, the narrator implies here, is to violate it in some way, to tear it, or perhaps change it, for narratives are fragile structures whose beautiful effects must be accepted at face value. However the "beautiful . . . effect" that the writer works to produce is that which invites the very violence he deplores, for it is the "gleam of beauty" that "induce[s] the beholder to attempt unravelling" the "scheme and purport" (306) of its figures. In a postlapsarian world there is no innocent reading, no intuitive understanding that can grasp the "inestimable something, that constitutes the life and soul" (60) of the work of art without disturbing its surface. There is, in short, no Gentle Reader. That "all-sympathizing critic" (1), that "Gentle, Kind, Benevolent, Indulgent, and most Beloved and Honored Reader" (2) belongs to that time of lost plenitude, that "Golden Age, before mankind was burdened with sin and sorrow" (84). He has now "withdrawn to the Paradise of Gentle Readers" and is available if at all only in the form of "some mossy gravestone, inscribed with a half-obliterated name, which I shall never recognize" (2). The death of the Gentle Reader, then, is the equivalent for the narrator of the loss of sympathy that he recounts in his narrative, a loss which in his case as in those of his characters complicates the problems of representing and interpreting. He, too, is an exile who looks to "ceremony" to help replace the "apprehensive sympathy" (2) that once bound writer and reader together and in the process discovers that ruin must be the source of his creativity.

The story of his loss is narrated in the preface to *The Marble Faun*, which is, like the novel itself, a nostalgic lament for a lost world of sympathetic involvement. It begins with a backward glance toward earlier prefaces that were "addressed nominally to the Public at large," but were really intended for that "one congenial friend . . . that all-sympathizing critic" (1) who was to receive the "scrolls which I flung upon whatever wind was blowing in the faith that they would find him out" (2). But now since he no longer is able to "presume upon the existence of that friend of friends, that unseen brother of the soul, whose apprehensive sympathy . . . encouraged [him] to be egotistical in [his] Prefaces," he will replace the "familiar" with the ceremonial and curtain himself off from the reader. "I stand upon ceremony, now, and, after stating a few particulars about the work which is here offered to the Public, must make my most reverential bow, and retire behind the curtain" (2).

However, it is worth noting that the pre-texts, which from Hawthorne's present perspective seem to embody a lost plenitude, specifically reject that possibility. In "The Old Manse" he denies being one of those writers who "serve up their own hearts delicately fried, with brainsauce, as a tidbit for their beloved public" (*MOM*, 33), and in "The Custom House" he rejects the practice of those authors who "indulge themselves in such confidential depths of revelation as could fittingly be addressed, only and exclusively, to the one heart and mind of perfect sympathy; as if the printed book, thrown at large on the wide world, were certain to find out the divided segment of the writer's own nature, and complete the circle of his existence by bringing him into communication with it" (*SL*, 3–4). Indeed, as I have argued elsewhere, most of Hawthorne's prefaces suggest that the creative energy of romance derives from a tension between the hidden and the shown, that it, like the scarlet A, can reveal and conceal simultaneously, thereby making it possible for a writer to speak to a potentially hostile audience about matters of which silence is the safest form of expression and for the reader to respond to his words without the fear of becoming his mystified victim.[7]

In the preface to *The Marble Faun* these earlier strategies of indirection are replaced by a myth of original innocence and loss that nostalgically posits a moment when writer and reader were free of the burden of interpretation and reduces the present to a barren world of ruins and fragments that cannot be shaped into an ordered and consistent form and hence precludes any interpretive dialogue between writer and reader. Although this preface echoes earlier ones in denying any attempt "to describe local manners" (*HSG*, 3) and in pointing to the importance of establishing a "poetic or fairy precinct" (*MF*, 3) that will provide a "foothold between fiction and reality" (*BR*, 2) the emphasis is significantly different. The focus falls not on the question of how to "dream strange things, and make them look like truth" (*SL,* 36), not on the mysterious process of "creating the semblance of a world out of airy matter" (37), but rather on the more prosaic problem of revision. The romance is "sketched out" in Italy, is "rewritten and prepared for the press in England" (*MF,* 2), and it is this process of "reproducing the book, on the broad and dreary sands of Redcar, with the gray German Ocean tumbling in upon me, and the northern blast always howling in my ears" (3) that dominates the preface. And this process is not one of transforming substance into shadow, of building castles in the air but of trying to manage the "realities of the moment" (*HSG,* 3). For the "actual reminiscences," which in earlier work had been used simply to give a "more lifelike tint to the fancy-sketch" (*BR,* 1) now become primary. The "various Italian objects, antique, pictorial, and statuesque" that "fill the mind everywhere in Italy . . . cannot easily be kept from flowing out upon the page" (*MF,* 3), and it is these "Italian reminicences" (3), "reminiscences . . . broken into fragments, and hopelessly intermingled" (24), that dominate in *The Marble Faun.* As Thomas Woodson has observed, the novel is pervasively indebted to *The French and Italian Notebooks.* Nine-tenths of its chapters include material taken directly from the *Notebooks,* and some consist almost entirely of such material.[8] Moreover, the notebooks themselves are filled with the same sense of weariness and despair that pervades the novel, a weariness brought on both by the Roman scene and the act of writing itself.

From the beginning of his writing career Hawthorne had associated romance with the "old countries" (*BR,* 1) and with the idea of a "Faery Land, so like the real world, that, in a suitable remoteness, one cannot well tell the difference . . . " (*BR,* 2), but he now comes to see that such a realm depends on ruin and death. "Romance and poetry . . . need ruin to make them grow" (*MF,* 3), and "there is reason to suspect that a people are waning to decay and ruin, the moment that their life becomes fascinating either in the poet's imagination or the painter's eye" (296). Moreover, if any "gloom within the heart corresponds to the

spell of ruin, that has been thrown over the site of ancient em-
pire," if there is "ruin in your heart" (409), then "all of the ponderous gloom of the Roman Past will pile itself upon that spot,
and crush you down" (410), as a "mean reality" thrusts itself
"through life's brightest illusions" (303).

> Standing amid so much ancient dust, it is difficult to spare the
> reader the commonplaces of enthusiasm, on which hundreds
> of tourists have already insisted. Over this half-worn pave-
> ment, and beneath this Arch of Titus, the Roman armies had
> trodden in their outward march, to fight battles, a world's
> width away. Returning, victorious, with royal captives and
> inestimable spoil, a Roman Triumph, that most gorgeous pag-
> eant of earthly pride, had streamed and flaunted, in hundred-
> fold succession, over these same flag-stones, and through this
> yet stalwart archway. It is politic, however, to make few allu-
> sions to such a Past; nor, if we would create an interest in the
> characters of our story, is it wise to suggest how Cicero's foot
> may have stept on yonder stone, nor how Horace was wont to
> stroll near by, making his footsteps chime with the measure of
> the ode that was ringing in his mind. The very ghosts of that
> massive and stately epoch have so much density, that the ac-
> tual people of to-day seem the thinner of the two, and stand
> more ghostlike by the arches and columns, letting the rich
> sculpture be discerned through their ill-compacted substance.
> (159–60)

This passage is interesting because of the way that it both suggests and reverses a number of familiar Hawthornian themes.
Here, as in the prefaces to *The Scarlet Letter* and *The Blithedale
Romance*, Hawthorne focuses on the problem of the ontological status of his characters and the nature of his reader's response
to them. But the difficulties here do not derive from the writer's
attempt to "fling [himself] back into another age" (*SL*, 37) or
from his concern that the "beings of imagination will be com-
pelled to show themselves in the same category as actually
living mortals; a necessity that generally renders the paint and

pasteboard of their composition too painfully discernible" (*BR*, 2). The reverse is true. Here the past imposes itself with the same insistence that the present had done at the Custom House. There the "petty and wearisome incidents" of "daily life" had "tarnished" the "mirror" of the writer's "imagination" (*SL*, 34), making it impossible for him to give life to "dead corpses" (34) "imparted" to him by Surveyor Pue's "ghostly hand" (33). But here it is the past that renders the present fragile and insubstantial that fills the mind and flows upon the page with such mass and density that it makes a ghost of the writer's own voice. "Side by side with the massiveness of the Roman Past, all matters, that we handle or dream of, now-a-days, look evanescent and visionary alike" (*MF,* 6). So it is that the "four individuals . . . whose fortunes" are "to interest the reader" (5) seem inconsequential in Rome, for, like the "Demon of Weariness, who haunts great picture-galleries," the city possesses the "magic that is the destruction of all other magic" (336).

The romancer, then, becomes the victim of that city that gives romance its name, as his art is overwhelmed and disenchanted by the objects that "fill the mind everywhere in Italy," objects that possess a "malignant spell" (338) that "puts people in mind of their earthly necessities and incites them to defile therewith whatever temple, column, ruined palace or triumphal arch may be nearest at hand" (*FIN,* 480–81). In this context the creatures of the imagination lose their interest and significance. The characters whose fortunes are to interest the reader are introduced "standing in . . . the sculpture-gallery in the Capitol, at Rome" (5), a place Hawthorne describes in the *Notebooks* as having "always had a dreary and depressing effect on me" (*FIN,* 511) and their story is concluded (in a parallel chapter that bears the same title as the first) in the Pantheon which "stands almost at the central point of the labyrinthine intricacies of the modern city, and often presents itself before the bewildered stranger, when he is in search of other objects" (*MF,* 456).[9] The setting, in short, overwhelms the story, the fragmented events of which "never explain themselves, either as regards their origin or their tendency" (455). The text that is discontinuously woven from fragmentary sentences may have no magic in its web, and its reader, therefore, may be led to unravel it motivated only by the "idle purpose of discovering how its threads have been knit together" (455).

THREE

The Entangled Text:
Pierre *and the*
Romance of Reading

Every book is a quotation; and
every house is a quotation out
of all the forests and mines and
stone quarries; and every man is a quotation from all his ancestors.

The originals are not original. There is imitation, model, and suggestion, to the very archangels, if we knew their history. The first book
tyrannizes over the second. Read Tasso, and you think of Virgil; read
Virgil, and you think of Homer; and Milton forces you to reflect
how narrow are the limits of human invention. The Paradise Lost
had never existed but for these precursors.

—Ralph Waldo Emerson, "Quotation and Originality"

I shudder at the idea of the ancient Egyptians. It was in these pyramids that was conceived the idea of Jehovah . . . Moses learned in all
the lore of the Egyptians. The idea of Jehovah born here.

Man seems to have had as little to do with it as Nature. It was that
supernatural creature, the priest. . . . And one seems to see that as out
of the crude forms of the natural earth they could evoke by art the
transcendent mass & symtry & . . . . . of the pyramid so out of
the rude elements of the insignificant thoughts that are in all men,
they could rear the transcendent conception of a God.

—Herman Melville, *Journal Up the Straits*

For Melville, as for Hawthorne, romance is the formal expression of a thematics of reading and writing, but Melville is free of the Hawthornian nostalgia for a "Gentle," "Indulgent" reader and a "prim old author." For him both writers and readers seek to break free of the prescriptions of generic conventions and literary institutions. "Hawthorne and His Mosses" unambiguously celebrates both writing and reading as distinguished, productive, and unconventional activities. The narrator is "seized" by Hawthorne's "wild, witch voice" (HHM, 556), "spun . . . round about in a web of dreams" by his "soft ravishments" (537–38), but the "spell" (538) of his first reading response generates a sense of Hawthorne's "dimly-discernible greatness" rather than a "blind, unbridled admiration" (542). And this is an insight "mostly, insinuated to those who may best understand it, and account for it; it is not obtruded upon every one alike" (543). It is the "eagle-eyed reader" (549) who, on second reading, will "[pick] up many things here and there" (548) that "deceive . . . the superficial skimmer of pages" (549) and use these "clews" (539) to initiate a "curious and elaborate analysis" (540).

Creative reading, in short, leads to creative writing. Composed during the period when Melville was hard at work on *Moby-Dick*, "Hawthorne and His Mosses" implies a direct and unambiguous link between Shakespeare and Hawthorne and records the positive effects of both writers on Melville, effects that are clearly discernible in the novel he was about to dedicate to Hawthorne. However, important if unacknowledged problems exist in the essay. At the same time that Melville records the effects of Hawthorne's spell on his imagination and celebrates Shakespeare's "Great Art of Telling the Truth" (542), he also "boldly contemn[s] all imitation, though it comes to us graceful and fragrant as the morning; and foster[s] all originality, though, at first, it be crabbed and ugly as our own pine knots" (546). The essay, then, raises, only to ignore, the problems of derivation: authority and priority, tradition and the individual talent, literary fathers and sons.

These issues become, I will argue, the enabling themes that

generate the troubling eccentricities of *Pierre*. And they continue as the central concerns of "The Piazza" (Melville's subversive version of Hawthorne's "familiar kind of preface"), a sketch that situates itself not only in relation to the stories it introduces but also in reference to Melvilles' previously published works. A revaluation by Melville of his personal and literary past, including his ambivalent relation to Hawthorne, it offers a detailed critique of conventional romance and provides a useful entrance to the labyrinths of *Pierre*. The sketch is filled with echoes and allusions, haunting presences from Hawthorne's prefaces—in particular the preface to *Mosses from an Old Manse*[1]—from Melville's earlier enthusiastic review of that volume, from Shakespeare's plays, from *The Faerie Queene*, from Tennyson's poetry, from Melville's own novels, from the Bible, from *The Pilgrim's Progress*. And all these blend together to disturb the clarity and meaning of the narrative voice. For almost every statement is twisted or redirected by the other voices that speak through it, with the result that the present seems troubled by a past that can only manifest itself as a disturbing ghostlike presence.

But, even in December, this northern piazza does not repel—nipping cold and gusty though it be, and the north wind, like any miller, bolting by the snow, in finest flour—for then, once more, with frosted beard, I pace the sleety deck, weathering Cape Horn.

In summer, too, Canute-like, sitting here, one is often *reminded* of the sea. For not only do long ground-swells roll the slanting grain, and little wavelets of the grass ripple over upon the low piazza, as their beach, and the blown down of dandelions is wafted like the spray, and the purple of the mountains is just the purple of the billows, and a still August noon broods upon the deep meadows, as a calm upon the Line; but the vastness and the lonesomeness are so oceanic, and the silence and the sameness, too, that the first peep of a strange house, rising beyond the trees, is for all the world like spying, on the Barbary coast, an unknown sail.

And this *recalls* my inland voyage to fairy-land. A true
voyage; but take it all in all, interesting as if invented. (P, 3)

This curious passage (italics mine) suggests one of the movements of the sketch. At work here is a process of recall and substitution that results in a progressive movement or turning from
literal toward figurative meaning. Initiating the movement is the
desire to use the memories of an adventurous past to revitalize a
"time of failing faith and feeble knees" (2). But the effect of the
turn is to emphasize the distance that separates that past from a
wearisome present, for words here seem used in improper
senses, to have wandered from their rightful places.[2] The beginning of the passage is governed by the substitution of ship for
piazza, made possible by an analogy that emerges from the
phrase "sleety deck," to bridge the gap between imagination and
action. But that association is introduced by another composed
of elements that are less compatible. The figure that associates
the north wind with a miller is borrowed by Melville from *The
Winter's Tale,* where a lady's hand is described as "soft and white
as fann'd snow that's bolted / By northern blasts twice o'er"
(4.4.373–75); but he changes Shakespeare's figure in a way that
disturbs its logic and initiates a series of asymmetrical substitutions. In Melville's rearrangement the primary meaning of the
word "bolting" seems to be that of moving suddenly or quickly,
and the sense of "bolting" as sifting that controls the logic of
Shakespeare's figure is present here as a secondary meaning only
because of the proximity of the words "miller" and "flour." The
image suggested is that of a figure covered with snow in the
same way a miller is covered by the flour he sifts, and that
figure, in turn, suggests the narrator with his "frosted beard."
But this is a series of associations generated by a sort of sliding
process rather than by poetic logic, and the result is to reduce
the persuasive power of the figures. Hence the passage goes on
to acknowledge that the seagoing past belongs exclusively to
memory, and the attempt to reexperience and represent that
past can only lead to disenchantment as the author's strained

attempt to turn landscape into seascape is linked to King Canute's effort to stop the rising tide. The reference here is probably to Thackeray's satirical ballad on the subject in his parody of *Ivanhoe,* entitled *Rebecca and Rowena,* where the "sick and tired and weary" king surrounded by flatterers, tormented by a troubled conscience and visions of his approaching death, sinks into his "great chair" and tests the power of his divine authority by commanding the ocean to retreat.[3] Many of the complexities surrounding the reference to Canute must await the consideration of a set of related allusions, but we can notice at this point that it contaminates the narrator's attempt poetically to transfigure the landscape by suggesting that his effort has its source not in the memory of a lived experience but in other texts. The emphasis in the passage falls on the relations among literary works (*The Winter's Tale,* Thackeray's satire, *Ivanhoe,* Melville's sketch) and on the power these entities possess to generate others that displace and represent them. This process of displacement is a major issue in the account of the inland voyage that is the subject of "The Piazza."

As the title of the collection suggests, the piazza is a figure for the creative source or origin of the tales, and the journey recounted in the introductory sketch is a metaphor for the experience of the writer during the act of creation. In this sense it clearly follows the example of Hawthorne in the "Custom House" and "Old Manse" sketches, both of which focus on the complex motives behind the acts of writing and reading. But whereas Hawthorne's explanation of these issues is carried out in the "transparent obscurity" of a nostalgia for a lost Spenserian world of enchantment and for an "honored reader" who, having been "ushered into [the author's] study" (*MOM,* 34) graciously receives the "bouquet" of "tales and essays" which had "blossomed like flowers in the calm summer of [his] heart and mind" (35), Melville's explanation sweeps away the "mirage haze" created by that perspective and replaces it with an atmosphere that systematically disenchants.

The Hawthornian point of view is suggested by Melville's

epigraph from *Cymbeline,* the introductory lines to a sentimental, elegiac speech:

> With fairest flowers,
> Whilst summer lasts and I live here, Fidele,
> I'll sweeten thy sad grave: thou shalt not lack
> The Flower that's like thy face, pale primrose;
> The azur'd harebell, like thy veins; no, nor
> The leaf of eglatine, whom not to slander,
> Out-sweeten'd not thy breath: the ruddock would,
> With charitable bill,—O bill sore shaming
> Those rich-left heirs that let their fathers lie
> Without a monument.—bring thee all this;
> Yea, and furr'd moss besides, when flowers are none,
> To winter-ground thy corse.
>
> (4.2.219–28)

These lines would seem to suggest that the sketch and the tales
that it introduces are, like Hawthorne's "tales and essays,"
which remind him of "flowers pressed between the leaves of a
book" (34), reminiscences that commemorate the spirit of a
place or person. However, the scene in *Cymbeline* to which Melville alludes is richly ironic, filled with delusions and misread-
ings. The speaker in the passage is Arvirigus, a king's son who
believes himself a "rustic Mountaineer" (4.2.100) and who mis-
takenly mourns the death of a man who is his sister in disguise
and who is drugged but not dead. Even his words are equivocated in his brother's answer:

> Prithee, have done;
> And do not play in wench-like words with that
> Which is so serious. Let us bury him,
> And not protract with admiration what
> Is now due debt to the grave.
>
> (4.2.230–33)

The relation between these two speeches suggests the movement and theme of "The Piazza," for it points to the inauthenticity of literary language, and the sketch both invokes and subverts such a language. The artificial and conventional nature of its world is apparent in the description of the landscape as a "picture" that is in turn copied by the "sun-burnt painters painting there" (1). And the sense of the cultivated picturesque is enhanced by the narrator's assertion that the piazza serves much as a bench in a picture gallery, "for what but picture-galleries are the marble halls of these limestone hills?—galleries hung, month after month anew, with pictures ever fading into pictures ever fresh" (2). The piazza, in short, is a structure that represents an artistic or literary point of view and suggests the sentimental possibility of a happy reciprocity between man and nature. It is a place that combines the "coziness of indoors with the freedom of outdoors," an "easy chair" that allows a leisurely and appreciative view of nature's "purple prospect." Seen from the piazza land becomes landscape as the viewer seems in unison with grass, birds, flowers, and moutains. Nature here, to paraphrase Sartre, is social and literary myth, for natural objects easily become intentional ones by way of figurative language.

Whoever built the house, he builded better than he knew; or else Orion in the zenith flashed down his Damocles' sword to him some starry night, and said, "Build there." For how, otherwise, could it have entered the builder's mind that, upon the clearing being made, such a purple prospect would be his?—nothing less than Greylock, with all his hills about him, like Charlemagne among his peers. (1)

The narrator's language here suggests an authority that is at once creative and benevolent, but he then goes on to undermine that sense of an originating power by extending the dimensions of his metaphor.

During the first year of my residence, the more leisurely to witness the coronation of Charlemagne (weather permitting, they crown him every sunrise and sunset), I chose me, on the hill-side bank nearby, a royal lounge of turf—a green velvet lounge, with long, moss-padded back; while at the head, strangely enough, there grew (but, I suppose, for heraldry) three tufts of blue violets in a field-argent of wild strawberries; and a trellis, with honeysuckle, I set for canopy. Very majestical lounge, indeed. So much so, that here, as with the reclining majesty of Denmark in his orchard, a sly ear-ache invaded me. But, if damps abound at times in Westminster Abbey, because it is so old, why not within this monastery of mountains, which is older?

A piazza must be had. (2)

Worth noting here is the fact that the earlier association of Greylock with Charlemagne has solidified into a mode of vision that affects the narrator's view of himself no less than his view of the surrounding landscape. For he has come to associate himself and his authorship with the authority of emperors and kings who "had the casting vote, and voted for themselves" (3). However, as the above passage goes on to suggest, the metaphor that generates the elaborate images of royalty and heraldry and suggests an idyllic relation between man and nature is not sufficient to maintain the autonomy of the figurative perspective. The allusion to *Hamlet* introduces an association that sharply subverts the sense of stately dignity and authority.

> Sleeping within mine orchard,
> My custom always of the afternoon,
> Upon my secure hour thy uncle stole,
> With juice of cursed hebona in a vial,
> And in the porches of mine ears did pour
> The lep'rous distilment; whose effect
> Hold such an enmity with blood of man
> That swift as quicksilver it courses through
> The natural gates and alleys of the body,
> And with a sudden vigour it doth posset

And curd, like eager droppings into milk,
The thin and wholesome blood; so it did mine,
And a most instant tetter bark'd about,
Most lazar-like, with vile and loathsome crust,
All my smooth body.

(1.5.59–73)

This ghostly voice discloses others, for the orchard of the "reclining majesty of Denmark" at once invokes and contaminates
Hawthorne's description of the one at the Old Manse, where
the trees possess a "domestic character" and suggest an "infinite
generosity and exhaustless bounty on the part of our Mother nature" (12); as well as Melville's interpretation of that orchard in
"Hawthorne and His Mosses" as the "visible type of the fine
mind that described it." The "spell" operating in the "The
Piazza" differs markedly from the one Melville earlier had
found working in "The Old Manse."

Stretched on that new mown clover, the hill-side breeze blowing over me through the wide barn door, and soothed by the
hum of bees in the meadows around, how magically stole over
me this Mossy Man! And how amply, how bountifully, did he
redeem that delicious promise to his guests in the Old Manse,
of whom it is written—"Others could give them pleasure, or
amusement, or instruction—these could be picked up anywhere—but it was for me to give them rest. Rest, in a life of
trouble! What better could be done for weary and world-worn
spirits? What better could be done for anybody, who came
within our magic circle, than to throw the spell of a magic
spirit over him?" So all that day, half-buried in the new clover,
I watched this Hawthorne's "Assyrian dawn, and Paphian sunset and moonrise, from the summit of our Eastern Hill."
(HHM, 537)

The horrible transformation described in the *Hamlet* passage
stands in stark contrast to and undermines the idyllic language
of the texts to which it is linked metaleptically. As we move

from the body of the leprous king to the guests at the Old Manse "stretched among the shadows of the orchard" (28), then to the reclining narrator of "Hawthorne and His Mosses," and, finally, to the lounging figure in "The Piazza," a ghostly presence moves with us, disordering stable worlds of similitudes with the intrusion of horrifying and unnatural differences. And this sense of sinister transformations is not relieved by the possibility of establishing a mediating piazza perspective, for in nineteenth-century America, "porch" and "piazza" were used interchangeably to refer to a verandah. In short the figurative use of "porch" in the *Hamlet* passage puts into question both the literal and figurative aspects of the piazza in the sketch and suggests a contagion spreading through language in the same way that the "lep'rous distilment" courses through the body of the king. The piazza, it appears, can offer neither the protection nor the perspective that the narrator expects, for he finds himself, like the weary and troubled Canute in his "great chair" weakened and disenchanted.

At length, when pretty well again, and sitting out, in the September morning, upon the piazza, and thinking to myself, when, just after a little flock of sheep, the farmer's banded children passed, a-nutting, and said, "How sweet a day"—it was, after all, but what their fathers call a weather-breeder— and, indeed was become so sensitive through my illness, as that I could not bear to look upon a Chinese creeper of my adoption, and which, to my delight, climbing a post of the piazza, had burst out in starry bloom, but now, if you removed the leaves a little, showed millions of strange, cankerous worms, which, feeding upon those blossoms, so shared their blessed hue, as to make it unblessed evermore—worms, whose germs had doubtless lurked in the very bulb which, so hopefully, I had planted: in this ingrate peevishness of my weary convalescence, was I sitting there; when, suddenly looking off, I saw the golden mountain-window, dazzling like a deep-sea dolphin. Fairies there, thought I, once more; the queen of fairies at her fairy-window; at any rate, some glad mountain-girl; it will do me good, it will cure this weariness, to look on her. No more; I'll launch my yawl—ho, cheerly, heart! and push away for fairy-land, for rainbow's end, in fairy-land.

(6–7)

Here is a world where man is not at home, where rest and peace are impossible, for nature is experienced as a feeling of threatening change and contagion brought on by the encounter with deception and difference. The phrase "weather-breeder" implies an analogy of proportion—fathers are to children as the sweet September day is to subsequent storms—but in a manner that ironizes and contaminates the linkage. And the example of the Chinese creeper subverts the possibility of a relation based on a positive acceptance of difference. As a parodic version of the adopted child whose tainted blood resists the hopes and efforts of the substitute parent, the plant undermines any idea of a cultivated decorative nature. Hence in an act of poetic defiance the narrator determines to begin an ascending movement toward another realm nearer to the sky, toward a mixed transitional landscape that is the product of the magical forces of the imagination. Promising relief from weariness is the golden glow of the "mountain window," a "fairy sign" of romance that had appeared like a Hawthornian birthmark as a "small, round, strawberry mole upon the wan cheek of northwestern hills" (5) on an autumn afternoon when the air seemed "sick" and the "sky was ominous as Hecate's cauldron." As a sign of a "haunted ring where fairies dance" that promises a cure from weariness, the glow recalls Hawthorne's description of the "Enchanted Ground" of the Old Manse that offers rest to those "weary and world-worn spirits" who come "within [the] magic circle" (*MOM*, 29), and it recalls, too, Melville's citation of that description in "Hawthorne and His Mosses" (noted earlier). But Melville does not recall the magic spell of Hawthornian romance and its earlier effect on him in order to celebrate unambiguously the positive effects of such enchantments, nor to suggest that the "witching conditions of light and shadow" (4) he experiences on the piazza duplicate those of the Old Manse. Here recall takes the form of a new, more negative reading of Hawthorne's text, one that brings to the foreground details that earlier analysis had ignored. It is the dark aspect of enchantment suggested by Hawthorne's reference to the Enchanted Ground of *Pilgrim's Progress* but never developed in his preface that troubles the text of "The Piazza." The reference to Hecate's cauldron, for example, reminds us that she and the other witches in *Macbeth* "about the cauldron sing, / Like elves and fairies in a ring, / Enchanting all that you put in" (2.1.257–58), and hence suggests that enchanters have complicated, perhaps sinister, motives. And sleep, of course, does not always bring relief from weariness, as the example of Lady Macbeth makes clear; a point also suggested by the narrator's reference to *A Midsummer Night's Dream*, a play where fairies "following darkness like a dream" (5.1.393) "streak" the eyes of sleepers with enchanted juice and fill their minds "full of hateful fantasies" (2.1.257–58).

Quite clearly, the narrator's description of his interest in fairy land, his desire to seek out the "queen of fairies at her fairy window," is disturbed by a series of allusions suggesting some of the dismaying dangers such a pursuit involves. And these unsettling suggestions continue to accumulate as the narrator describes his search for "rainbow's end, in fairy-land." For unlike the voyages of Melville's earlier first-person narrators, the writer's journey here takes him "inland" (4), and his search is rendered from the beginning in terms of strained metaphors that call attention to their figurative or merely fanciful nature and, at the same time, nostalgically invoke real adventures of the past. The "golden mountain window" dazzles "like a deep-sea dolphin"; his "yawl" is a "high-pommeled, leather one"; the guiding stars are present in the forms of a "wigged old aries, long-visaged, and with a crumpled horn," a "milky way of white weed," and "Pleides and Hyades, of small forget-me-nots" (7). But this is a pattern that cannot be long sustained. The "yawl" is soon disenchanted (it becomes a horse) and is eventually left behind like Una's lamb when the narrator reaches a point where "none might go but by himself" (8). Indeed, by the time he approaches fairy-land, "foot-sore enough and weary" (8), the voyaging ideal persists only in improper or displaced reminders of earlier adventures. "A sultry hour, and I wore a light hat, of yellow sinnet, with white duck trowsers—both relics of my tropic sea-going. Clogged in muffling ferns, I softly stumbled, staining the knees a sea-green" (10).

Following this fall, the narrator sees "the fairy queen sitting at her fairy window," and although she starts "like some Tahiti girl" (10) she is obviously no Fayaway. Nor does she suggest Spenser's Gloriana. Rather she recalls the deserted and isolated figure of Tennyson's poem "Mariana." Like her poetic name-sake, Melville's Marianna sits alone in an isolated, dreary house and laments her weary existence. Unlike the enchanted ground of Hawthorne's retreat, Marianna's surroundings possess no "slumberous influence" (*MOM,* 39), for she is tormented by "weariness and wakefulness together" (P, 14). And the pictur-esque "veil of woodbine" (*MOM,* 33) that adds to the idyllic at-mosphere of the Old Manse is here the sign of decay: "This old house is rotting. That makes it so mossy" (P, 11).

The house that from the piazza had appeared as "one spot of radiance" has its "golden sparkle" (5) disenchanted by the "strange fancies" of Marianna. Hers is a world of enigmatic shad-ows that lead not to essential forms but to other shadows. "The invading shadow gone the invaded one returns" (12). Indeed, for Marianna "shadows are as things," as loving friends, for they are valued in themselves rather than as signs pointing to the things that cast them.

But the friendliest one, that used to soothe my weariness so much, cooly quivering on the ferns, it was taken from me, never to return, as Tray did just now. The shadow of a birch. The tree was struck by lightning, and brother cut it up. You saw the cross-pile out-doors—the buried root lies under it, but not the shadow. That is flown, and never will come back, nor ever anywhere stir again. (13)

This astonishing passage suggests the depth of Marianna's despair, for her lament ignores as irrelevant both the natural and human aspects of the "cross-pile of silver birch." Neither the lightning strike nor the act of cutting has significance for her. And if the "cross-pile" with the "buried root" beneath it suggests to her, as it does to the narrator, "some sequestered grave" (9), it is neither an indication of a nostalgia for the natural object nor a sign that the influences of nature can sooth us when "death is in our thoughts."[4] Her interest is not in evidences of past life, for what was important to her was not alive. Indeed what is now poignantly missing in her world might be said itself to be simply the sign of an absence.

Marianna, however, is not completely without hope. For although all other possible cures have failed to relieve her weariness, she believes that it would leave her if she could once "look upon whoever the happy being is" (14) who lives in the gleaming house at the bottom of the mountain. Ironically it is her belief in the power of that happy house that permanently disenchants the narrator.

—Enough. Launching my yawl no more for fairy-land, I stick to the piazza. It is my box-royal; and this amphitheatre, my theatre of San Carlo. Yes, the scenery is magical—the illusion so complete. And Madam Meadow Lark, my prima donna, plays her grand engagement here; and, drinking in her sunrise note, which, Memnon-like, seems struck from the golden window, now far from me the weary face behind it.

But, every night, when the curtain falls, truth comes in with darkness. No light shows from the mountain. To and fro I walk the piazza deck, haunted by Marianna's face, and many as real a story. (14–15)

Once the narrator sees that Marianna's view of his "happy house" (14) is as poetic to her as her "fairy mountain house" (10) has been to him, he comes to understand the way the imagination seeks to relieve the weariness and boredom of life by establishing the authority of illusion. And this understanding disenchants forever the fiction of a fairy land by exposing it as a cruel and empty pretense. Gone now is the desire for adventure that had transformed the piazza into the "sleety deck" of a ship and generated the "inland voyage to fairy land," with the pleasant, haunted, picturesque perspective of the early paragraphs of the sketch. The piazza is no longer seen as a substitute pew, easy chair, or cozy lounge where the writer can sit, like Hawthorne, in his "familiar room" and "dream strange things and make them look like truth" (*SL*, 36). It has become a theatre-box, a place of deceiving appearances, of unreal falsifications. And with that change comes the return of a discredited authority. The narrator sits comfortably, even self-indulgently, in his "box-royal" enjoying the perspective of a privileged consciousness for whom both nature and other people have become merely elements in a representation. But along with this disenchanted vision comes a reversal of the traditional metaphorics that makes truth analogous to light and creativity to the act of seeing. "Truth comes in with darkness," the darkness that follows the fall of the stage curtain; and with it come ghostly presences quite unlike those that appear "without affrighting us" in Hawthorne's "familiar room." These are the presences that haunt the world of *Pierre*.

Dearest Lucy!—well, well;—'twill be a pretty time we'll have this evening; there's the book of Flemish prints—that first we must look over; then, second, is Flaxman's Homer—clear-cut outlines, yet full of unadorned barbaric nobleness. Then Flaxman's Dante;—Dante! Night's and Hell's poet he. No, we will not open Dante. Methinks now the face—the face—minds me a little of pensive, sweet Francesca's face—or, rather, as it had been Francesca's daughter's face—wafted on the sad dark wind, toward observant Virgil and the blistered Florentine. No, we will not open Flaxman's Dante. Francesca's mournful face is now ideal to me. Flaxman might evoke it wholly,— make it present in lines of misery—bewitching power. No! I will not open Flaxman's Dante! Damned by the hour I read in Dante! more damned than that wherein Paolo and Francesca read in fatal Lancelot! (*P*, 42)

Woven and entangled in this passage are most of the thematic strands of *Pierre:* the problem of reading; the questions of relatedness, of genealogical continuity and intertextuality (family structures and narrative forms); and, linking them all, the larger issues of repetition and representation. The generative energy of the passage (and the novel) is a story, the story of the face, a story that Pierre can narrate but cannot read because it exists for him in the form of a "riddle" (37) or "mournful mystery" whose meaning is "veiled" behind a "concealing screen" (41). Nevertheless, he is determined to understand it fully, to confront its meaning, as he says, "face to face" (41). But as the labyrinthine quality of the above passage suggests, the meaning of the story is difficult to decipher, and Pierre's attempt to read it will generate a second and even more entangled and problematic narrative, that of the novel itself.

Many of the complexities must be put aside to be gathered up later, but we can notice at this point that although the face "was not of enchanted air" but had been "visibly beheld by Pierre" (43), it nevertheless exists for him in an ambiguous representational mode. The "wretched vagueness" (41) that haunts his memory stands not in the place of its "mortal lineaments" (43) but in the place of something else: in this instance Dante's description of Francesca's face, or, perhaps, in the place of Flaxman's graphic representation of Dante's description, or, more problematically, in the place of Pierre's imaginary conception of Francesca's daughter's face. Pierre's initial encounter with Isabel, then—an encounter that he is later to see as the central and authenticating one of his life—is cast in terms of signs rather than substances. It is derived not immediate. Any sense of the face as a living reality dissolves before the "long line of dependencies" (67) implied in the passage. The focus here is on purely textual entities, on questions of the relations between literary works (the chivalric tale, Dante's poem, Melville's novel), between graphic and linguistic signs (Flaxman's illustrations, Dante's poem) and on the bewitching power these entities possess to produce others that displace and represent them. In this sense the story of the face, and by extension Pierre's own story, is necessarily written and read from the perspective of the "already written." The Paolo and Francesca episode implies that not even passion itself is natural in the sense of being an underived and spontaneous emotion (it comes from books)[5] and hence suggests an entangled relation between one's natural genealogy and the inherited texts of one's culture.

This problem of relatedness raised by Pierre's imaginatively creating literary parents for the mysterious face is the first one to appear in the novel which begins with a celebration of the apparent differences between the "great genealogical and real-estate dignity of some families in America" (12) and the "winding and manufactured nobility" of the "grafted families" (10) of the old world. Unlike the English Peerage, which is kept alive by "restorations and creations" (10), Pierre's pedigree seems straight and unflawed. We meet the young hero "issuing from the high gabled old home" of his father and entering a world where the "very horizon [is] to him as a memorial ring," where all the "hills and swales seemed as sanctified through their long uninterrupted possession by his race" (8). Unlike the orphaned Ishmael, he seems to find himself in a world where he truly belongs, a world where his identity, place, and destiny are confirmed by the self-reflecting environment of a "powerful and populous family" (7). Moreover, his position as the only "surnamed Glendinning extant" and the "solitary head of his family" seems to assure him that his only "duplicate" is the "one reflected to him in the mirror" (8). Pierre, in other words, seems to enjoy the security of a family circle within which he can define and fix himself and at the same time remain free of any challenge to his originality or authority. He can possess at once the feeling of belonging enjoyed by the son and the procreative power of the father as well, hence his dream of achieving a "monopoly of glory in capping the fame-column, whose tall shaft had been erected by his noble sires" (8).

However, this is a dream based on the assumption of an absolute correspondence between the natural and the human, on the notion that institutions and language possess the characteristics of the biological structure of generation. But families are not trees even though they may seem to "stand as the oak" (9) for they do not originate and develop in the same way. The permanence, stability, and order implied by a genealogical chart or by the metaphor of the family tree conceals a host of discontinuities, disjunctions, entanglements, and desires that mark human relationships. The seemingly unentangled lines of the Glendinning genealogy are actually twisted and interwoven by the young heir's problematic relation to his family. Pierre's relation to his mother, for example, equivocates the orderly process whereby the father and mother produce a son who marries and continues the line: "In the playfulness of their unclouded love, and with that strange license which a perfect confidence and mutual understanding at all points, had long bred between them, they were wont to call each other brother and sister" (5). The entangling and confusing of relationships implied by this behavior is further complicated by their domestic practice that anticipates the "sweet dreams of those religious enthusiasts, who paint to us a Paradise to come, where etherealized from the drosses and stains, the holiest passion of man shall unite all kindreds and climes in one circle of pure and unimpairable delight" (16). Pierre's relation to his mother, in short, is an only partially disguised expression of a set of inhibited desires generated by a genealogical system that condemns the son to a derived and secondary existence. These desires, partially displaced here by the religious language in which they are manifested, are more concretely expressed in Pierre's "strange yearning . . . for a sister" as well as by the narrator's smug observation, "He who is sisterless, is as a bachelor before his time. For much that goes to make up the deliciousness of a wife, already lies in the sister" (7). This barely concealed expression of brother-sister incestuous desire, like the more deeply displaced mother-son relationship, suggests the extent to which Pierre unconsciously resists the defining authority of the father as well as the sense that he is no more than his father "transformed into youth once again"

(73). Both his relation to his mother and his longing for a sister constitute a challenge to the parental role by subtly entangling the genealogical line and disrupting its temporal development. The "striking personal resemblance" between Pierre and his mother—she sees "her own graces strangely translated into the opposite sex"—makes it seem as if the mother has "long stood still in her beauty, heedless of the passing years" and Pierre seems to "meet her half-way," to have "almost advanced himself to that mature stand-point in Time, where his pedestaled mother so long had stood" (5).

But it is Pierre's response to the phantom face that is haunting and enchanting him with its suggestions of dark foreignness that is the most obvious expression of his desire to free himself from a family prison. Its magnetic quality derives in part from the fact that it is at once "wholly unknown to him" (49) and yet somehow familiar, thus making him aware of a "certain condition of his being, which was most painful, and every way uncongenial to his natural, wonted self" (53). The nature and speed of Pierre's response to Isabel's disruptive note, of course, makes explicit the status of these hidden desires. In Pierre's mind the note completely undermines the dignity and authority of the father and forces him to abandon all the "hereditary beliefs" (87) he has been unconsciously resisting all along. "I will have no more father" (87), he says, as he rejects all "earthly kith and kin" and orphan-like "stagger[s] back upon himself and find[s] support in himself" (89). "Henceforth, cast-out Pierre hath no paternity, and no past . . . twice-disinherited Pierre stands . . . free to do his own self-will and present fancy to whatever end" (199). Because he feels himself "divinely dedicated," he decides that he can abandon all "common conventional regardings," including his "hereditary duty to his mother" and his "pledged worldly faith and honor to the hand and seal of his affiancement" (106). Personal faith will replace hereditary beliefs, and the result will be a more orderly as well as more authentic life, for the genealogical tradition that seems to promise continuity and unity is actually intertwined in the "infinite entanglements of all social

79

things" (191). From the "long line of dependencies" that constitute it come the "thousand proprieties and polished finenesses"
(83) that characterize the social. Like Christ, Pierre believes that
he can free himself from these "myriad alliances and crisscross-
ings" (191) and disentangle himself from "all fleshly alliances"
(164) by substituting for the genealogical imperative a new and
celebate enterprise.

> Not that at present all these things did thus present them-
> selves to Pierre; but these things were foetally forming in him.
> Impregnations from high enthusiasms he had received; and
> the now incipient offspring which so stirred, with such pain-
> ful, vague vibrations in his soul; this, in its mature develop-
> ment, when it should at last come forth in living deeds,
> would scorn all personal relationship with Pierre, and hold
> his heart's dearest interests for naught.
>   Thus, in the Enthusiast to Duty, the heaven-begotten Christ
> is born; and will not own a mortal parent, and spurns and
> rends all mortal bonds. (106)

In the place of inherited values and relations Pierre places an
orphaned, self-begotten identity and that in turn generates a
miraculous conception. In effect a spiritual genealogy supplants
the physical one, apparently making possible a new family
structure.[6] For both Isabel and Lucy, Pierre seems capable of ful-
filling all the traditional familial roles. "I want none in the
world but thee" (312), Isabel tells him, and Lucy insists that he is
"my mother and my brothers, and all the world, and all heaven,
and all the universe to me—thou *art* my Pierre" (311). Moreover,
the new relationships, as Pierre sees them, are free from the ambiguities of the more traditional ones: he and Isabel are "wide
brother and sister in common humanity" (273) and he and Lucy
spiritual cousins with "no declaration; no bridal" (310) who
"love as angels do" (309).

Pierre, then, seems to have made himself his "own Alpha and
Omega," to have reached a point where he can "feel himself in
himself and not by reflection in others" (261). Moreover, having

freed himself from the defining relationships of the patriarchal tradition he has also made himself independent of its economic imperatives. When he abandons his "fine social position" and "noble patrimony" he boldly asserts that he will "live on himself"; that is to say that he will become an author and support himself by putting his "soul to labor . . . and pay his body her wages" (261). In the place of fathering a natural son who will be his unwilling copy even as he was his father's, he will give the world a book, "a child born solely from one parent" (259), that through its radical originality will "gospelize the world anew" (273).

Pierre assumes that as an author he will wield an authority that is not subject to the confining and restricting definitions from the past. However, behind the differences that seem to separate the act of authoring from that of physical engenderment is a notion common to both, that what one makes is one's offspring, legacy, and representative. This element of sameness puts into question Pierre's claims of absolute authority and originality.[7] As the Paolo-Francesca passage implies, the process of representation involves questions of inherited tendencies as well as originating intentions. These issues appear in their most obvious form in the novel's focus on painted images of the father, an especially likely association, for as Paul de Man has shown, it is in painting (and especially in eighteenth-century theories of painting) that the process of representation appears in its most unambiguous aspects. Conceived of as imitation, painting (as de Man points out) has the effect of seeming to restore the represented object to view as if it were present, miraculously bringing back into existence a presence that existed in another time and in another place. This duplication of the objects of perception, however, does not exhaust the power of the painted image. Even more impressive is its apparent ability to transform inward and ideal experiences into objects of perception and, by making them visible, confer upon them the ontological stability of objective existence.[8] The military portrait of Pierre's grandfather, for example, at once captures the image of the original so completely that Pierre feels "a mournful longing to meet his living aspect in real life" and possesses the "heavenly persuasiveness of angelic speech; a glorious gospel framed and hung upon the wall, and declaring to all people, as from the Mount, that man is a noble, god-like being, full of choicest juices; made up of strength and beauty" (30) This description, of course, equivocates Pierre's decision to "gospelize the world anew" by associating it with a related and prior originating act, but it also undermines the assumption that imitation duplicates presence. The "mournful longing" that the painting generates in Pierre is a reminder of one problematic aspect of representation since it points to the absence of the represented entity, and the disquieting effects of that absence are strengthened by the irony implicit in the fact that a military portrait seems to the young man to be a concrete expression of the ideals of Christ's Sermon on the Mount.

The painted image of the old Pierre Glendinning points to an absence rather than a presence, to "once living but now impossible ancestries in the past" (32) and raises the problem of genealogy as representation by illustrating what the narrator calls the "endless descendedness of names" (9). Not only is Pierre his father's "namesake" (73) but his grandfather's as well, hence from one point of view doubly derived, the copy of a copy and as such a diminution, a smaller, weaker version of the authoritative original:

The grandfather of Pierre measured six feet four inches in height; during a fire in the old manorial mansion, with one dash of his foot, he had smitten down an oaken door, to admit the buckets of his negro slaves; Pierre had often tried on his military vest, which still remained an heirloom at Saddle Meadows, and found the pockets below his knees. . . . (29)

Pierre in his "most extended length measures not the proud six feet four of [his] John of Gaunt Sire," and as the "stature of the warrior is cut down" so is the "glory of the fight" (271).

Pierre's assumption, however, is that his position in the genealogical chain is a matter of "empty nominalness," not "vital realness" (192); for if his name on the one hand seems to bind him to his paternal precursors, on the other it suggests a means of escape. The French origins of his Christian name allow him through a series of substitutions to link himself to another tradition that counters the democratic, revolutionary one represented by his ancestors. This is the one suggested by the mysterious "foreigner" of "noblest birth" and "allied to the royal family" (76) who enchants Pierre's father and perhaps becomes the mother of Isabel. Although the signs of this "foreign feminineness" (76) are less objective, less concrete, than the portrait of Pierre's grandfather—they consist of a "subtle expression of the portrait of [Pierre's] then youthful father" (112), the word "Isabel" written in the interior of a guitar, and a "touch of foreignness in the accent" (113) of the mysterious Isabel—Pierre is so convinced of her reality and her spiritual link to him through Isabel that he willingly breaks the lines linking him to his forefathers and, by a process of substitution based on the French meaning of his Christian name, becomes Peter, the rock on which Christ builds his church rather than the grandson of the old warrior.[9]

At first glance his progress seems significant. Replacing the authority of the grandfather and the father is that of Christ as expressed in "those first wise words, wherewith [he] first spoke in his first speech to men" (91), the Sermon on the Mount. Although Christ's words come to Pierre in the secondary form of the biblical text, he at least no longer has to receive them indirectly and ambiguously by way of the military portrait of his grandfather. And just as he seems to have replaced a physical genealogy with a spiritual one and an interpreted, metaphoric "gospel" by the actual one, so he seems to have turned from the socially and conventionally determined aspects of his name toward its literal meaning. A detailed analysis of this remarkable process of substitution must await a discussion of a set of similar acts, but one can note at this point that Pierre's career is developing in the context of a series of conflicting but related representations.

   This is a process that is at once complicated and illuminated by the narrator's discussion of Pierre's attitudes toward several other portraits that represent the father and associate his authority and power with biblical models. The most interesting of these are the two paintings of his dead father: the one, the drawing room portrait, commissioned by Pierre's mother, painted by a "celebrated artist," portraying the father "during the last and rosiest days of their wedded union" (82–83); the other, the chair portrait, noncommissioned, the product of an amateur, portraying an "unentangled, young bachelor, gayly ranging up and down in the world" (73). The dissimilarity of these "precious memorials" (73) of his father, who is "now dead and irrevocably gone," presents young Pierre with a set of teasing interpretive problems that call for a "careful, candid estimation" (73) and "cunning analysis" (82). Unlike his mother who simply asserts that the chair portrait is not her husband because it does not "correctly . . . convey his features in detail" (72), Pierre is unwilling to reject either portrait and wonders if in some mysterious way the "two paintings might not make only one." Neither is "all of [his] father" (83) but if regarded intertextually, if the "family legend" (73) of the smaller painting is read in the context of the "tales and legends of . . . devoted love" that are "rehearsed" (83) by the other portrait, then the father may be restored to view as if he were actually present. Hence the chair portrait seems to Pierre to contain a strange mystery that he can fancifully solve.

Thus sometimes in the mystical, outer quietude of the long country nights; either when the hushed mansion was banked round by the thick-fallen December snows, or banked round by the immoveable white August moonlight; in the haunted repose of a wide story, tenanted only by himself; and sentineling his own little closet; and standing guard, as it were, before the mystical tent of the picture; and ever watching the strangely

concealed lights of the meanings that so mysteriously moved
to and fro within; thus sometimes stood Pierre before the portrait of his father, unconsciously throwing himself open to all
those ineffable hints and ambiguities, and undefined half-
suggestions, which now and then people the soul's atmosphere, as thickly as in a soft, steady snow-storm, the snow-
flakes people the air. (84)

In this passage the "precious memorial" (73) combines with
Pierre's "revered memory of [his] father" (81) to confirm, perhaps to bring back, the plenitude of the dead father. Pierre's ancestral home is figured as a carefully enclosed monument that
sustains history and embalms memory by preserving deep inside itself the sign of an authoritative presence even as the Taber-
nacle of the Hebrews held within a central tent the veiled Ark
of the Lord, the Tables of Stone, God's testimony to man (Exod.
25:10–16). While the meanings of the painting remain hidden,
the mode of concealment seems, paradoxically, a form of revelation, in the same manner that God remains hidden in the
Cloud of Glory that is the sign of his immediate presence and
that at times surrounds and protects the sacred Ark. Nor are
these impressions simply mystifications, the results of "reveries
and trances" that give to the painting the quality of "legendary
romance" (85). The arrival of Isabel's letter seems to confirm the
portrait's power and to "rip . . . open as with a keen sword" all
the "preceding . . . mysteries" (85). "Now his remotest infantile
reminiscences—the wandering mind of his father—the empty
hand, and the ashen—the strange story of Aunt Dorothea—the
mystical midnight suggestions of the portrait itself; and, above
all, his mother's intuitive aversion, all, all overwhelmed him
with reciprocal testimonies" (85). The problem, then, is not that
the letter undermines the power and authority of the painted
image but rather that it confirms it in a particularly disturbing
way, validating the "story of the picture" (74) as narrated by his
aunt. For that story had implied that the artist in "stealing" the
portrait had "detected" the subject's "innermost secrets" and

"published them in a portrait" (79), thereby conferring upon mental experience the stability of a perceived object. It is precisely because the portrait presents an image of the father in such a palpable and immediate way that Pierre first reverses it on the wall and then removes it entirely, hoping in that way to "banish the least trace of his altered father." However, "in a square space of slightly discolored wall, the picture still left its shadowy, but vacant and desolate trace" (87), apparently maintaining its validity and influence even while locked away in Pierre's trunk.

In the strange relativeness, reciprocalness, and transmittedness, between the long-dead father's portrait, and the living daughter's face, Pierre might have seemed to see reflected to him, by visible and uncontradictable symbols, the tyranny of Time and Fate. Painted before the daughter was conceived or born, like a dumb seer, the portrait still seemed leveling its prophetic finger at that empty air, from which Isabel did finally emerge. There seemed to lurk some mystical intelligence and vitality in the picture; because, since in his own memory of his father, Pierre could not recall any distinct lineament transmitted to Isabel, but vaguely saw such in the portrait; therefore, not Pierre's parent, as any way rememberable by him, but the portrait's painted *self* seemed the real father of Isabel; for, so far as all sense went, Isabel had inherited one peculiar trait nowhither traceable but to it.

And as his father was now sought to be banished from his mind, as a most bitter presence there, but Isabel was become a thing of intense and fearful love for him; therefore, it was loathsome to him, that in the smiling and ambiguous portrait, her sweet mournful image should be so sinisterly becrooked, bemixed, and mutilated to him. (197)

Here, as in the Paolo-Francesca passage, the usual view of human life as a linear, natural, biological process of generation and procreation is replaced by one that portrays it as a confusing play of images. Although an "unsolid duplicate" of a "vanished

solidity" (198), the portrait seems to preserve the power of the
dead father. But the procreative authority manifests itself in the
form of a "strange transfer" of its own represented "lineaments"
to the "countenance of Isabel" (196). The result is that she seems
to exist not as a "thing of life . . . but a thing of breath, evoked
by the wanton magic of a creative hand" (169) that is itself a
representation. The portrait functions, then, to undermine the
substantiality of both Pierre's own and Isabel's existences, and
for that reason he decides to destroy it along with all other external signs of the paternal past.

Since it is the portrait that carries the disturbing trace of the
father's presence, Pierre assumes that his problems will vanish
when he burns it and "urn[s it] in the great vase of air" this being the second and final time that he will see his father's "obse-
quies performed" (198). To escape from the burden of the past
and from ordinary historical and genealogical principles, he believes that he has only to destroy their signs and refuse any
longer "to reverse the decree of death, by essaying the poor perpetuating image of the original" (197-98). This plan of action,
however, is based on the assumption that the individual exists
independently of and has control over the "mementoes and
monuments of the past" (197), an assumption that ignores the
"myriad alliances and criss-crossings among mankind, the infinite entanglements of all social things, which forbid that one
thread should fly the general fabric, on some new line of duty,
without tearing itself and tearing others" (191). It is not surprising that the act of burning the portrait and the other contents
of the trunk—"packages of family letters and all sorts of miscellaneous memorials in paper" (198)—does not free Pierre from
the influence of the past. The entangled aspects of his predica-
ment are implied in the contradictory language he uses to express it. "Thus, and thus, and thus! on thy manes I fling fresh
spoils! pour out all my memory in one libation!—so, so, so,
lower, lower, lower; now all is done and all is ashes" (198-99).
Needless to say Pierre's metaphors are hopelessly mixed and entangled, implying that he at once feeds the fire and extinguishes

it, rejects his father and celebrates him. And adding to the ambiguity is the fact that in Melville's day it was generally assumed that the word "pyramid" derived from πύρ, fire. Since fire ascends in the figure of a cone, it was generally accepted that a pyramid imitates the shape of a flame.[10] So in a certain sense to burn the portrait is but to "mummy it in a visible memorial for every passing beggar's dust to gather on" (197), or, as Pierre says, to "urn [it] in the great vase of air."

Subsquent events mark the ambiguity present here. Late in the novel Pierre discovers in a "gallery of paintings recently imported from Europe" (349) a portrait that undermines his assumption that he can free himself from the mediation of all signs and relics. Belonging to another heritage, painted by an "Unknown Hand" (351), portraying a stranger, hence tied to the Glendinning family neither by legend nor by personal reminiscence, the portrait nevertheless represents the father to both Isabel and Pierre. Because Isabel "knew nothing of the painting Pierre had destroyed," she sees the foreign portrait as signifying the "living being who—under the designation of her father—had visited her at the cheerful house" (352) and also as containing "certain shadowy traces of her own unmistakable likeness" (351). To Pierre, however, it seems a "resurrection of the one he had burnt at the inn" (351). But no matter how the painting is regarded—whether it is seen as the sign of a sign or the sign of a once-living being—it signals the nonpresence of the origin, the ambiguity of any inscription of an origin in the present. "Then, the original of this second portrait was as much the father of Isabel as the original of the chair-portrait. But perhaps there was no original at all to this second portrait; it might have been a pure fancy piece" (353). This insight undoes once and for all Pierre's belief that the presence of his father can ever be located in or constituted by a sign that can then be either worshiped or destroyed. The "resurrection" of the chair portrait in the form of the *Stranger's Head* is a repetition that places the entangled issues of genealogy and representation within the context of loss and thereby substitutes a notion of meaning as presence and plenitude with one of meaning as void.

The themes of loss and absence, of course, are woven thickly into the fabric of *Pierre*. The language of the novel is heavy with images of devastating earthquakes, flowing rivers of lava, piles of drifting sand, ruined cities, abandoned excavation sites, and empty and desecrated burial places, all of which associate culture with man's vain attempts to resist the ravages of time and death and situate Pierre's career in a context that robs it of its uniqueness by making it no more than a minor repetition of a process as old as civilization itself. His early naive view of the world is expressed partially by his idealization of his dead father, a process represented by a figurative "shrine of marble" in which stands the perfect marble form of his departed father, a shrine as imposing as that of "Prince Mausolus," one that manages to take things "evanescent" and make them "unchangeable" and "eternal" (68) and one that remains "spotless and still new as the marble tomb of his of Arimathea" (69). These references to the ruins of Helecarnassus and to Joseph, the rich man of Arimathea who claims Christ's body and buries it in his own tomb, subversively link pagan and Christian burial practices and indirectly introduce the theme of ruined and empty tombs, a theme that becomes explicit with the arrival of Isabel's letter, which had the destructive force of a volcanic eruption rolling "down on [Pierre's] soul like melted lava, and [leaving] so deep a deposit of desolation, that all his subsequent endeavors never restored the original temples to the soil, nor all his culture completely revived its buried bloom" (67–68). That "one little bit of paper scratched over with a few small characters by a sharpened feather" obliterates the meaning of characters inscribed in marble, for it strips Pierre's "holiest shrine of all overlaid bloom" and "desecrates" that "casket, wherein he had placed [his] holiest and most final joy" (69). At issue here is the complicated relation between the acts of interment and inscription, both of which seem to mark the point separating man from nature by expressing his humanity.[11] It is significant, for example, that Pierre's first response to the mysterious Isabel, who comes from a world without tombs or inscriptions–"No name; no scrawled

or written thing; no book . . . no one memorial . . . no gravestone, or mound, or any hillock around the house, betrayed any
past burials of man or child" (115)–is to seek out a "remarkable
stone, or rather, smoothed mass of rock" (131) bearing the mysterious inscription S ye W. The first of two such objects to occupy his attention, the Memnon Stone or Terror Stone marks
the first stage of Pierre's career as the rock of Enceladus does the
final one. From one point of view the stone is no more than a
"natural curiosity" (133), but the mysterious writing on it gives it
a privileged position (one both scriptural and natural), associating it with a remote but human past and investing it with a mystery that seems to justify Pierre's poetical interpretation of its
significance.

When in his imaginative ruminating moods of early youth,
Pierre had christened the wonderful stone by the old resound-
ing name of Memnon, he had done so merely from certain associative remembrances of that Egyptian marvel, of which all
Eastern travelers speak. And when the fugitive thought had
long ago entered him of desiring that same stone for his headstone, when he should be no more; then he had only yielded
to one of those innumerable fanciful notions, tinged with
dreamy painless melancholy, which are frequently suggested to
the mind of a poetic boy. But in aftertimes, when placed in
far different circumstances from those surrounding him at the
Meadows, Pierre pondered on the stone, and his young
thoughts concerning it, and, later, his desperate act in crawling
under it; then an immense significance came to him, and the
long-passed unconscious movements of his then youthful
heart, seemed now prophetic to him, and allegorically verified
by the subsequent events.

For, not to speak of the other and subtler meanings which
lie crouching behind the colossal haunches of this stone, regarded as the menacingly impending Terror Stone . . . consider
its aspects as the Memnon Stone. . . .

Herein lies an unsummed world of grief. For in this plaintive fable we find embodied the Hamletism of the antique
world; the Hamletism of three thousand years ago: "The

flower of virtue cropped by a too rare mischance." And the English Tragedy is but Egyptian Memnon, Montaignized and modernized; for being but a mortal man Shakespeare had his fathers too. (135)

This suggestive passage focuses directly on two important and related themes: the problematic aspect of funerary monuments and the nature of interpretation. When Pierre first contemplates the "ponderous inscrutableness" (134) he reads its meaning in terms of "associative remembrances" of his Occidental culture's fascination with the Orient, in particular with the myth of the singing monument said to produce a dirgelike sound at sunrise in the memory of the young boy it commemorates; and then he personalizes his poetic reverie by associating that "sweet boy long since departed in antediluvian times" (134) with himself and imagines that the "imposing pile" will provide him with a fitting headstone.[12] This is a process of thought that derives directly from the tradition of romantic nature inscriptions, a tradition expressed by Wordsworth in his "Essays upon Epitaphs," where he argues that inscribed monuments imply a faith that man is an immortal being by expressing on the one hand the desire of the individual "to survive in the remembrance of his fellows" and on the other a "wish to preserve for future times vestiges of the departed." This double desire is present in man's attempt "to give to the language of senseless stone" a voice that assures "that some part of our nature is imperishable." [13] However, as Geoffrey Hartman has noted, inscribing and naming are secondary and elegiac acts that can produce the death feeling they try to deny.[14] Pierre's poetic melancholy is painless precisely because it ignores the elegiac aspects of the stone and imbues it with the force of a living presence.

Nevertheless the stone has a darker side even for the dreamy youth, and that aspect is acknowledged by the other name with which Pierre designates it, the Terror Stone. This is an aspect that emphasizes its anonymous, natural side, for if at times there seems to "lurk" about the stone "some mournful and lamenting plaint," at others it seems merely a "Mute Massiveness" (134), a "ponderous mass" balanced in such a way as to create beneath itself a "vacancy" (132), a "horrible interspace" (134). Considered from this point of view, its "music . . . is lost among . . . drifting sands" (136) and it becomes the "monument of a lost significance."[15]

The juxtaposition of the apparently opposing designations— Memnon Stone and Terror Stone—has the effect of suggesting other, "subtler meanings which lie crouching behind the colossal haunches" (135) of the sphinxlike stone. Read from the perspective of his future recollections, Pierre's "young thoughts concerning [the stone]" seem to him at once prophetic and allegorical; and to say that recollection is prophecy, that one's life is an allegory, is to say that every individual act derives its meaning or significance from an earlier one that it displaces and repeats (often unconsciously) in much the same way that the son displaces the father in the genealogical chain. Hence in the "plaintive fable" of Memnon "we find embodied the Hamletism of the antique world," the English tragedy being nothing but the "Egyptian Memnon, Montaignized and modernized; for being but a mortal man Shakespeare had his fathers too"; and Pierre's story, by extension, is yet another repetition of that "melancholy type" (136).

The implications of this repetition are spelled out in the second of the two symbolic stones that mark the stages of Pierre's career. The "spinx-like" (345) shape of Enceladus appears in the text first in the form of a "remarkable dream or vision" that Pierre experiences during a "state of semi-unconsciousness" (342), but the dream represents the unwilled return of earlier experiences and reconstitutes them as a form of repetition. The dream returns him once again to the "blue hills encircling his ancestral manor" and surrounds him with another confining and defining relationship. Since "Nature is not so much her own ever-sweet interpreter, as the mere supplier of that cunning alphabet, whereby selecting and combining as he pleases, each man reads his own peculiar lesson according to his own peculiar mind or mood" (342), Pierre now sees the "familiar features" of the landscape in a new and different way. In the same way that the Christian name (The Delectable Mountain) of the Mount of the Titans is displaced by the apparently more appropriate pagan one, so the "hills and swales" of Saddle Meadows that had once seemed to Pierre "sanctified through their long uninterrupted possession by his race" (8) are now read in the context of an older genealogy, that of "Coelus and Terra . . . incestuous Heaven and Earth" (347).

In Pierre's vision the landscape of the New World duplicates that of the Old: "curtained by [a] cunning purpleness," there is "stark desolation; ruin, merciless and ceaseless; chills and gloom,—all here lived a hidden life" (344).

And, as among the rolling sea-like sands of Egypt, disordered rows of broken Sphinxes lead to the Cheopian pyramid itself; so this long acclivity was thickly strewn with enormous rocky masses, grotesque in shape, and with wonderful features on them, which seemed to express that slumbering intelligence visible in some recumbent beasts—beasts whose intelligence seems struck dumb in them by some sorrowful and inexplicable spell. (343)

Among these "spinx-like shapes" (345) is a rock wrought by the "vigorous hand of nature's self" (346), a natural rather than an intentional object, that is partially uncovered and designated Enceladus by a "strolling company of young collegian pedestrians" (345). As Pierre recalls the "Titan's armless trunk," he suddenly sees "his own duplicate face and features" gleaming "upon him with prophetic discomfiture and woe" (346).

This dream vision is the final manifestation of a pattern of doubling that has tormented Pierre from the beginning of the novel. He has resisted being merely the "likeness" (73) and the namesake of his father, the "glass" (90) in which his mother sees her own reflected beauty, and the "personal duplicate" (289) of his hated cousin. But in resisting these familial doublings he is led at last to see his life as a fated repetition of certain tragic types, first Christ, then the Memnon-Hamlet type, and finally the Enceladus one. This development, moreover, is one that moves from a sense of repetition as a willed reappropriation of the past (as in the cases of Pierre's associating himself with Christ, Memnon, and Hamlet) toward a sense of repetition as an inevitable and unwilled nonhuman movement (as in the case of the dream of Enceladus). And this shift from one mode of repetition to another mirrors a movement at the level of language from the lyricism of the gospels to the silence of senseless stone.

Both of these developments are marked in the novel by the shifting meanings of Pierre's name, which, like his face, would seem to contain and express his uniqueness but which instead suggests to him the extent to which he is contained and defined by others. As we have seen, he attempts to resist being no more than Pierre Glendinning the Third by dedicating himself to what he perceives as a Christ-like duty and associating himself with Peter, the rock on which Christ builds his church. However, this act as well as his assertion that "I am Pierre" (373) calls attention to the literal meaning of his name, and it becomes his fate to live out that meaning, to become at the end a rock "arbored . . . in ebon vines" (362).

The implications of this movement from name to thing are important concerns of *Pierre*, and they are symbolized most clearly in the related figures of the mountain and the pyramid, a natural object and an intentional representation of it. As I have noted elsewhere, the mountain is a recurring image in *Pierre*.[16] The novel is dedicated to the "majestic mountain, Greylock," the "sovereign lord and king" of the "amphitheatre over which his central majesty presides," and important functions are given to Mount Sinai, meeting place of God and Moses; the "divine mount," site of Christ's famous sermon; Bunyan's Delectable Mountains, from which the Celestial City may be seen; and Pelion and Ossa, mountains of Thessaly used by the Titans in the war against the gods' stronghold on Mount Olympus. These "crude forms of the natural earth" are the "cunning alphabet, whereby selecting and combining as he pleases, each man reads his own peculiar lesson according to his own peculiar mind or mood" (342). Hence divine speech is associated with mountain tops as first Moses and then Christ, following their pagan predecessors, interpret that "profound Silence," that "divine thing without a name."

This process is emblematized in the figure of the pyramid, regarded by Melville as the source of the idea of Jehovah as well as the first work of art. Metaphysically the pyramid seems to suggest permanence, to proclaim a tenacious resistence to the pillages of time, and yet inside it contains decayed human ruins or, more frighteningly, absolutely nothing. "By vast pains we mine into the pyramid; by horrible gropings we come to the central room; with joy we espy the sarcophagus; but we lift the lid— and no body is there" (285). Like Hegel, Melville is fascinated by the pyramid because it offers him an external man-made form that represents the "forms of the natural earth." It has the appearance of a natural product and yet conceals as its meaning a hollow void, the sign perhaps of the "horrible interspace" (134) of the Memnon Stone and the "Hollow" (139) of God's hand. For as Hegel points out, this is the "realm of death and the invisible."[17] The pyramid, in other words, aptly symbolizes the process of representation itself, for it points to the absence that all signs carry within them. Contained within language is a "Silence" that "permeates all things" (204) and within all man-made objects and inscriptions a hollow void. Hence that "all-controlling and all-permeating wonderfulness, which, when imperfectly and isolatedly recognized by the generality, is so significantly denominated The Finger of God" is not "merely the Finger, it is the whole outspread Hand of God; for doth not Scripture intimate, that He holdeth all of us in the hollow of His Hand?—a Hollow, truly!" (139).

It is the finger of god that inscribes the Tablets of Stone given to Moses on Mount Sinai (Exod. 31:18) and that furnishes Christ with the power to give speech to the dumb (Luke 11:14–20).

Inscribed within all cultural constructs and within language itself is a radical absence suggesting an original loss. It is the pyramid situated in the cradle of civilization and the birthplace of the gods that marks the point beyond which it is impossible to go and that at the same time indicates that the moment of origin is not one of plenitude and presence but the sign of a loss. At the beginning for Melville there is already an unrecoverable past signified by the empty sarcophagus, and it is the burden of the present and future architects that no matter how hard they may seek to establish an original relation to the forms of the natural earth, they must inscribe that empty tomb within all their monuments. Implied in the voice of culture is the silence of the tomb.

What then of the acts of writing and reading? How does the reader in the silence of his solitude define his relation to the verbose narrator of *Pierre* and to his "book of sacred truth" (107). This is a problem that is inscribed in the text of *Pierre*. The life of its hero is the story of a reader who attempts to become a writer. His growth is rendered in terms of the development of his interpretive faculties, and his maturity is defined by his decision to "give the world a book" (283). As a youth Pierre is a naive, unquestioning reader of novels, impatient with the "sublime . . . Dante" because his "dark ravings . . . are in eternal opposition to [his] own free-spun shallow dreams" (54) and incapable of understanding even the "superficial and purely incidental lessons" of *Hamlet,* much less of glimpsing the "hopeless gloom of its interior meaning" (169).

The extent to which the content and mode of Pierre's reading constitute his world is suggested by the fact that the act of reading provides the grid through which all aspects of his early life are seen. His life is an "illuminated scroll" (7); love is a "volume bound in rose-leaves, clasped with violets, and by the beaks of humming-birds printed with peach juice on the leaves of lilies" (34); grief is "still a ghost story" (4); and human relations are intertextual: "'Read me through and through,'" says Lucy to Pierre, "'I am entirely thine'" (40). The arrival of Isabel's letter, the "fit scroll of a torn as well as a bleeding heart" (65) reveals to Pierre the artificial and conventional structure of this world and produces a new understanding of reading and interpretation: "Oh, hitherto I have but piled up words; brought books, and bought some small experiences and builded me in libraries; now I sit down and read" (91).

One result of this new view of things is that Pierre is able to recuperate a number of memories that to this point in his life have existed as unreadable and meaningless details of his inner world. His dying father's delirious ravings, his mother's ambiguous reaction to the chair portrait, and other "imaginings of dimness" that "seemed to survive to no real life" (71) are suddenly rendered intelligible by Isabel's letter, the pretext that "puts the chemic key of the cipher into his hands; then how swiftly and how wonderfully, he reads all the obscurest and most obliterate inscriptions he finds in his memory; yea, and rummages himself all over, for still hidden writings to read" (70). Nor is the effect limited to the inscriptions of memory. The letter also allows Pierre to read Dante and Shakespeare in a deeper, more profound way, and this rereading leads him to see that "after all he had been finely juggling with himself, and postponing with himself, and in meditative sentimentalities wasting the moments consecrated to instant action" (170).

Isabel's letter, then, seems to provide a context that renders intelligible textual details that to this point have been unreadable or misread. The full implications of this complicated process, however, are not immediately obvious. But a number of them are illuminated by the narrator's account of Pierre's reading of two apparently contradictory texts: the gospel of Matthew and the pamphlet "Chronometricals and Horologicals." Matthew, of course, is an important text for Pierre, since in his enthusiasm he has decided to model his life on Christ's, to be directed by those "first wise words, wherewith our Savior Christ first spoke in his first speech to men" (91), the Sermon on the Mount. His "acts" then will be a "gospel" (156) perfectly intelligible and natural if read in the context of his scriptural model.

However, in the darkness and silence of the coach that carries him and his "mournful party" (104) away from his ancestral home, Pierre begins to question his conduct, and to escape from the "evil mood" that becomes "well nigh insupportable," he "plunge[s] himself" (207) into a mysterious pamphlet that he has found.

> There is a singular infatuation in most men, which leads them in odd moments, intermitting between their regular occupations, and when they find themselves all alone in some quiet corner or nook, to fasten with unaccountable fondness upon the merest rag of old printed paper—some shred of a long-exploded advertisement perhaps—and read it, and study it, and re-read it, and pore over it, and fairly agonize themselves over this miserable, sleazy paper-rag, which at any other time, or in any other place, they would hardly touch with St. Dunstan's long tongs. So now, in a degree, with Pierre. But notwithstanding that he, with most other human beings, shared in the strange hallucination above mentioned, yet the first glimpse of the title of the dried-fish-like, pamphlet-shaped rag, did almost tempt him to pitch it out of the window. . . . .
>
> Nevertheless, the silence still continued; the road ran through an almost unplowed and uninhabited region; the slumberers still slumbered before him; the evil mood was becoming well nigh insupportable to him; so, more to force his mind away from the dark realities of things than from any other motive, Pierre finally tried his best to plunge himself into the pamphlet. (206–7)

Here reading appears as a form of "infatuation" or "hallucination" the nature of which is "strange" and "unaccountable." Nevertheless, its function is to fill the voids of doubt, silence, and loneliness, for it is either that which we do to escape the "dark realities of things" or that which we do in the face of nothing to do. Pierre, as he slowly unfingers, unbolts, unrolls, and smooths out the piece of "waste paper" "accidentally left there by some previous traveller" (206), resembles the person alone at breakfast intensely studying the back of an empty cereal box or the one absorbed in a year-old magazine in a doctor's office, for that which fascinates him is a discarded fragment of the past that now exists independently of its original intent and content. Here then is a situation that seems to promise a totally naive and innocent reading: on the one hand a displaced reader seeking only relief from the loneliness and boredom of everyday life; on the other an orphaned and abandoned text picked up unconsciously and accidentally; a situation, in other words, that seems removed from the vicious cycle of the return of repressed and inhibited desire that previously has marked Pierre's reading.

Once Pierre becomes absorbed in the pamphlet, however, he discovers that he cannot "master [its] pivot-idea" (292). Indeed, the "more he read and re-read, the more [his] interest deepened, but still the more likewise did his failure to comprehend the writer increase. He seemed somehow to derive some general vague inkling concerning it, but the central conceit refused to become clear to him" (209). Moreover, not only is the pamphlet unreadable but the reason for its being so is itself undecidable.

If a man be in any vague latent doubt about the intrinsic correctness and excellence of his general life-theory and practical course of life; then, if that man chance to light on any other man, or any little treatise, or sermon, which unintendingly, as it were, yet very palpably illustrates to him the intrinsic incorrectness and non-excellence of both the theory and the practice of his life; then that man will—more or less unconsciously—try hard to hold himself back from the self-admitted comprehension of a matter which thus condemns him . . . Again. If a man be told a thing wholly new, then—during the time of its first announcement to him—it is entirely impossible for him to comprehend it. For—absurd as it may seem— men are only made to comprehend things which they comprehended before (though but in the embryo, as it were). Things new it is impossible to make them comprehend, by merely talking to them about it. . . . Possibly, they may afterward come, of themselves, to inhale this new idea from the circumambient air, and so come to comprehend it; but not otherwise at all. It will be observed, that neither points of the above speculations do we, in set terms, attribute to Pierre in connection with the rag pamphlet. Possibly both may be applicable; possibly neither. (209)

Two possible explanations are offered here for Pierre's inability to comprehend the pamphlet, but neither is presented as absolutely applicable. Worth noting, however, is that both have the effect of seriously limiting the dimensions of reading as an activity. We can read only the old and the familiar, the narrator seems to suggest, that which confirms and supports our normal assumptions and expectations. This is an insight that is confirmed later in the novel when Pierre meets Plotinus Plinlimmon the "ostensible author" (HHM, 536) of the pamphlet, and seeks to re-read and understand it by the "commentary of [his] mystic-mild face" (*P*, 239). For now having found the "author" he has lost the text.

Pierre must have ignorantly thrust it into his pocket, in the stage, and it had worked through a rent there, and worked its way clean down into the skirt, and there helped pad the padding. So that all the time he was hunting for this pamphlet, he himself was wearing the pamphlet. . . .
Possibly this curious circumstance may in some sort illustrate his self-supposed non-understanding of the pamphlet, as first read by him in the stage. Could he likewise have carried about with him in his mind the thorough understanding of the book, and yet not be aware that he so understood it? (294)

To say that Pierre wears the pamphlet even as he searches for it and that his understanding is an unconscious one is to imply that the act of reading is not so much one of recovery or discovery of an original meaning as it is one of becoming aware of relationships between texts. This is an insight confirmed by the fact that the narrator interrupts and delays his account of the fascinating pamphlet in order to discuss what appears to be another kind of reading and a completely different sort of text,

the earnest reperusal of the Gospels: the intense self-absorption into that greatest real miracle of all religions, the Sermon on the Mount. From that divine mount, to all earnest-loving youths, flows an inexhaustible soul-melting stream of tenderness and loving-kindness; and they leap exulting to their feet, to think that the founder of their holy religion gave utterance to sentences so infinitely sweet and soothing as these; sentences which embody all the love of the Past, and all the love which can be imagined in any conceivable Future. Such emotions as that Sermon raises in the enthusiastic heart; such emotions all youthful hearts refuse to ascribe to humanity as their origin. This is of God! cries the heart, and in that cry ceases all inquisition. (207–8)

Here, of course, the focus is on a sacred text rather than a "sleazy pamphlet"; here reading seems an activity directed toward action in the world rather than a mystified escape from the "dark realities of things." The particular text in question is gospel of St. Matthew, and within it, the account of Christ's "first wise words . . . in his first speech to men" (91) words that Christ speaks "as one having authority, and not as the scribes" (Matt. 7:29) and that are transcribed by the author with unusual instructions: "whoso readeth, let him understand" (Matt. 24:15). The written text is presented as an authoritative and unambiguous record of speech, thereby restoring for the reader the full presence of Christ's words. Christ, however, presents himself as Son, as the representative of God the Father, who speaks through him. In that sense his words have a secondary quality, and this aspect of his message is underlined when it is given printed form. As Melville is well aware, Matthew, like the other gospels, was written years after the death of Christ; the identity of its author is questionable; and it is uncertain whether the Greek text is the original or a translation from an earlier Hebrew text. All these aspects signal nonpresence and remind us that Christ, like Moses, his Old Testament precursor, insists that he can get a voice out of silence and hence resembles certain philosophers who pretend to have found the "Talismanic Secret" that will reconcile man's desire for full presence with the fact of his orphaned existence. "That profound Silence, that only Voice of our God, which I before spoke of; from that divine thing without a name, those impostor philosophers pretend somehow to have got an answer; which is as absurd, as though they should say they have got water out of stone; for how can a man get a Voice out of Silence?" (208).

The sacred text, then, has inscribed within it the very silence and absence that motivates Pierre to plunge himself into the sleazy pamphlet he finds in the coach, a text that seems to offer a model for human action directly contradicting that of the Sermon on the Mount since it emphasizes the incompatibility of Christian ideals and the practical demands of life in this world. However, as the narrator points out, the pamphlet is more of a "restatement of a problem, than the solution to the problem itself" (210). And, indeed, the apparent differences between the two texts are equivocated by a set of ironic similarities. The pamphlet's parobolic structure—based on a "strange conceit . . . apparently one of the plainest in the world; so natural a child might have originated it" and yet "again so profound, that scarce Juggalarius himself could be the author" (210)—and the fact that it exists not as the product of the author who appears to have signed it but is rather his "verbal things, taken down at random, and bunglingly methodized by his young disciples" (290) tie it to its biblical pretext. And this knotted relationship appears to be inevitable rather than accidental since it is the product of a law as basic as that of gravity itself.

Thus over the most vigorous and soaring conceits, doth the cloud of Truth come stealing; thus doth the shot, even of a sixty-two pounder pointed upward, light at last on the earth; for strive we how we may, we cannot overshoot the earth's orbit, to receive the attractions of other planets; Earth's law of gravitation extends far beyond her own atmosphere. (261)

All words and conceits are subject to an "insensible sliding process" (7) that mixes and entangles their paths and destines them to return at last to their silent source. Reading consequently is an activity controlled by conceits that promise both wonderment and enlightenment but produce disenchantment and confusion by entangling man in such a complex web of relationships that the "three dextrous maids themselves could hardly disentangle him" (175). Such is Isabel's experience when she reads a "talismanic word" (147) inscribed in the center of a booklike handkerchief. Before she can decipher the mysterious inscription, she must teach herself to read, and that process radically changes her relation to the world. Up to this point in her life the relation to the man who calls himself her father has been a special and unconventional one.

The word father only seemed a word of general love and endearment to me—little or nothing more; it did not seem to involve any claims of any sort, one way or the other. I did not ask the name of my father; for I could have had no motive to hear him named, except to individualize the person who was so peculiarly kind to me; and individualized in that way he already was, since he was generally called by us *the gentleman,* and sometimes *my father.* (145)

For Isabel, at this point, "father" is simply the "word of kindness and of kisses" (124), a word that raises neither the problem of origins nor of authority, for it implies only the "tenderness and beautifulness of humanness" (122). Although when she looks in the pool of water behind the house, she sees the "likeness—something strangely like, and yet unlike, the likeness of his face" (124), the play of images does not generate sinister ambiguities but simply confirms her sense of the value of the human "in a world of snakes and lightnings, in a world of horrible and inscrutable inhumanities" (122). Her father, however, on the last visit to her before his death, leaves behind a handkerchief bearing in its middle a "small line of faded yellowish writing" that becomes for her a "precious memorial."

But when the impression of his death became a fixed thing to me, then again I washed and dried and ironed the precious memorial of him, and put it away where none should find it but myself . . . and I folded it in such a manner, that the name was invisibly buried in the heart of it, and it was like opening a book and turning over many blank leaves before I came to the mysterious writing, which I knew should be one day read by me, without direct help from any one. Now I resolved to learn my letters, and learn to read, in order that of myself I might learn the meaning of those faded characters. . . . I soon mastered the alphabet, and went on to spelling, and by-and-by to reading, and at last to the complete deciphering of the talismanic word–Glendinning. I was yet very ignorant. *Glendinning,* thought I, what is that? It sounds something like *gentleman;*–Glen-din-ing;–just as many syllables as gentleman; and–G–it begins with the same letter; yes, it must mean *my father.* I will think of him by that word now:–I will not think of the *gentleman,* but of *Glendinning.* . . . as I still grew up and thought more to myself, that word was ever humming in my head; I saw it would only prove the key to more. (146–47)

The inscribed handkerchief that is abandoned by "chance" and found "lying on the uncarpeted floor" (146) is an object totally separated from its originating source, cut loose from the authority who could testify to the meaning of the "faded yellowish writing" on it. (Is its author the gentleman's wife, his sister who initials his neckcloths, or some anonymous seamstress like those who sew "in concert" at Miss Pennies's house?) Consequently the meaning of the word does not lie behind or within it but in its relation to other words and social conventions. For Isabel the word "Glendinning" does not stand first in the place of a person but in the place of another word, "gentleman," which it echoes, supplements, and particularizes. Ironically, it is this orphaned sign that leads Isabel to the second and even more problematic key to her origins, the word "Isabel" "gilded" in the "heart of [her] guitar" (148). Even more than the handkerchief the guitar, having been purchased by Isabel from a peddlar who had "got it in barter from the servants" (152) at the Glendinning estate, is a free-floating object, and the origins and meaning of the word in its interior are more mysterious than that of the one written on the handkerchief. Does it refer to the guitar's maker, to its owner, or to neither? As a given name rather than a patronym it is more clearly an object in its own right, its signification determined completely by the circumstances in which it functions, a truth that is confirmed by the fact that Isabel claims the name as her own only after she has read it in the guitar, having to this point "always gone by the name of Bell" (148).

These two words, concealed in the interiors of the handkerchief and guitar and associated by Isabel with her absent parents, function for her as the keys that unlock and reveal a previously hidden set of relationships. These keys, however, are ambiguously inside the objects whose meanings they are supposed to unlock, and their significance derives from a set of purely arbitrary associations. In this sense Isabel as a reader may be said to be the author of her own parentage, since she has arrested the motion of two free-floating words and placed them within a genealogical order that is partially discovered, partially invented. And Pierre, through his reading and interpretation of the note that proclaims Isabel's relation to this order, entangles himself in a "fictitious alliance" (175) that will lead him at last to his decision to "gospelize the world anew" (273).[18]

This process is the one the narrator refers to when he insists that "to a mind bent on producing some thoughtful thing of absolute truth, all mere reading is apt to prove an obstacle hard to overcome" (283). Since the only nontextual reality is the silence of the crude forms of the natural earth, any act of speaking and

writing is bound to be a repetition, a displacement or a representation of a purely textual entity and necessarily derived, secondary, and inessential. This is the perception that marks the text
of *Pierre*, a book that is written against the "countless tribes of
common novels and countless tribes of common dramas" as
well as against those "profounder emanations of the human
mind" (141); yet it is doomed to absorb and repeat them. Empty
conventions from the domestic sentimental novel—the country-
city setting, the incest theme, the dark and light ladies, the romantic symbols of guitar and portrait—combine with references to Dante, Spenser, Shakespeare, Milton, and others to
produce a text that undermines the notion of writing as original
creation and reading as an authentic act of discovery. "Had
Milton's been the lot of Casper Hauser," the narrator insists,
"Milton would have been as vacant as he" (259). Hence the
writer is portrayed as a whore who sells herself for money—
"careless of life herself, and reckless of the germ life she contains"; as an actor in an empty melodrama performing a part
not written by him— "only hired to appear on the stage, not vol-
untarily claiming the public attention" (258); and as an improvis-
ator, echoing the music of others and creating off-hand, on the
spur of the moment, variations on any proposed subject—"it is
pleasant to chat . . . ere we go to our beds; and speech is further
incited, when like strolling improvisators of Italy, we are paid
for our breath" (259). Correspondingly the reader is portrayed as
a victim of this "lurking insincerity . . . of written thoughts,"
the enchanted dupe of books whose leaves "like knavish cards"
are "covertly packed" (339). For that "wonderful" and mysterious "story" of the illegitimate and orphaned child may have
been "by some strange arts . . . forged for her, in her childhood,
and craftily impressed upon her youthful mind; which so—like
the mark in a young tree—had enlargingly grown with her
growth, till it had become the immense staring marvel" (354).
Her story like all stories is inevitably genealogical; it resembles a
family tree that "annually puts forth new branches" (9), but it
also bears a "mark" that at once implies the activity of an

originating intention and signifies our distance from it. For it points not to the authoritative source but to the tangle of other such inscriptions scattered throughout the text of *Pierre,* inscriptions that haunt both writer and reader as do the faces of Marianna and Isabel.

FOUR

The Image in the Mirror: James's Portrait and the Economy of Romance

It arrived, in truth, the novel, late at self-consciousness; but it has done its utmost ever since to make up for lost opportunities. The flood at present swells and swells, threatening the whole field of letters, as would often seem, with submersion. It plays, in what may be called the passive consciousness of many persons, a part that directly marches with the rapid increase of the multitude able to possess itself in one way and another of the *book*. The book, in the Anglo-Saxon world, is almost everywhere, and it is in the form of the voluminous prose fable that we see it penetrate easiest and farthest. Penetration appears really to be directly aided by mere mass and bulk. There is an immense public, if public be the name, inarticulate, but abysmally absorbent, for which, at its hours of ease, the printed volume has no other association. This public—the public that subscribes, borrows, lends, that picks up in one way and another, sometimes even by purchase—grows and grows each year, and nothing is thus more apparent than that of all the recruits it brings to the book the most numerous by far are those that it brings to the "story."

—Henry James, "The Future of the Novel"

For Henry James, as for Herman Melville, Nathaniel Hawthorne is a writer who must be both acknowledged and absorbed. James's *Hawthorne* like Melville's "Mosses" is a work that at once celebrates and questions the force of Hawthornian romance. Indeed, as John Carlos Rowe perceptively suggests, "*Hawthorne* might be considered a critical preface to the realization in *The Portrait of a Lady* of James's early aim to transume his predecessor, Hawthorne."[1] Rowe's insight both acknowledges and gives a negative turn to Richard Chase's earlier observation that the *Portrait* is a supreme example of James's attempt to assimilate "romance into the substance of the novel" [2] by rejecting its conventional devices while preserving its wonder and beauty. And in so doing it points to the way James's process of selective absorption is accomplished by a reading that associates Hawthorne and his text with the innocence and naiveté of childhood. Significantly, James describes the importance of the publication of *The Scarlet Letter* by recording the effect that its appearance had had on his own childish imagination.

The writer of these lines, who was a child at the time, remembers dimly the sensation the book produced, and the little shudder with which people alluded to it, as if a peculiar horror were mixed with its attractions. He was too young to read it himself; but its title, upon which he fixed his eyes as the book lay upon the table, had a mysterious charm. He had a vague belief, indeed, that the "letter" in question was one of the documents that came by the post, and it was a source of perpetual wonderment to him that it should be of such an unaccustomed hue. Of course it was difficult to explain to a child the significance of poor Hester Prynne's blood-coloured A. But the mystery was at last partly dispelled by his being taken to see a collection of pictures (the annual exhibition of the National Academy), where he encountered a representation of a pale, handsome woman, in a quaint black dress and a white coif, holding between her knees an elfish-looking girl, fantastically dressed, and crowned with flowers. Embroidered on the woman's breast was a great crimson A, over which the child's fingers, as she glanced strangely out of the picture, were maliciously playing. I was told that this was Hester Prynne and little Pearl, and that when I grew older I might read their interesting history. But the picture remained vividly imprinted on my mind; I had been vaguely frightened and made uneasy by it; and when, years afterwards, I first read the novel, I seemed to myself to have read it before, and to be familiar with its two strange heroines.[3]

The most striking aspect of this scene of reading is the way the figure of the child/reader at once suggests and displaces that of the famous author. The passage clearly echoes that moment in "The Custom House" when Hawthorne with a "perplexed" shudder "fastened" his "eyes" upon the "scarlet symbol" (*SL*, 31–33) which "strangely interested" him but which remained a "riddle which . . . [he] saw little hope of solving" (31). But the figure of the author contemplating an "ornamental article of dress" (31) is displaced by the child studying the title of the book, an initial substitution that leads to another when the words suggest to the child's innocent mind a postal communication of "unaccustomed hue." But if Hester Prynne's "blood-coloured A" is unreadable to the child, its mystery is partially "dispelled" by the painting, which offers an interpretation of the book that at once troubles and enlightens him by violating his sexual innocence. For him the book becomes the story of "two strange heroines" whose images are at once seductive and vaguely troubling. But this response, too, is a mystified one, as much the result of a childish misunderstanding as was the initial naive reaction to the book's title. For as James, the mature author of *Hawthorne*, goes on to suggest, the story of *The Scarlet Letter* "is in a secondary degree that of Hester Prynne; she becomes, really, after the first scene, an accessory figure; it is not upon her the *dénoûment* depends."[4] But, of course, James's account of the success of *The Scarlet Letter* has not been the story of either Hester or her guilty lover. It has been the story of his own artistic growth, the narrative of *his* learning to read the A, a process that absorbs and transforms the account of the publication of *The Scarlet Letter,* "a literary event of first importance"[5] in a young and provincial country.

This strategy of interpretation and absorption that marks James's relation to Hawthorne characterizes his treatment of romance in general. In the preface to *The American,* where he examines the "art or mystery" by which a "given picture of life appear[s] to us to surround its theme, its figures and images, with the air of romance," he associates the "stuff of romance" with the "infancy of art;"[6] and he links his own flirtation with its charms with the innocence and naiveté of youth. Taken together the prefaces form a "thrilling tale," a "wonderous adventure" of the artist's "unfolding," of the "growth of his whole operative consciousness"[7] as he moves from the "old stupidities of touch" that characterize *The American* to the "altogether better literary manners of 'The Ambassadors' and 'The Golden Bowl.'"[8] From the point of view of the mature artist "redreaming on many of [his] gathered compositions,"[9] the charm of the earlier pieces derives from his remembered sense of the "blest absence of wonder at [observation's] being so easy" and his current recognition that he had been "plotting archromance without knowing it." This is the "truth" that emerges from "reading the book over" and it is one that the author finds both interesting and rewarding, for it brings with it the memory of the "joy" and "eagerness" of youthful "ingenuity."[10]

The thing is consistently, consummately–and I would fain really make bold to say charmingly–romantic; and all without intention, presumption, hesitation, contrition. The effect is equally undesigned and unabashed, and I lose myself, at this late hour, I am bound to add, in a certain sad envy of the free play of so much unchallenged instinct. One would like to woo back such hours of fine precipitation. They represent to the critical sense which the exercise of one's *whole* faculty has, with time, so inevitably and so thoroughly waked up, the happiest season of surrender to the invoked muse and the projected fable: the season of images so free and confident and ready that they brush questions aside and disport themselves, like the artless schoolboys of Gray's beautiful Ode, in all the ecstasy of the ignorance attending them. The time doubtless comes soon enough when questions, as I call them, rule the roost and when the little victim, to adjust Gray's term again to the creature of frolic fancy, doesn't dare propose a gambol till they have all (like a board of trustees discussing a new outlay) sat on the possibly scandalous case.[11]

From the perspective of the mature "critical sense" the creatures of the youthful artistic fancy, "images . . . free and confident," suggest an ingenuous point of view, one associated with the "careless childhood" of Gray's "little victims" who play in ignorance of the fact that they are surrounded by the "ministers of human fate."[12] This is a mode of vision that is the result of a complete surrender to "muse" and "fable," one undisturbed by complicating questions involving human relationships. The power of observing, in short, is taken for granted as the writer gives himself over to the charm of his subject happily ignorant of verisimilitude's demands that the subject be placed and defined relationally.

It is the fond memory of this youthful vision that the mature writer most values and uses as the "occasion" to explore the "art or mystery" of romance, the "determining condition" of which, being "latent,"[13] is available only to the mature critical intelligence through an act of rereading. That is to say that romance appears as such only in retrospect "only after the particular magic . . . has thoroughly operated" (30) and its appearance produces both an "amusing and even touching" sense of the "serenity" (35) of youthful "ingenuity" (34) and a newly awakened awareness that the "way things happen is frankly not the way in which they are represented as having happened" (34–35). James at once glories in the memory of his youthful vision of his hero and acknowledges that in the real world the Bellegardes would "have jumped . . . at my rich and easy American" (35) would have taken "everything he could give them" (36). It is this double sense of the artist's youthful commitment to the unity and integrity of his subject, his desire to preserve it as a *"centre,"* to "economise its value" (37–38), and his mature understanding that the law of the novel demands that the subject be placed and defined relationally, hence tied to our "vulgar communities" (33), that becomes a central concern of the prefaces. And it is a concern, too, that echoes an important preoccupation within the novels themselves, that of the conflict between youthful dreams of absolute freedom and the restricting realities of social intercourse.

There is, then, for James an "intimate connection" between the "story" of his hero or heroine and the "story of [his] story itself,"[14] and this is a latent connection that appears when, during the act of "reading over, for revision, correction and republication," the "process of production" itself suddenly becomes a "thrilling tale," a "wondrous adventure."[15] In this sense romance for James is a sign for a certain form of interpretation or understanding that occurs when the writer through the process of revision becomes the reader of his own work. For "to revise is to see, or to look over, again—which means in the case of a written thing neither more nor less than to reread it."[16] And the effect of the rereading is to reveal an inherent instability between the principles of production and the realities of consumption, between the nature of the writer's relationship to his art and the form of this relationship to his reader. For the art of the novel is one involving economics as well as aesthetics. Novels are merchandise, commodities produced to be exchanged for something else, hence the relationship between writer and reader is in part a contract relation, a fact that gives rise to problems of intention and meaning. Are the novel's words used in a "moral or financial sense" (*PL*, 24)? Is the novelist motivated by the "sublime economy of art"[17] or by the crass desire to "put money in [his or her] pocket" (*PL*, 431)? And are readers appreciators or merely consumers? Do they devour the book driven only by the childish appetite for story or do they read carefully and slowly with an eye to effect and style? The problem of figurative language, the question of representation, the issue of the relation between writer and reader: these are the recurring concerns in all of James's prefaces, but they are especially prominent in the preface to the *Portrait,* a novel at once marked by the "conscious assimilation of romance"[18] and directly concerned with the relation between the aesthetic and the economic, between works of art and money.

The preface focuses on a double problem: the nature of the writer's relation to his art and the form of his relation to his reader, that is to say on the problem of representing and reading. The figure of the reader haunts the preface to the *Portrait,* infusing its ghostly presence into the essay's metaphoric details and interrupting and delaying James's attempt to recover the "germ" of his idea for the novel. This spectre is the representative of an exterior realm, a world outside the writer's sanctuary, and he threatens to compromise the writer's artistic ideals and to violate his solitude. The essay begins with the figure of the novelist at the window of his Venice apartment "driven in the fruitless fidget of composition" to seek inspiration in the "sight of a wondrous lagoon" (*PL,* 3). However, his appeal to that "romantic and historic" site fails, and that failure is expressed in figures that question the dignity and value of the act of writing.

They are too rich in their own life and too charged with their own meanings merely to help him out with a lame phrase ... so that, after a little, he feels, while thus yearning toward them in his difficulty, as if he were asking an army of glorious veterans to help him arrest a peddlar who has given him the wrong change. (3–4)

The writer's search for "some better phrase," some "true touch for his canvas" (3) is associated with acts of haggling and cheating, and this chain of association is lengthened as James goes on to discuss the effect of beautiful places on the writer's imagination in terms of attention's being "wasted," "squandered," and "cheated" (4). The act of writing, then, from its beginning seems to depend on but also to be contaminated by a world outside the writer's study. The relation between these external and internal spaces is expressed by a set of commercial metaphors that imply a series of exchanges destined to frustrate the writer's dream of creating a self-sufficient and autonomous world.

Nevertheless, as James goes on to insist, the writer's "subject" appears to him pure and alone, free of the "tangle, to which we look for much of the impress that constitutes an identity" (8), a vivid individual yet one independent of the "cluster of appurtenances" (172) that normally represent the self. But if the writer's subject comes to him free of social tangles, it does not completely liberate him from a world of exchange. However it does appear to make his relation to that world marginal and eccentric.

The figure has to that extent, as you see, *been* placed–placed in the imagination that detains it, preserves, protects, enjoys it, conscious of its presence in the dusky, crowded, heterogeneous backshop of the mind very much as a wary dealer in precious odds and ends, competent to make an "advance" on rare objects confided to him, is conscious of a rare little "piece" left in deposit by the reduced, mysterious lady of title or the speculative amateur, and which is already there to disclose its merit afresh as soon as a key should have clicked in a cupboard-door.

That may be, I recognize, a somewhat superfine analogy for the particular "value" I here speak of . . . but it appears to fond memory quite to fit the fact—with the recall, in addition, of my pious desire but to place my treasure right. I quite remind myself thus of the dealer resigned not to "realise," resigned to keeping the precious object locked indefinitely rather than to commit it, at no matter what price, to vulgar hands. For there are dealers in these forms and figures and treasures capable of that refinement. (8)

Although James carefully conceals the circumstances of his actual acquisition of the image of Isabel Archer, this elaborate figurative description of his relation to it suggests a host of complicating factors. The image is not yet surrounded by the "envelope of circumstances" (172) that constitute society. Instead it remains at home within the writer's imagination, which, like Mr. Venus's shop in *Our Mutual Friend*, is a dusky, crowded place filled with heterogeneous objects. There it retains its independence, for its relation to its surroundings is that of one discrete and unique object among others. For the artist, like the "wary dealer in precious odds and ends," enjoys an unconventional relation to the ordinary world of social and economic intercourse. With an eye for the unusual and the "genuine" (6) the artist seems free of the confining and defining forces that constitute society. Still, the "value" of the treasure remains an entirely subjective one until it is placed, and to place it means to remove it from the confines of the imagination and to locate it within the tangle of human relationships where its value and meaning will be determined relationally. Moreover, because the act of placing the treasure is one of social and commercial engagement, the writer must leave the protective solitude of his eccentricity and enter a more conventional world.

This is a world of tradition, history, and established conventions that threatens to devalue the treasure by destroying its uniqueness. The artist's first "problem" (9), therefore, is one of distinguishing the "slim shade of an intelligent but presumptuous girl" (8) from the "Juliets and Cleopatras and Portias," the "Hettys and Maggies and Rosamonds and Gwendolens" (9) of romance who have "their inadequacy eked out with comic relief and underplots . . . when not with murders and battles and the great mutations of the world" (9). This will be accomplished by making her the center of interest and focusing on her sense of her "mild adventure" (14), for her consciousness will convert it "into the stuff of drama or, even more delightful word still, of 'story'" (14), thereby making it "'interesting' as the surprise of a caravan or the identification of a pirate" (14). In this way the author will generate the interest of romance but remain independent of its tawdry trappings, be able to place the treasure without committing it to vulgar hands. Moreover the account of the way this process of "conversion" is managed becomes itself a marvelous adventure of difficulties "braved" and dangers "intensified," a story of "evasion," "retreat," and "flight" (10). This is to say that both Isabel's story and James's story of that story are energized by process that absorbs and transforms the conventions of romance by using them to construct a system of metaphor, and this system is designed to make possible an interchange between different orders of experience.

These orders are represented, on the one hand, by the image of Isabel and on the other by the "ado" that the novelist must organize around her, since the "novel is by its very nature an ado about something" (9) The "ado" is provided by the characters who surround Isabel, "satellites" who are to function as the "rockets, the roman candles and Catherine-wheels of a 'pyrotechnic display'" (11) and who are "like the group of attendants and entertainers who come down by train when people in the country give a party; they [represent] the contract for carrying the party on" (12). These are the "other lights, contending, conflicting" with the "light in which Isabel Archer had originally dawned" but expressing the author's "anxiety" to "provide for the reader's amusement" (11), an anxiety that reveals another view of creative authority. No longer can the author envision himself as an eccentric pawnbroker, a dealer in precious odds and ends who relates only to mysterious aristocrats and speculative amateurs. These other metaphors suggest, rather, the professional entertainer and party-giver whose primary obligation is to the felt need "to be amusing" (15). In this case there is no question of protecting precious objects or avoiding vulgar hands. Here the emphasis falls on the "benefit" that can be expected from the reader, and that is a form of enchantment resulting from a spell cast "upon the simpler, the very simplest form of attention." The "quantity of attention" that is required for consciousness of spell is the "living wage" for which the novelist works and any act of "reflexion" or "discrimination" on the reader's part must be regarded as a "tip" or "gratuity 'thrown in'" (12). No longer is the novelist privileged as the owner of money always is over the owner of commodities. The balance of power has shifted. Now it is the novelist who is in the inferior position both economically and socially. As George Simmel has noticed, the principle of supplement whereby the buyer demands and receives an extra measure points to the superior position of the owner of money. (It is precisely an effort to provide an extra measure of amusement that caused James, as he says, to *"over-treat"* (15) in his portrayal of Henrietta Stackpole.) Moreoever, as Simmel further notes, when the supplement is provided by the owner of money, as in the case of a gratuity, the act simply expresses the social superiority of the giver.[19]

The preface to the *Portrait*, then, offers a vision of the "artist doubled with a man of business" and this "monstrous duality"[20] implies two apparently incompatible theories of writing, the one associated with the pure vision of the artist and founded on the love of form, the other directed toward the uncontrolled "appetite" for adventure of an "unreflective and uncritical"[21] reader and based on a love of gain. And this conflict between the demands of art and those of the marketplace is thematized within the novel itself which, like *Our Mutual Friend*, is about "money, money, money and what money can make of life." Both Dickens and James are interested in the problems resulting from the inheritance of a great fortune and in the effects that the presence or absence of money has on human lives. For almost all the characters in the *Portrait* the "money question [is] always a trouble" (*PL*, 368). The lack of money has narrowed the expectations of Osmond, Madame Merle, and the Countess Gemini and threatens the happiness of Rosier and Pansy. Indeed the world of the *Portrait* is one where the relations of people to one another, to social institutions, and to works of art are marked by monetary interests. All human activities, in short, are regulated by paradigm of exchange. As the expression and equivalent of all values, money becomes the center of the novel's action, the secular god of its world.[22]

Ralph Touchet, fascinated by the figure of his attractive cousin, decides to make her independent in a "financial" as well as in a "moral" (24) sense in order that she be able to "meet the requirements of her imagination" (158), but in so doing he becomes the "beneficent author of infinite woe" (351) for in making her free "to choose" he makes her free to fall and thus condemns her to a life of "darkness and suffocation (355). This chain of association is lengthened by similar figures that echo *Paradise Lost* and *Aeropagitica* and mix together the theological metaphor of the Fall with the apparently unrelated economic metaphor of money. Feeling the new freedom that comes with her inherited fortune, the "absolute boldness and wantonness of liberty" (267), Isabel bids farewell to her visiting American relatives and prepares to begin her new life.

The world lay before her—she could do whatever she chose. There was a deep thrill in it all, but for the present her choice was tolerably discreet; she chose simply to walk back from Euston Square to her hotel. The early dusk of a November afternoon had already closed in . . . our heroine was unattended and Euston Square was a long way from Picadilly. But Isabel performed the journey with a positive enjoyment of its dangers and lost her way almost on purpose, in order to get more sensations, so she was disappointed when an obliging policeman easily set her right again. (267)

One effect of this allusion to *Paradise Lost* is to emphasize the reduction and impoverishment of the Christian myth which has become completely socialized and trivialized. Here Isabel appears most obviously as that "frail vessel" of which James writes in the preface, one of the "smaller female fry" (9) whose familiar adventures can hardly be seen as possessing epic dignity. Nevertheless, James also insists that his "frail vessel" possesses the "high attributes of a subject" (9) more in keeping with the Miltonic model. And in extravagantly elevating one of the "smaller female fry" (3) to the status of the subject (a "task unattempted" (9) by Scott, Dickens, and Stevenson), James himself assumes a Miltonic dignity. Once again, however, the central issue is the extent to which the writer's artistic ideal is undermined by the demands of his story. And indeed James's description of Isabel as a "rare little piece" calls attention to a set of similar figures within the novel itself that seem to copy and hollow out the one in the preface. Its world is filled with such valuable pieces that are bought, sold, collected, and admired for a variety of reasons. Isabel, alone in the gallery at Gardencourt near the end of the novel, offers a suggestive reading of the significance of such objects.

> She envied the security of valuable "pieces" which change by no hair's breadth, only grow in value, while their owners lose inch by inch youth, happiness, beauty; and she became aware that she was walking about as her aunt had done on the day she had come to see her in Albany. She was changed enough since then—that had been the beginning. It suddenly struck her that if her aunt Lydia had not come that day in just that way and found her alone, everything might have been different. She might have had another life and she might have been a woman more blest. She stopped in the gallery in front of a small picture—a charming and precious Bonington—upon which her eyes rested a long time. But she was not looking at the picture; she was wondering whether if her aunt had not come that day in Albany she would have married Casper Goodwood. (464)

At issue here, of course, is a question of *value,* a word that appears repeatedly in the *Portrait* in a variety of contexts but almost always in a mode that entangles ideas of aesthetic value and economic value. For example, the value of a "real collector's piece" (296) is a double one: it possesses qualities that give it an inherent worth and that grant a certain dignity and authority to its owner; but it also enjoys an economic value that has little or nothing to do with its inherent qualities but that is established by the expenditure of another object in exchange for it. Economic objects have meaning only in terms of exchange. Appropriately, money, the medium of exchange, possesses no content of its own.[23] In the above passage these two very different notions of value are mixed and confused. The pieces are valuable, first, because, like Keats's urn, they belong to an immutable world of art that is "all breathing human passion far above." Their beauty remains while that of their owner tragically fades. Nevertheless in their changelessness they grow in value, for while their beauty and meaning remain the same, their exchange value increases. But Isabel, who according to James's plan for the novel, will be primarily concerned with "her relationship to herself" (11) measures the value of the pieces in purely subjective terms. Characteristically she gazes at the "precious Bonington," without seeing it, her attention caught by her own inner life, and her meditation reminds the reader of Isabel's own representational status.

Isabel's meditation on these valuable pieces echoes not only James's description of her in the preface as a "rare little piece" but also Ralph's appreciative reaction to her as "an interesting little figure" (62). For her ill and bored cousin, she is "entertainment of a high order . . . finer than the finest work of art–than a Greek bas-relief, than a great Titian, than a Gothic cathedral" (62–63). In a sense Ralph's decision to "put money in her purse" (158) is an attempt to make Isabel's economic value equal to her aesthetic value for it is designed to "facilitate the execution of good impulses" (160). The effect, however, is to cause her "ruin" (470) for it results in her becoming one of Osmond's "fine pieces" (302).

Osmond, of course, is another collector of "pictures . . . medallions and tapestries" (219), a few "good things" that "hint that nothing but the right 'values' was of any consequence" (215). Initially, Osmond sees Isabel as a "present of incalculable value," a fine object that will reflect his thought "on a polished elegant surface" (290). Her value for him is that of a representation but in a social rather than an aesthetic sense. Like his other "treasures" she is esteemed because she will "extract" from the "base, ignoble world . . . some recognition of [Osmond's] own superiority" (353). On the one hand he wants to dissociate himself from the vulgar world of commerce, to insist that he has never "scrambled or struggled" (88) for money, that his interest in others is only for their "advantage, not for any profit to a person already so generally, so perfectly provided as Gilbert Osmond" (391). On the other hand, however, his social relations are valued entirely for the "prospect of gain" (391) that they promise. This aspect of Osmond is rendered brilliantly by James both in his description of him as a "fine gold coin" but with "no stamp nor emblem of the common mintage that provides for general circulation; he was the elegant complicated medal struck off for a special occasion" (194) and by the picture of him alone in his study meticulously copying from a book the "drawing of an antique coin," transferring the image of the "delicate, finely-tinted disk" to a "sheet of immaculate paper" (436). Here at once is an indication of Osmond's "exquisite" taste and a sign that that taste has commercial origins. His "box of water colours and fine brushes" (436), his immaculate paper, and the delicate disk cannot conceal the fact that he is reproducing a copy of a copy of an object that may itself have been mechanically reproduced, and that object is a token of money. Isabel's sense of her husband's "blasphemous sophistry" (439) seems exactly to the point since both Plato and Aristotle associate the sophist with the exchange of apparent wisdom for money. Like the sophist Osmond insists that "what I value most in life is the honour of a thing" (438) while demonstrating through his words and action that like the monetary token whose image he copies his values are the product of an external impress.[24] All other objects have a content from which they derive value, but money derives its content from its value—it represents the values of things without the things themselves. Osmond's words are like coins because while they seem to represent "something transcendental and absolute, like the sign of the cross or the flag of one's country" (439), they are, in fact, forms without a content.

In contrast to Osmond is Edward Rosier, another collector of "pretty things" (299) who, with his "eye for decorative character, his instinct for authenticity," and a "sense of uncatalogued values" (303), is capable of appreciating both people and objects of art in a way that Osmond is not. His fascination with Pansy echoes with a difference Osmond's interest in Isabel. Initially she seems to him a "consummate piece"–"he thought of her in amorous meditation a good deal as he would have thought of a "Dresden-China shepherdess" (296). But Rosier's attitude toward his things–"I love my things"–and toward Pansy–"I care more for Miss Osmond than all the *bibelots* in Europe" (396)– indicates a sense of relation that Osmond never experiences. Osmond cares only for "one's money" (310), and Rosier's "forty thousand francs a year and a nice character" (299) fail to qualify him as a son-in-law. Recognizing that in Osmond's eye he is not a "real collector's piece" (296), Rosier exchanges his beloved *bibelots* for money: "I have the money instead–fifty thousand dollars" (431). Although he is careful to "put them in good hands," he gives them up in order to "put money in [his] pocket" (431). His interest, however, is not in money but in Pansy, whom he loves. Earlier he had insisted that he can "buy very well, but . . . can't sell" since it takes "much more ability to make other people buy than to buy yourself" (184), but now his love for Pansy introduces another and higher system of values that re-directs and changes the meaning of his commercial transactions.

Isabel's relation to Ralph, Osmond, and Rosier–all of whom are collectors of interesting figures–develops in a context that echoes suggestively James's rereading of the novel in the preface. This echoing effect serves to contaminate the purity of his aes-thetic ideal by associating him with the desires and limitations of his characters, and it serves to confuse the ontological status of the characters, thereby breaking the spell of art and disen-chanting the reader. Once we see that the "figure" of Isabel is transferred from hand to hand–from an unknown source to James, to Ralph, to Osmond–we are caught in a sliding process that is impossible to stop at any one particular point or mean-ing. The characters like the author become for us irreducibly double, at once "authentic and elusive [people] moving through visible and tangible territories"[25] and painted portraits, valuable pieces in a tasteful collection of good things. And this sense of troubling doubleness is echoed by the theory of representation that governs the logic of both preface and novel and shapes the relation between James and his reader.

"The most fundamental and general sign of the novel," James writes in "The Lesson of Balzac," "is its being everywhere an effort at *representation*."[26] Indeed, the "only reason for the existence of a novel is that it does attempt to represent life."[27] However, as James recognizes, "people differ infinitely as to what . . . constitutes representation"[28] for the concept is more complicated than it first appears. James's model for his idea of representation is the painted image. For him the "analogy between the art of the painter and the art of the novelist is . . . complete."[29] A "community of method" exists between the "artist who paints a picture and the artist who writes the novel"; hence the novel can best be thought of as a "prose picture."[30]

This analogy between painting and the novel informs James's literary and critical vocabulary and seems to provide a familiar and comfortable foundation for creative and interpretive activities, for it suggests not only a clear and unambiguous relationship between the image and the represented entity, but a perfect compatibility between language and vision as well. For James, however, representation is a more problematic process than the analogy between painting and writing at first suggests. For him the act of representing involves more than the mere duplication of sense data and hence cannot be thought of simply as imitation: "But the affair of the painter is not the immediate, it is the reflected field of life, the realm not of application, but of *appreciation*. . . . My report of people's experience—my report as a 'story-teller'—is essentially my appreciation of it. . . ."[31] Representation, in other words, is a constructive, interpretive act that derives from an "impression of life,"[32] life seen as an image, in a glass darkly, not face to face. The novelist does not depict the real but a represented or interpreted version of the real. Consequently, the art of the novel unlike that of lyrical poetry, is not one of immediacy and presence.

The Poet is most the Poet when he is preponderantly lyrical, when he speaks . . . most directly from his individual heart, which throbs under the impressions of life. It is not the *image* of life that he thus expresses, so much as life itself, in its sources—so much as his intimate, essential states and feelings. By the time he has begun to collect anecdotes, to tell stories, to represent scenes, to concern himself, that is, with states and feelings of others, he is well on the way not to be the Poet pure and simple.[33]

As "lovers of the image of life" novelists seem to prefer distance and difference to a sense of unmediated presence. The novel is precisely a "monument,"[34] a "bequest,"[35] that is the record of an absence, a deferred and indirect account of a direct exposure. James writes that "There is, to my vision, no authentic, and no really interesting and no *beautiful,* report of things on the novelist's, the painter's part unless a particular detachment has operated, unless . . . the observant and recording and interpreting mind in short, has intervened and played its part—and this detachment, this chemical transmutation for the aesthetic, the representational, end is wanting in autobiography brought, as the horrible phrase is, up to date."[36]

James's view of representation, then, complicates that of the one traditionally associated with realism. For him the novel is not simply the verbal representation of social reality, a standing for or standing in place of something that exists somewhere else and in another time. Prior to the act of verbally representing is the "power of life to project itself upon [man's] imagination" and to produce the "impressions" that are "experience," the "very air we breath."[37] And since "experience" for James is "our apprehension and our measure of what happens to us as social creatures,"[38] the source of that "power" is the figure of the other. Consequently the act of literary representation is subsequent to and dependent on another form of representation, one that comes into play whenever the self confronts the other.[39]

Selves for James are not accessible to one another in direct or obvious ways. His novels insist on the importance of "feel[ing] one's relation . . . to others" (*PL*, 286) and at the same time emphasize the distance and difference that disturb and problematize any attempt to establish meaningful relations to others. His characters come to see that selfhood depends on the presence of others and yet that presence is experienced as a kind of absence. Others appear to me—they are there—but they appear as aliens; they present themselves as unpresentable. They cannot, in other words, be present to me in their own persons, and hence some form of representation is called for.[40] To represent the self is to offer something to stand in its place, something that is not the self but that is, perhaps, analogous to it. For this reason the self always appears as a sign, an image necessitating reading, appreciation, interpretation. Hence the concept of identity itself is a form of representation to the extent that it is a social category and is defined in terms of "career . . . name . . . position . . . fortune . . . past . . . future" (*PL*, 169). For Madame Merle, Ralph Touchet's selfhood is represented by his disease, which is a "kind of position." Ralph's father, on the other hand, "represents a great financial house" (169), while Gilbert Osmond may be defined in terms of his painting or the fact that he is a father. This attitude is not simply the expression of Madame Merle's cynicism, for most of the characters in the *Portrait* exist in such a representational mode. Henrietta Stackpole is the "representative of the *Interviewer*" (175); Lord Warburton, "a fine specimen," is a "representative of the British race" (242); Isabel represents Gilbert Osmond and Pansy "represents" Isabel's "responsibility" (292).

As Laurence Holland has noticed, this form of representation differs in obvious ways from the model of representational painting that is suggested by the title of the *Portrait* and the association of sketching and writing within the novel.[41] However, the two models are related, and the form of the relationship is suggested by Lord Warburton's assertion that "You can't see ideas" (23). Like feelings and emotions, ideas belong to inward experience and depend on some form of representation to make them visible. The more complicted the idea, of course, the more difficult the problem of representing it becomes. "The two words in the language [Mrs. Touchet] most respects are Yes and No" (230), presumably because in each case the distance between the concept and the sound image that represents it is bridgeable and remains stable. But Ralph's more complicated vision results in such a "fanciful, pictorial way of saying things" that his mother feels that she is being addressed in a "deaf mute's alphabet" (230). "'I don't know what you mean' she said, 'You use too many figures of speech: I never could understand allegories'" (230).

James, of course, shares Mrs. Touchet's dislike of allegory, a process he describes as a "story told as if it were another and very different story."[42] Nevertheless, as he recognizes, metaphor has its allegorical aspects in the sense that it is an attempt to represent in words that which we experience, and experience for James consists of impressions, of seeing. Hence his ideal of the "prose picture" expresses a desire to be able to say what he sees, to render exactly with words the image that appears in the mirror of consciousness. However, as the examples of Ralph and his mother make clear, the realms of vision and language are not equivalents. What is seen, of course, is itself a sign, and Ralph's highly metaphoric language problematizes rather than clarifies the relation between the human hieroglyph and its verbal signifier by making the primary question one of the nature of the relation between the figures themselves. What, for example, does a tender young rose have in common with a bird, an encastled princess, a physician, a steam ship, or a sailing vessel, all of which are figures that Ralph uses to describe Isabel?

Ralph's difficulty in representing his vision of Isabel is mirrored by that of his creator. James's description of Isabel's vigil as the "best thing in the book" and a "supreme illustration of the book's general plan" points directly to the problem, for the chapter as a "representation simply of her motionless *seeing*" is designed to offer a verbal image of her "inward life" that will have "all the vivacity of incident and all the economy of picture" (14). It will be a moment of pure vision but will also have the interest of the sequential aspects of narrative. Few critics would quarrel with James's assessment of this admirable chapter. Nevertheless, in some ways it, like Ralph's pictorial way of speaking, points to the incompatibility between language and vision. To be sure the chapter is in some sense a "portrait of a lady," but it is also a revelation of the differences that exist between words and pictures, since it demonstrates that neither can be reduced to the other's terms.

It is true that Isabel, motionless and alone, seems to occupy a space where she is free only to look, but it is equally true that that space is filled both for her and the reader by signs of an intrusive temporality. Her vision is of a tangle of relationships that are represented by her departed husband's words: "She had answered nothing because his words had put the situation before her and she was absorbed in looking at it. There was something in them that suddenly made vibrations deep, so that she had been afraid to trust herself to speak. After he had gone she leaned back in her chair and closed her eyes; and for a long time, far into the night and still further, she sat in the still drawing-room given up to her meditation" (347). Osmond's words seem at first to have been transformed into a picture, thereby placing Isabel's situation within the space of her vision. This moment of insight, however, has been generated partially by the "strange impression she had received in the afternoon of her husband's being in more direct communication with Madame Merle than she suspected" (349), and hence does not occur in the form of an unambiguous flash of meaning; rather, it manifests itself as a series of readings or interpretations that take the form of successive moments in a narrative. Isabel must "read" (348) the signs of Warburton's attitude in order to grasp the relation between his past desires and present intentions; place those interpretations within the context of her knowledge that her problems with Osmond derive from the fact that "she had not read him right" (351) as well as her sense that she can now "read" him "as she would have read the hour on the clock-face" (356); and, finally, decide how her current reading of Osmond is to shape her relations to Warburton, Ralph, and Pansy.

Isabel's vision, then, is both the result and expression of an uninterrupted and irresistible flow of time, and James's portrayal of that "motionless seeing" reveals time's erosive power. Movement persists in spite of the illusion of simultaneity, for the moment of insight is spread out across a temporal field marked by Warburton's arrival at ten at night, his departure half an hour later, Osmond's appearance at eleven, and the clock's striking four at the end of the chapter.

The attempt in this chapter to synthesize the spatial and temporal, stasis and motion, the "economy of picture" and the "economy of interest"[43] is an effort to reconcile the acts of writing and reading by placing both within the same closed system. But the painterly model for narrative that James emphasizes in this chapter and in the title of *Portrait* is partially subverted by a paradigm of textuality. The alternating motion of reading violates the sense of "motionlessly seeing" and disturbs the illusion of unmediated experience by introducing the problem of the other. Against the notion of the novel as a "sketch" or prose picture and against the ideal of moments of pure vision James sets the suggestion that both characters and novelist are readers of a text caught within a system of signs that, like one of Mrs. Touchet's puzzling telegrams "admit of so many interpretations" (24). Isabel seems to her brother-in-law to be "written in a foreign tongue. I can't make her out" (37). Warburton must be "read" by Isabel "more or less between the lines" (390), while Ralph, in his dealings with Henrietta Stackpole, who "challenged all his ingenuity of interpretation," finds it easier "to read between the lines ... than to follow the text" (109). Pansy, in her innocence, is like a "blank sheet of paper," a "fair and smooth page" (233) that Isabel hopes will be "covered with an edifying text" (262), while the well-used Countess Gemini "has been written over in a variety of hands" and has a "number of unmistakable blots ... upon her surface" (233).

If the textuality paradigm offers a model of intelligiblity for dealing with the interpersonal world of social relations, it also puts into question both Mr. Touchet's traditional assumption that he is able to receive "information in the natural form" (57) rather than through books and Isabel's dream of being free and open to pure experience. The primary problem in James's world is not the problem of the book. Although Isabel's initial situation seems to echo that of Scott's Waverley, her blindness differs from his in important ways. Like him she is "spoiled and neglected as a child," has "no regular education and no permanent home" (40), the "foundation of her knowledge [being] laid in the idleness of her grandmother's house, where . . . she had uncontrolled use of a library full of books" (33). But as a daughter of the Puritans, Isabel reads not to escape from the reality of things but in an innocent attempt to "fix her mind" (33), to "transfer the seat of consciousness to the organ of pure reason" (92). Although she has a bookish reputation and is found by her aunt "reading a heavy book and boring herself to death" (47), Isabel, like her uncle, "really preferred almost any source of information to the printed page" (41). Her eyes characteristically "wander from the book in her hand to the open window" (475). Books for Isabel are little more than distractions, and while she often holds them and fingers them, she seldom reads them. We see her holding a book but "without going through the form of opening the volume" (143), find her "seated in a library with a volume to which her attention was not fastened" (176) or "holding a volume of Ampere . . . in her lap with her finger vaguely kept in the place" (255). Indeed in the world of the *Portrait* all books, like those "rare and valuable volumes" (475) in Ralph's library, are objects to be held, their pages fingered, their bindings admired, and then to be carefully set aside. Like Madame Merle's "pastimes" books are "laid down" (165) as easily as taken up and reading as an activity is neither more nor less valuable than letter writing, painting, "touching the piano," or any other "cultivated and cultured" (164) activity.

As the textuality paradigm suggests, however, these bound volumes are parts of a larger socially given text, and it is this larger one that characteristically draws Isabel's attention from the printed ones.

Seated toward nine o'clock in the dim illumination of Pratt's Hotel and trying with the aid of two tall candles to lose herself in a volume she had brought from Gardencourt, she succeeded only to the extent of reading other words than those printed on the page—words that Ralph had spoken to her that afternoon. Suddenly the well-muffled knuckle of the waiter was applied to the door, which presently gave way to his exhibition, even as a glorious trophy, of the card of a visitor. When this memento had offered to her fixed sight the name of Mr. Casper Goodwood she let the man stand before her without signifying her wishes.

"Shall I show the gentleman up, ma'am?" he asked with a slightly encouraging inflexion.

Isabel hesitated still and while she hesitated glanced at the mirror. "He may come in," she said at last; and waited for him not so much smoothing her hair as girding her spirit. (133–34)

Spoken discourse no less than the written text must be read. Like calling cards, those "oblong morsels of symbolic pasteboard" (59), or like one's image in the mirror, spoken words as a form of representation imply that the subject is not present in his or her own person. As Isabel holds her book she is confronted first by the image of Ralph's vision of her future—the "world interests you and you want to throw yourself into it" (132)—then by the calling card, a sign that stands for another person and yet another version of her destiny, and, finally, by her own mirror image, a two-dimensional reflection of her body on glass that manages nevertheless to represent her ambivalent relation to Goodwood, the extent to which she wishes both to attract and resist him. Following their conversation and Goodwood's departure, Isabel "takes up her book, but without going through the form of opening the volume" (143) and enjoys the memory of what she takes to be the first "exercise of her power," the expression of her "love of liberty," only to be reminded by Henrietta that her ideas of happiness resemble those of the heroine of an "immoral novel" (144).

This episode is an interesting one because it opens up the problem of the book, setting experience and natural information against secondary book knowledge but also putting such a formulation into question by revealing the textual nature of ordinary discourse. This is, of course, an important issue for James as well as for Isabel as the emphasis on reading in the prefaces makes clear. Like Isabel, James at times seems to privilege direct experience over written accounts of it: "One can read when one is middle-aged or old," he writes to his brother, William, "but one can mingle in the world with fresh perceptions only when one is young. The great thing is to be *saturated* with something, that is in one way or another with life; and I chose the form of my saturation. Moreover you exaggerate the degree to which my writing takes it out of my mind, for I try to spend only the interest of my capital."[44] This interesting observation parallels Isabel's attitude and situation in a variety of ways. James, too, insists that he "wants to see for [himself] (*PL*, 132), to experience direct impressions rather than to secure them second-hand by way of books. However his interest is not in life for its own sake, nor with his liberty or personal independence, but rather with the act of writing, which depends upon his being saturated with life. Writing demands a direct involvement with life, but as productive, active economic activity it refines and improves life.

Life being all inclusion and confusion, and art being all discrimination and selection, the latter, in search of the hard latent *value* with which alone it is concerned, sniffs round the mass as instinctively and unerringly as a dog suspicious of some buried bone. The difference here, however, is that, while the dog desires his bone but to destroy it, the artist finds *his* tiny nugget, washed free of awkward accretions and ham-

mered into a sacred hardness, the very stuff for a clear affirmation, the happiest chance for the indestructible. It at the same
time amuses him again and again to note how, beyond the
first step of the actual case, the case that constitutes for him
his germ, his vital particle, his grain of gold, life persistently
blunders and deviates, loses herself in the sand. The reason is
of course, that life has no direct sense whatever for the subject
and is capable, luckily for us, of nothing but splendid waste.
Hence the opportunity for the sublime economy of art,
which rescues, which saves, and hoards and "banks," investing
and reinvesting these fruits of toil in wondrous useful "works"
and thus making up for us, desperate spendthrifts that we all
naturally are, the most precious of incomes.[45]

This suggestive passage nicely illuminates the complexities of
James's double economy. It begins with what seems to be a clear
explanation of the special "value" of the prose picture that is
based on an unambiguous distinction between the realms of art
and life. Like the textuality figure, however, the economic metaphor contaminates the ideal of pure vision by way of notions of
equivalence and exchange. As a product, this passage implies,
the novel must submit itself to an economic system and become
merchandise subject to desires other than those that produced
it. Unlike the writer the reader is often concerned with the "fact
of consumption"[46] and regards the novel as a "good dinner"
with a happy ending being a "course of dessert and ices and the
artist in the fiction . . . as a sort of meddlesome doctor who for-
bids agreeable aftertastes."[47] This is the reader who will "con-
sume" fiction "on the scale and with the smack of lips that mark
the consumption of bread-and-jam by a children's school-feast."[48]
It is perhaps this aspect of the reading process that leads James
to write that "I am a wretched person to *read* a novel—I began
so quickly and concomitantly, *for myself,* to write it rather—
even before I know clearly what it's about! The novel I can *only*
read I can't read at all!"[49]
Nevertheless writing and reading are inextricably entangled,
the one act inevitably conditioned by and dependent on

the other. In this sense the art of the novelist like that of the physician is the result and expression of the flawed human condition. From the reader's point of view the novel is an "anodyne" that like the "dentist's ether, muffles the ache of the actual"[50] by offering us another world. It is precisely that "ache" that is responsible for man's "appetite for a picture," a vicarious desire for the derived and secondhand.

And if we are pushed a step farther backward, and asked why the representation should be required when the object represented is itself mostly so accessible, the answer to that appears to be that man combines with his eternal desire for more experience an infinite cunning as to getting his experience as cheaply as possible. He will steal it whenever he can. He likes to live the life of others, yet is well aware of the points at which it may too intolerably resemble his own. The vivid fable, more than anything else, gives him this satisfaction on easy terms, gives him knowledge abundant yet vicarious. It enables him to select, to take and to leave; so that to feel that he can afford to neglect it, he must have a rare faculty, or great opportunities for the extension of experience . . . at first hand.[51]

Because fiction creates the illusion that "for a time . . . we have lived another life," it allows us to "live at the expense of someone else,"[52] to satisfy our desire for experience but to avoid being "exposed and entangled"[53] ourselves. Hence there are those—especially children and the "innumerable women who, under modern arrangements, increasingly fail to marry"—who "live in a great measure by the immediate aid of the novel." These are, one hardly needs to add, the traditional readers of romance, "irreflective and uncritical," concerned with "the fact of consumption alone."[54] Clearly the principles of economy and representation implied by this perspective differ in obvious and important ways from the "sublime economy of art" and the notion of the prose picture that James associates with the act of writing. Writing as an activity is usually linked to saving, investing, and reinvesting, to the production of the "most princely of incomes." Reading on the other hand is an activity engaged in by someone too poor, too lazy, or too young to approach experience directly and is associated with a lower class world of haggling and cheating. Moreover, the overwhelming "appetite for a picture" establishes a "demand" that threatens the "splendid . . . economy"[55] of the novel by causing it to become an "object of easy manufacture," an article of commerce. The result is a flood of "monstrous multiplications" and the "bankrupt state"[56] of the novel as a form.

The acts of reading and writing, then, appear, paradoxically, to be mutually dependent but incompatible activities. The "object" of the novel is to represent life but the "effect" is to "entertain,"[57] and the "effect" seems to contaminate the "object." *The Portrait of a Lady* represents James's attempt to harmonize these two opposing principles. However, the artist is governed by one economic law and the reader by another, so that the two economies can never be congruous. The principle of composition is always dislocated by the principle of consumption, the act of reading in perpetual conflict with the act of writing. It is this incompatibility that becomes for James the very mark of the novel as a form, at once the sign of its flawed nature and the source of its enormous energy. He writes in "The Future of the Novel" that man will renounce fiction "only when life itself too thoroughly disagrees with him. Even then, indeed, may fiction not find a second wind, or a fiftieth, in the very portrayal of that collapse. Till the world is an unpeopled void there will always be an image in the mirror."[58]

FIVE

Faulkner and the Sepulcher of Romance: The Voices of Absalom, Absalom!

But still her love clings to her and increases
And grows on suffering; she cannot sleep,
She frets and pines, becomes all gaunt and haggard,
Her body dries and shrivels till voice only
And bones remain, and then she is voice only
For the bones are turned to stone. She hides in woods
And no one sees her now along the mountains,
But all may hear her, for her voice is living.

Ovid, *Metamorphoses*

Faulkner's conception of fiction, like those of Hawthorne, Melville and James, is linked to the acts of writing and reading. For him as for his American precursors the writer is at first a reader. Asked what is the best training for writing he replies, "Read, read, read. Read everything—trash, classics, good and bad, and see how they do it. Just as a carpenter who works as an apprentice and studies the master. Read. You'll absorb it. Then write."[1] However, Faulkner's reading does not seem to generate the anxiety of influence that troubles earlier American writers. Nor does it appear to make him more sensitive to his own relationship to a reader. He happily acknowledges the fact that "any writer is a thief and robber" who will "steal from any source," and maintains that a writer's only obligation is "to get the work done the best he can do it," a responsibility that is so demanding that "he has no time to think of the reader." Because the writer is a "creature driven by demons,"[2] "demon driven with something to be said,"[3] the act of writing is his only concern and the product of primary importance. "The artist is of no importance," he asserts. "Only what he creates is important. . . . "[4] Hence Faulkner prefers to speak of books rather than authors. "I have no favorite authors. I have favorite books," he insists.[5] And he insists too on maintaining an absolute distinction between his personal existence and the world of his novels. Unlike Hawthorne and Melville he denies that there is any significant relation between his biographical and literary selves and ignores the question of his personal identity and the form of its manifestation to the world. "It is my ambition to be, as a private individual abolished and voided from history, leaving it markless, no refuse save the printed book," he writes to Malcolm Cowley.[6] As David Minter suggests, this attitude is consistent with Faulkner's sense that the creative act is one "in which the hackneyed accidents which make up his world—love and life and death and sex and sorrow—brought together by chance in perfect proportions, take on a kind of splendid and timeless beauty."[7] Faulkner, then, will write no familiar or critical prefaces exploring the origin and status of his fiction in the manner of Hawthorne and James. About the process of creation and the nature of the relation between the fictive and real he prefers to remain silent. And yet as Minter acutely observes, these personal and aesthetic issues are explored indirectly in his work[8] and nowhere more clearly than in *Absalom, Absalom!*, where the situations of the writer and reader and the question of the nature of the fictive world are inscribed within the novel in the situations of the characters. With its "marks" we may begin an investigation of Faulknerian romance.

Read it if you like or don't read it if you like. Because you make so little impression, you see. You get born and you try this and you don't know why only you keep on trying it and you are born at the same time with a lot of other people, all mixed up with them, like trying to, having to, move your arms and legs with strings only the same strings are hitched to all the other arms and legs and the others all trying and they don't know why either except that the strings are all in one another's way like five or six people all trying to make a rug on the same loom only each one wants to weave his own pattern into the rug; and it cant matter, you know that, or the Ones that set up the loom would have arranged things a little better, and yet it must matter because you keep on trying or having to keep on trying and then all of a sudden it's all over and all you have left is a block of stone with scratches on it provided there was someone to remember to have the marble scratched and set up or had time to, and it rains on it and the sun shines on it and after a while they dont even remember the name and what the scratches were trying to tell, and it doesn't matter. And so maybe if you could go to someone, the stranger the better, and give them something—a scrap of paper—something, anything, it not to mean anything in itself and them not even to read it or keep it, not even bother to throw it away or destroy it, at least it would be something just because it would have happened, be remembered even if only passing from one hand to another, one mind to another, and it would be at least a scratch, something that might make a mark on something that *was* once for the reason that it can die someday, while the block of stone can't be *is* because it can never become *was* because it can't ever die or perish. (*AA*, 127–28)

Like *Pierre* and *The Marble Faun, Absalom, Absalom!* is a text that tangles together issues of generation, representation, and interpretation. The above passage, like the novel, knots together life lines, family lines, and narrative lines into a labyrinthine entanglement of language that both characters and readers seek to unravel or untie by tracing a thread of logic through its bewildering complexity and by reading anonymous "scratches on stone" and letters without "salutation or signature" (129). We seek the design hidden by the surface tangles, the denouement that will solve, dissolve, resolve.[9] This is a process that Faulkner seems to have in mind when he describes the story and its climax: "The story is an anecdote which occurred during and right after the civil war; the climax is another anecdote which happened about 1910 and which explains the story. . . . Quentin Compson of the Sound and Fury tells it, or ties it together; he is the protagonist so that it is not complete apocrypha."[10] One anecdote it appears is the resolution or the denouement of the other in the sense that it explains by untying or unraveling as the mystery of the life and death of the Sutpen family is solved by the revelation of the identity of the mysterious figure "living hidden in that house" (172) at Sutpen's Hundred. This seemingly definitive ending, however, leaves behind the confused figure of Quentin, who, as Faulkner says, ties it all together, but certainly not in the sense of a neat fold or clear design. Indeed, once we see that Quentin himself is deeply and personally involved in the story its lines are rewoven, the fabric of narrative like the rug of life tangled by the impress of self. "Everytime any character gets into a book," Faulkner has said, "he's actually telling his biography, talking about himself, in a thousand different terms, but himself."[11] In other words, Quentin attempts to weave his own pattern into the rug by telling and interpreting the drama of Thomas Sutpen and in the process tangles his own story with those of Sutpen, Rosa Coldfield, and Shreve. And these tangles are further ensnarled by the fact that Quentin himself belongs to the "old ghost-times" that he describes; "too young to deserve yet to be a ghost, but nevertheless having to be one for all of that" (9), not only in the figurative sense of living in the past but in a literal one as well since his suicide is recorded in *The Sound and the Fury* written seven years before *Absalom, Absalom!* The fact of death, the desire to say "No" to it by leaving a "record"[12]: these generate the tangles of life and narrative and make the acts of reading and writing examples of man's attempts "endlessly to express himself and to make contact with other human beings."[13]

In *Absalom, Absalom!* as in *Pierre* the problem of genealogy is primary. Sutpen's story is that of a "man who wanted a son through pride; and got too many of them and they destroyed him,"[14] and the mystery at its center is a mystery of relatedness. Sutpen's design is born when he and his family "fall" by "sheer altitude, elevation and gravity" (222) from a world characterized by animal desires that are easily and immediately satisfied— "everybody had just what he was strong enough or energetic enough to take and keep, and only that crazy man would go to the trouble to take or even want more than he could eat or swap for powder and whiskey" (221)—into one of "Tidewater splendor" (222), where desires are mediated and personal worth and value are determined by the recognition of others. When Sutpen is turned from the front door of the plantation house by the Negro butler and made to realize that he has no significance for the man—*"there ain't any good or harm either in the living world that I can do to him"*—his human identity is born in the form of a "bright glare that vanished and left nothing, no ashes nor refuse" (238). And with this sense of self-consciousness comes an awareness of the importance of his freedom, his history, and his historicity. He abandons his family with its sliding, skating movement, "such as inanimate objects sometimes show" (223), its houses with no back doors but only windows, and its entropic drifting, "a kind of accelerating and sloven and inert coherence like a useless collection of flotsam on a flooded river" (223).

So he knew neither where he had come from nor where he was nor why. He was just there, surrounded by the faces, almost all the faces which he had ever known (though the number of them was decreasing, thinning out, despite the efforts of the unmarried sister who pretty soon, so he told Grandfather, and still without any wedding had another baby, decreasing because of the climate, the warmth, the dampness) living in a cabin that was almost a replica of the mountain one . . . where his sisters and brothers seemed to take sick after supper and die before the next meal. (227)

It is this uncertainty, this drifting, this lack of direction and meaning that Sutpen hopes to conquer through his design. He will map the destiny of his family by establishing a heritage. By making himself the point of reference and imposing his will, he will give the history of his descent the weight and dignity of necessity. "All of a sudden he discovered . . . what he just had to do . . . because if he did not do it he knew that he could never live with himself for the rest of his life, never live with what all the men and women that had died to make him had left inside of him for him to pass on, with all the dead ones waiting and watching to see if he was going to do it right, fix things right so that he would be able to look in the face not only of the old dead ones but all the living ones that would come after him when he would be one of the dead" (220).

Sutpen's design is grounded on an image of himself as founding father who not only will breed successive and genealogically related offspring whose lives take the form of a natural, logical sequence of events but will also become his own origin recreating the past as he establishes the direction of the future. His life and that of the family he founds will be a sequence of intelligible developments, a sequence of personal achievements connected by a dynamic of their own.

now he would take that boy in where he would never again
need to stand on the outside of a white door and knock at it:
and not at all for mere shelter but so that that boy, that whatever nameless stranger, could shut that door himself forever
behind him on all that he had ever known, and look ahead
along the still undivulged light rays in which his descendants
who might not even ever hear his (the boy's) name, waited to
be born without even having to know that they had once
been riven free from brutehood just as his own (Sutpen's) children were— (261)

So it is that he appears in Jefferson, builds a "house the size of a
courthouse" and calls it "Sutpen's Hundred as if it had been a
king's grant in unbroken perpetuity from his great grandfather—
a home a position" (16).

Needless to say, the simplicity, permanence, and stability implied by Sutpen's design, his sense of a family dynasty, does not
adequately reflect the discontinuities of human life, which cannot be described fully by a model that implies a natural sequence
of events. As Sutpen's experience in the West Indies suggests,
one's own design is subject to the desires and expectations of
others, desires that complicate and tangle ordinary lines of relations. Moreover once lines of relation have been formed, they are
not so easily undone. Sutpen finds it impossible to incorporate
his first wife and child into his design because in his world the
parent with black blood determines the race of the child. Bon is
legally black, not his father's son but his mother's, and, hence,
cannot be part of the patriarchal design: getting land, building a
house, founding a dynasty.[15] And so, having devoted some four
years establishing the trajectory for the linear procession of the
"ones that would come after him" (220) toward the "forwarding
of the design" (262), he is forced to halt his "advance" (264) and remove himself from the sequence that he has initiated. He resigns
all "right and claim" (264) belonging to him as the original
author of the family line and seeks to cut and tie off the line by
providing his son with a name that associates him with no family
and with a "legal guardian rather than parents" (74).

But the unwanted products of one's sexual/procreative life cannot be "clean[ed] up" as are the "exploded caps and musket cartridges after the siege" (265). Paternity involves two acts, generation and acknowledgment, one biological, the other social, and it is the second that is the source of the father's authority granted by society, as Levi Strauss argues, in order to prohibit and prevent incest.[16] But for Sutpen paternity is an entirely symbolic act, a means only of self-perpetuation and expansion, with the mother merely "incidental" and the offspring "replicas of his face" (23). Hence when he tries to deny that other self outside the self he represses it and guarantees its reappearance in other forms. The fact of Bon's generation becomes the repressed content in Sutpen's history, and it returns with a vengeance to disturb the pattern of his design.

There is, then, an ironic incompatibility between Sutpen's conscious design, the pattern that he wished to impose on his life, and the actual design that he is in the process of weaving. And, as we shall see, that irony permeates every part of the novel. (Worth noting at this point, however, is the fact that Sutpen's repeated attempts to accomplish his wild design provide a sort of genetic pattern for the novel itself as the story gets told over and over again in a futile effort to get it right.) At the simplest level it manifests itself in the fact that Sutpen "helped to bring about the very situation which he dreaded" (268), unwittingly repeating the affront that he had suffered as a child when he turns his son from the family mansion. More suggestively, by refusing to acknowledge his offspring he releases a force that removes from his hands the power of determining the pattern of his life.

Bon, who seems to have been "fathered" on his mother not by a "natural process" but to have been "blotted onto and out of her body by the old infernal immortal male principle of all unbridled terror and darkness" (313), appears and immediately confuses traditional family relationships bringing about a "fateful intertwining" of the threads of the Sutpen family line and causing a *fatal snarly climax* (167), a "horrible and bloody mischancing of human affairs" (101). Seducing brother and sister "almost simultaneously" (92) "without any effort or particular desire to do so" (93), he initiates an "abnegant transference" (105) causing brother to "metamorphose into, the lover, the husband" (96). Unacknowledged by his father, he appears as a hidden genetic disorder, "some effluvium of Sutpen blood and character" (104) that provokes fatal interminglings and mergings, both miscegenation and incest.

The tangles of the Sutpen genealogy become those of the novel itself, for the history of his family does not come to us through his children but by way of strangers whose knowledge is based on communal gossip and who are narrating the history only as a way of telling their own stories, thereby entangling the weave of Sutpen's design with that of their own. Hence the "boy-symbol at the door" (261), which marks the beginning of Sutpen's design by establishing its purpose and direction, has its meaning equivocated and contaminated as it is entangled in a network of similar images. The entire novel is governed by a dialectic of inside and outside, its action regulated by doors and windows open and closed but not according to the geometry of Sutpen's design. Interiors in the book do not shelter as much as stifle as the example of Sutpen's great house makes clear. All who enter die there as individual family members seem doomed to cancel each other out. "So it took Charles Bon and his mother to get rid of old Tom, and Charles Bon and the octoroon to get rid of Judith, and Charles Bon and Clytie to get rid of Henry; and Charles Bon's mother and Charles Bon's grandmother got rid of Charles Bon" (377–78).

So it is that the last surviving member of Sutpen's line, a "hulking slack-mouthed saddle-colored boy" and a "dried up woman not much bigger than a monkey" (214) put into question his assumption that his descendants have been "riven free from brutehood." Indeed Sutpen himself, as he nears the end of his life, seems drawn back to that world he has tried to close out, back to "people whose houses didn't have back doors, but only windows" (233). Wash Jones's "rotting cabin" (285), site of

Sutpen's death, suggests the ones of his youth; Jones's grand-daughter is an ironic reminder of Sutpen's "unmarried sister" (227); and the young Sutpen himself seems somehow replicated in Jones when he is prevented by Clytie from entering the great house.

The tangling up of the family sequence, the collapse of the genealogical line into a series of unnatural relations contaminates the linear purity of Sutpen's design, and it also puts into question the idea that the forces operating in history are controlled by either destiny or human intentions. As a profusion of tangled events, the history of the Sutpen family is not the product of the "capabilities of a demon for doing harm" (181), not an example of "moral retribution," of the "sins of the father come home to roost" (267), not the result of a "minor tactical mistake" (269), but apparently is governed by "blind accident" (222), "sheer chance" (102). It appears as a "child's vacant fairy tale" (146), a "shadow realm of make-believe" (147) where there is a "curious lack of economy between cause and effect" (119). Indeed the entire novel suggests a condition of existence without origins. Sutpen himself as a phantom or shadow is not locatable, and the novel is filled with odd metamorphoses, abrupt transitions, characters sliding into other characters, identities merging, scenes and persons echoing one another, voices and words blending together "without comma or colon or paragraph" (280).

"Yes," Quentin said. "The two children" thinking *Yes. Maybe we are both Father. Maybe nothing ever happens once and is finished. Maybe happen is never once but like ripples maybe on water after the pebble sinks, the ripples moving on, spreading, the pool attached by a narrow umbilical water-cord to the next pool which the first pool feeds, has fed, did feed, let this second pool contain a different temperature of water, a different molecularity of having seen, felt, remembered, reflect in a different tone the infinite unchanging sky, it doesn't matter: that pebble's watery echo whose fall it did not even see moves across its surface too at the original ripple-space, to the old ineradicable rhythm* thinking

Yes, we are both Father. Or maybe Father and I are both Shreve, maybe it took Father and me both to make Shreve and Shreve and me both to make Father or maybe Thomas Sutpen to make all of us. (261–62)

This admirable passage offers a view of human life that differs markedly from the linear and sequential one implied by genealogical succession and transmission in a line descending from the father and at the same time puts into question the familiar view of birth as a loss of origin or a fall from a condition of pure presence into one of an individualized and derived existence. Here is a world where each person is linked umbilically to everyone else and all have an equal originality because the problem of priority in time does not exist: "nothing ever happens once and is finished," for this is a world of repercussions rather than events. What is important is not the sunken pebble but its watery echo, that ripple space that is the very rhythm of life. Here "Environment" transcends familial and individual differences, so that beings "born half a continent apart" are nevertheless "joined, connected after a fashion" by a sort of "giologic umbilical" which "laughs at degrees of latitude and temperature" (258). Individual differences are present as the repetition in the above passage of the word "different" emphasizes, but they don't "matter." The temperature, the molecularity, the reflecting qualities of separate pools, qualities that would characterize and individualize were the pools not joined, are subordinate to the rhythmic ripples that move across all their surfaces. Emphasized here is the *the* human family rather than a particular family line. And it is suggestive in this connection to recall Faulkner's remarks that Sutpen did not believe that he was a member of the human family. "He was Sutpen. He was going to take what he wanted because he was big enough and strong enough, and I think that people like that are destroyed sooner or later, because one has got to belong to the human family."[17]

And it is important also to remember the story of Echo and Narcissus for the passage (and the novel) knot together a number of thematic strands from the Ovidian version of that myth.[18] Like it, *Absalom, Absalom!* focuses on the relations between love and death, repetition and originality, visual and vocal forms of representation and suggests a world energized by motions and sounds from the past in such a way that the present moment becomes an effect that continues after its cause is gone. Faulkner, like Ovid, tells of "bodies changed / To different forms" as he reconstitutes a world that no longer exists. Like the voice of the bodiless nymph, those that speak in *Absalom, Absalom!* are echoes of beings who have faded away. But while Ovid's nymph vanishes into voice, Faulkner's disembodied voices metamorphose into text. As echoes of dead and disembodied voices, those of the characters of *Absalom, Absalom!* are haunted as Miss Rosa's is by a ghostly presence that at times seems to take it over: "Her voice would not cease, it would just vanish . . . not ceasing but vanishing into and then out of the long intervals like a stream, a trickle running from patch to patch of dried sand, and the ghost mused with shadowy docility as if it were the voice which he haunted where a more fortunate one would have had a house" (8). It is this ghostly presence that both is and is not there that makes the voices of all the characters sound alike, echo one another, although each stands for an individual who once tried desperately to tell his or her own story, to weave his or her own pattern into the rug of life. But the original voice in each case is displaced by its repetition, as the pebble is by its watery echo, and the primary relation becomes one between signs that echo each other. This is a process that at once puts into question the notions of originality and intentionality and suggests the way in which "texts eclipse voice and speak silence."[19] It is this sense of voice as the sign of absence rather than presence that so disturbs Quentin, for in spite of his momentary celebration of a world where everything is connected, he remains committed to the ideal of patriarchal design and is deeply disturbed by his failures to embody the buried voice of the father. It is that failure that seems to him to doom him to talk in the "long silence of notpeople in notlanguage" (9) and to bring to the entire novel the atmosphere of death.

Absalom, Absalom! is permeated by the odors and signs of death. Its title laments loss and absence, and that loss is repeated and echoed throughout the text.[20] It opens in the "dim coffin-smelling gloom" (8) of a room in Rosa Coldfield's house, closes in the "stale and static and moribund" (345) atmosphere of Quentin and Shreve's "tomblike room in Massachusetts" (336), and its "climax" is the revelation of a living "corpse" (373) in the "inviolate and rotten mausoleum" (350) that is the ruins of Henry Sutpen's great house. Even marriage and conception are shrouded by the presence of death. Sutpen's house is the *"cacoon-casket marriage bed of youth and grief"* (136) and Wash Jones's granddaughter the *"female flesh in which* [Sutpen's] *name and lineage should be sepulchered"* (134).

But if the book is centrally concerned with the "instant of dissolution" (191), with the "irrevocable and unplumbable finality" (173), it also, like *Wuthering Heights*, "performs a multiple act of resurrection, an opening of graves or a raising of ghosts."[21] The events that it records are those of a "dead time" (89), its voices are the sounds of "dead tongue[s] speaking" (129) from beyond the grave, and its characters and narrators "shades" and "phantoms" (97) who have long since been "graved and sepulchered" (130). The novel, in other words, insistently keeps before the reader the apparently contradictory assertions that death is total obliteration and that the dead in some way live on beyond the grave. If the dead person is one who no longer responds, who is absent, how are we to understand these voices that are themselves haunted by the voices of other ghosts?

One place to begin a consideration of such a question is the Sutpen family graveyard, with its "five headstones" among the "clump of cedars" (187), for Faulkner, like Melville, is fascinated by the relation between the acts of interment and inscription, with the attempt "to give to the language of senseless stone" a voice that assures "that some part of our nature is imperishable."²² From one point of view these "block[s] of stone with scratches on [them]" (127) are "little puny affirmations of spurious immortality" (191–92) which "pediment a forgotten and nameless effigy" (164), they and their silent inscriptions, like the ruins of Rome for Hawthorne or the pyramids for Melville, signs of a nonrecoverable absence. On the other hand, for women "who lead beautiful lives" (191), who *"draw meat and drink from some beautiful attenuation of unreality in which the shades and shapes of facts—of birth and bereavement, of suffering and bewilderment and despair—move with the substanceless decorum of lawn party charades, perfect in gesture and without significance or any ability to hurt"* (211), funeral rites and monuments are of "incalculable importance" (192), not because women believe that we are immortal beings or because they think that such rites and monuments will preserve for future time some vestige of the dead. No such flights from death are necessary, for they have a "courage and fortitude in the face of pain and annihilation which would make the most spartan man resemble a puling boy" (191). Funerals and graves for them are pure representations and possess an aesthetic rather than a metaphysical significance. Like the poetic worlds of Swinburne and the other late Romantics and Decadents that Faulkner admired, funerals and graves offer a realm of purity where human action becomes aesthetic gesture and death as death remains hidden. Hence the visit of Bon's octaroon mistress to his gravesite appears as an "interlude," the "ceremonial widowhood's bright dramatic pageantry" (192) resembling a "garden scene by the Irish poet, Wilde," or a sketch by the "artist Beardsley" (193), where even the heavy marble tombstones seem "cleaned and polished and arranged by scene shifters who with the passing of twilight would return and strike them and carry them, hollow fragile and without weight, back to the warehouse until they should be needed again" (193). The brute fact of Bon's death is not represented. There is only a *"closed door"* (150), the *"echo"* of a shot (150), and a *"shadowy...abstraction...nailed into a box"* (153). There is *"no corpse,"* no *"imprint of a body on a mattress"* (152), *"no trace of him, not even tears*" (152), only "*that mound vanishing slowly back into the earth, beneath which* [there is] *buried nothing*" (158). But if Judith, who remains "absolutely impenetrable, absolutely serene," displaying "no mourning, not even grief" (127), seems at times to draw her sustenance entirely from an unreal world of pure representation that is "all breathing human passion far above," she also recognizes that the significance of acts of ceremonial memorializing does not extend beyond the performance itself. Such pageants are precisely "interlude[s]" (193), and the pieces of marble that are left after the performance is over can convey none of its "dramatic pageantry" (192). All that remains are "two flat heavy vaulted slabs" that are "cracked across the middle by their own weight" and "three headstones leaning a little awry, with here and there a carved letter or even an entire word momentary and legible in the faint light" (188). As Judith acknowledges when she leaves the letter with Quentin's grandmother those stones scratched with a name and two dates signifying the beginning and end of life can only mark the absence of living speech and human presence because the words on them are "graved" (191), removed from the dynamic interplay of *is* and *was* that characterizes human life.

What Judith seeks, then, is a form of impress that will be more than aesthetic gesture but that will be free of the deadening weight of pure materiality. This pursuit leads her, finally, out of the family graveyard, for she discovers that the way to make a "scratch, that undying mark on the face of oblivion" (129), is to take some sign of the personal, the familial, the local and to give it to someone "the stranger the better . . . it not to mean anything in itself and them not even to read it or keep it, not even bother to throw it away or destroy it, at least it would be something just because it would have happened" (127). Directed toward a stranger, "to keep or not to keep, even to read or not to read" and without "date or salutation or signature," the letter is the sign neither of time, place, nor person. In that sense its "faint spidery script" differs importantly from the scratches on the tombstones in the Sutpen family graveyard.

There there is only silence; here a "dead tongue" speaks. And yet the script appears "not like something impressed upon the paper by a once-living hand but like a shadow cast upon it which had resolved on the paper the instant before he looked at it and which might fade, vanish, at any instant while he still read" (129). As Quentin reads he has access not to the presence of the letter's originating source but only to "the words, the symbols" (101), and the shadowy shapes that they invoke.

Like the fragmentary sentences that generate *The Marble Faun* or like the mysterious names in the guitar and handkerchief in *Pierre*, the surviving letter is an object separated from its originating source, removed from the authority who could fill in salutation and signature, establish the identities of the writer and the reader. Hence its meaning, its significance is problematic, and it forces us to "re-read, tedious and intent, poring, making sure that you have forgotten nothing, made no miscalculation" (101).

We have a few old mouth-to-mouth tales; we exhume from old trunks and boxes and drawers letters without salutation or signature, in which men and women who once lived and breathed are now merely initials or nicknames ... which sound to us like Sanscrit or Chocktaw; we see dimly people, the people in whose living blood and seed we ourselves lay dormant and waiting, in this shadowy attenuation of time possessing now heroic proportions. . . . They are there, yet something is missing, they are like a chemical formula exhumed along with the letters from that forgotten chest, carefully, the paper old and fading and falling to pieces, the writing faded, almost indecipherable, yet meaningful, familiar in shape and sense. (100–101)

The past persists not in the form of some grand, carefully woven design but in the form of these orphaned remnants, signs of human happenings which survive simply as a result of having passed from "one hand to another," kept perhaps merely out of whimsy or curiosity and rediscovered in some "accidental fashion" (49) in that "forgotten chest" by someone similarly motivated. These "rag-tag and bob-ends of old tales and talking" (303) suggest the way in which the past at once exists in and is created by the present and thereby implies a form of relatedness that differs markedly from the model of patrilineal descent. "The people in whose living blood and seed we ourselves lay dormant and waiting" are present only in the forms of initials and nicknames in letters without salutation and signature preserved perhaps by people who were strangers to their authors and exhumed and freely interpreted by numerous unrelated voices.

It was Shreve speaking, though save for the slight difference which the intervening degrees of latitude had inculcated in them (differences not in tone or pitch but of turns of phrase and usage of words), it might have been either of them and was in a sense both: both thinking as one, the voice which happened to be speaking the thought only the thinking became audible, vocal; the two of them creating between them, out of the rag-tag and bob-ends of old tales and talking, people who perhaps had never existed at all anywhere, who, shadows, were shadows not of flesh and blood which had lived and died but shadows in turn of what were (to one of them at least, to Shreve) shades too, quiet as the visible murmur of their vaporizing breath. (303)

In the same way that the tangle of human relationships resists the sequential simplicity implied in the idea of a *pater familias* who initiates successive generations of offspring, so it also equivocates the idea of narrative or story as the orderly unfolding of a plot from a single authoritative source as well as the notion of representation as a perfect mirroring of object and image. Shreve and Quentin are not blood relatives, but they are joined together by cords stronger than blood lines. And the "happy marriage of speaking and hearing (316) that unites them also creates the shadows in which they exist. Sitting in their "tomb-like room in Massachusetts in 1910" (336) they create and then merge with shadows from the 1860s. Not even aware of "which one had been doing the talking" (334), they at once tell and live the story of Charles and Bon and Henry Sutpen, become in a certain way both fathers and sons, creators and interpreters.

Shreve ceased again. It was just as well, since he had no listener. Perhaps he was aware of it. Then suddenly he had no talker either, though possibly he was not aware of this. Because now neither of them were there. They were both in Carolina and the time was forty-six years ago, and it was not even four now but compounded still further, since now both of them were Henry Sutpen and both of them were Bon, compounded each of both yet either neither, smelling the very smoke which had blown and faded away forty-six years ago. (351)

All seem like one another in blood and spirit: each is somehow repeated in the other, since the sharp boundaries separating one individual from another no longer exist. And the tale that they tell is not burdened by the unities of time, place, and action or by the demands of causal sequence. This is a realm of romance reminiscent of Hawthorne's description in "The Custom House" of "a neutral territory, somewhere between the real world and fairy-land, where the Actual and Imaginary Way meet, and each imbue itself with the nature of the other" (*SL*, 36). And also like Hawthornian romance it is a world partially generated by "popular rumors," what Hawthorne calls the "chimney-corner tradition" (HSG, 123), a world born of "a few old mouth-to-mouth tales" (100), "rag-tag and bob-ends of old tales and talking," that is to say communal gossip or idle talk. In Faulkner's world as in Hawthorne's gossip may be viewed as the true voice of the community since it transcends boundaries of self and family by being associated with no identifiable source and by having existed prior to the involvement of any single individual, or, to put it as Homer Brown does in his suggestive analysis, gossip "establishes an authority without an author."[23] It is, in effect, parentless and suggests displacement and disaffiliation.

Absalom, Absalom!, however, is not entirely the product of an endless round of old tales and talking. Framing and to some extent grounding the communal chatter about Thomas Sutpen are two letters, the one Judith leaves with Quentin's grandmother and the one Quentin's father writes announcing the death of Rosa Coldfield.[24] Now letters in novels usually differ from gossip in being private rather than public communications. They are written by a particular writer and are intended for the eyes of a particular reader. They are, in short, privileged communications and as such often name the source or provide the answer to the novel's puzzle and in so doing, to use Brown's formulations, "close the round of speculation that is gossip . . . [and] replace the substitute parent with a parent-Truth."[25] This is the sort of letter that Quentin and Shreve imagine that Bon dreams of receiving from Sutpen, the one that will confirm his origins and make events fall into a pattern "which would reveal to him at once, like a flash of light, the meaning of his whole life, past—the Haiti, the childhood, the lawyer, the woman who was his mother" (313). *"He would just have to write 'I am your father. Burn this' and I would do it. Or if not that, a sheet, a scrap of paper with one word 'Charles' in his hand, and I would know what he meant and he would not even have to ask me to burn it"* (326). But this letter is neither sent nor received in *Absalom, Absalom!* In its place stand two more ambiguous documents: one "without date or salutation or signature" and the other dated "Jefferson Jan 10 1919 Miss" (173), addressed to Quentin Compson, and signed by his father. As with many of the textual details of *Absalom, Absalom!* these two apparently unrelated communications bear a shadowy echoic relation to one another.

Because there was love Mr. Compson said *There was that letter she brought and gave to your grandmother to keep.* He (Quentin) could see it, as plainly as he saw the one open upon the open text book on the table before him, white in his father's dark hand against his linen leg in the September twilight . . . thinking *Yes. I have heard too much, I have been told too much; I have had to listen to too much, too long* thinking *Yes, Shreve sounds almost exactly like father: that letter.* (207)

This passage is the most obvious example of a series of troubling associations that link the two letters without disclosing any obvious reason for the linkage. Reading the passage, we recall the figure of Mr. Compson "his feet once more to the railing, the letter in his hand and the hand looking almost as dark as a negro's against his linen leg" (89); the letter that opens "*My dear son* in his father's sloped fine hand out of that dead dusty summer where he had prepared for Harvard so that his father's hand could lie on a strange lamp-lit table in Cambridge" (173); the figure of Quentin himself looking with "brooding bemusement upon the open letter which lay on the open text book, his hands lying on the table before him on either side of the book and letter" (238);[26] and, finally, the "faint spidery script not like something impressed upon the paper by a once-living hand but like a shadow cast upon it which had resolved on the paper the instant before he looked at it" (129). These curious repetitions suggest a number of questions: what is the relation between the "once-living hand" that authored the letter without "salutation or signature" (100) and the "dark" negro-like one that holds it, between its "spidery script" and the "sloped fine hand" of the other, between the "sardonic whimsical and incurably pessimistic" (129) voice of the one and the "whimsical ironic hand" (377) of the other, and, perhaps most curiously, between the literal and figurative uses of the word "hand"?

These are complicated tangles, but we can begin to unknot them by noticing that both letters are directly related to the act of narration. As Mr. Compson sits on his porch, which is illuminated by a single light, its "globe stained and bug-fouled" (89), holding the letter in his hand, he gives his account of the Sutpen family romance, and Shreve and Quentin spin out their version of the same tale seated at a "lamp-lit table" with Quentin "brooding . . . upon the open letter which lay on the open text book" (238). In neither case however does the letter serve as ground or source for the narrative. The one that Quentin reads at the conclusion of his father's account does not answer or substantiate Mr. Compson's version of the Sutpen story by providing privileged information. Indeed the letter seems less of a private and personal communication between lovers than a document, philosophical treatise, or "commentary" (129), a part of whose meaning is that it can be read later as a historical record of the moment. Moreover, without salutation or signature, it raises the question of who is speaking and to whom and introduces the theme of writing as a sort of disaffiliation, a disclosure of the absence of a single father.[27] As it passes from Mr. Compson's hand to those of his son it becomes in an obvious way a communication between someone who is not the writer and someone who is not the reader. It becomes a part of that anonymous world of "old tales and talking" (303) that Quentin has *"learned, absorbed . . . without the medium of speech somehow from having been born and living beside it, with it"* (212). And in so doing it breaks free of the tangles of Sutpen's failed design and out of the silence of the family graveyard.

Mr. Compson's letter announcing the death of Rosa Coldfield initiates and frames the action of the second half of *Absalom, Absalom!*, the first part of it being given at the opening of Quentin and Shreve's version of the story and the last delayed until the very end when, surrounded by the "pure snow-gleamed darkness," Quentin is at last able to "read it . . . finish it" (377). Its presence on the table, "lying at such an angle that [Quentin] could not possibly have read it, deciphered it" (217), provides one of the dominant motifs of the novel's second half, for the narrator returns to it repeatedly as if to suggest that it holds the answer to the novel's mystery.

There was snow on Shreve's overcoat sleeve, his ungloved blond square hand red and raw with cold, vanishing. Then on the table before Quentin, lying on the open text book beneath the lamp, the white oblong of envelope, the familiar blurred mechanical *Jefferson Jan 10 1910 Miss* and then, opened, *My dear son* in his father's sloped fine hand out of that dead dusty summer where he had prepared for Harvard so that his father's hand could lie on a strange lamp-lit table in Cambridge; that dead summer twilight—the wisteria, the cigar-smell, the fireflies—attenuated up from Mississippi and into this strange room across this strange iron New England snow. (173)

This passage introduces the details whose repetition will provide the setting for Quentin and Shreve's telling of Sutpen's story: the chilly Harvard dormitory room illuminated by the desk lamp and growing colder as they talk, the open letter upon the open book between Quentin's hands, and Quentin's brooding presence. As Quentin speaks, his voice "repressed" (218), "suffused restrained" (277), his tone "sullen, flat" (255), his attitude one of "brooding bemusement upon the open letter which lay upon the open text book, his hands lying on the table before him on either side of the book and the letter" (238), he seems to be "talking . . . to the letter lying on the open book on the table between his hands" (255). The insistent almost ritualistic quality of these repetitions suggests a direct relation between the letter and Quentin's narrative. John Irwin has argued that in narrating Sutpen's story Quentin is seeking to best his father by achieving temporal priority to him in the narrative act, and the narrator's insistence on the importance of the letter would seem to strengthen Irwin's argument.[28] But Quentin's "sullen bemusement" (280) does not express his problematic relation to his father; rather it signifies his "youthful shame of being moved" (280) by the events of his story. And the relation between the letter on the book between his hands and the "shadows . . . of shades" (303) that it in some way generates involves more than a struggle for authority.

To begin with, the letter serves as a sort of umbilical paper cord that links together a network of differences and distances. It first appears in the text five months before the date of its composition—"the odor, the scent, which five months later Mr. Compson's letter would carry up from Mississippi and over the long iron New England snow and into Quentin's sitting-room at Harvard" (31)—and in so doing disturbs the illusion that the narrative is a progressive unfolding of events in time. Like the history of the Sutpen family that it records, the novel's own events seem already both to have and have not occurred, or, rather, in some curious way to be happening all at the same time, and, hence, suggest a process that puts into question traditional assumptions about fictional representation. It is not just that the letter is able to bring back the moment and person that existed in another place and at another time and render them to the senses as if they were actually present but also that it is itself already there in the place and the moment.

Quite clearly, the creative power at work here is not the mimetic imagination that we usually associate with fictional representation. Significantly, the actual contents of the letter are unrelated to the time and place that it presents—it announces the death and burial of Rosa Coldfield on a frigid January day—and it accomplishes the presentation before it is fully read. Operating here is a process that changes our usual understanding of the relation between writing and reading, for when Quentin looks at the letter written in his father's "sloped fine hand" there is restored to view the September evening and the other letter "white in his father's dark hand." Here is a relational link that is the result not of an act of imitation but, as the above passage suggests, one of attenuation. Now the word "attenuate" suggests a process of refining, rarifying, thinning out and is used by Faulkner to describe not only the relation between writing and its effects but also those between past and present, reality and imagination, experience and memory. From the point of view of the present, the past is a "shadowy attenuation of time" (101); women are said to "live beautiful lives" because in their "very breathing they draw meat and drink from some beautiful attenuation of unreality in which shades and shapes of facts . . . move with the substanceless docorum of lawn party charades perfect in gesture and without significance or any ability to hurt" (211); and Sutpen's memory of his family's descent from the mountain in West Virginia is in terms of an attenuation rather than a period.

He didn't remember whether it was that winter and then spring and then summer that overtook and passed them on the road, or whether they overtook and passed in slow succession the seasons as they descended, or whether it was the descent itself that did it, and they not progressing parallel in time but descending perpendicularly through temperature and climate—a (you couldn't call it a period because as he remembered it . . . it didn't have either a definite beginning or a definite ending. Maybe attentuation is better) an attenuation from a kind of furious inertness and patient immobility, while they sat in the cart outside the doors of doggeries and taverns and waited for the father to drink himself insensible, to a sort of dreamy and destinationless locomotion after they had got the old man out . . . and loaded him into the cart again, and doing which they did not seem to progress at all but just to hang suspended while the earth itself altered, flattened and broadened out of the mountain cove where they had all been born, mounting, rising about them . . . and flowing past as if the cart moved on a treadmill. (224–25)

This moment in Sutpen's life is present to him as the fragments of his story are to Quentin and as the narrative events of *Absalom, Absalom!* are to the reader. It appears to memory not as a series of successive temporal moments marked by a definite beginning and end but as a process of moving from one to the other. The relationship between "furious inertness" and "dreamy and destinationless locomotion" like those between rising and falling, beginning and end, motion and stasis is not thought of in terms of opposition but rather as a process where one category is experienced as the result of or a sort of extension of the other. One condition or action becomes the shadow or echo of its opposite so that falling suggests rising, immobility, locomotion, and the space of visible reality, those of imagination and memory.[29]

The nature of the relationship implied in each of these cases is suggested by the examples that the O.E.D. provides for "attenuated": "The spider's most attenuated thread"; "As attenuated as parchment"; and "That most attenuated of all things, the shadow of a shade." The process implied in each of these cases is one of emptying out, becoming fainter, of losing substance to, but not beyond, the very point of expiration, suggesting a world that almost no longer exists, that seems about to fade at the very moment we experience it. And this sense of fragility and impermanence, of a dissolving reality, infects and disturbs the relations between object/image, shadow/substance, thing/word, and past/present so that one category seems the ghostly attenuation or echo of the other. Language itself is thought of as a "meager and fragile thread . . . by which the little surface corners and edges of men's secret and solitary lives may be joined for an instant now and then before sinking back into darkness" (251). Hence the writing of the letter without salutation or signature is "faded, almost indecipherable, yet meaningful, familiar in shape and sense" (101), a "faint spidery script not like something impressed upon the paper by a once living hand but like a shadow cast upon it which had resolved on the paper the instant before . . . and which might fade, vanish, at any instant while he still read" (129).

Words signify but not by standing unambiguously in the place of an object which they represent or by making possible a willed relation between a particular writer and a particular reader. Quentin gazes at his father's letter "lying at such an angle that he could not possibly have read it, deciphered it" (217) and sees the other letter "as plainly as he saw the one open upon the open text book on the table before him, white in his father's dark hand against his linen leg in the September twilight where the cigar-smell, the wisteria-smell, the fire-flies drifted" (207). Mr. Compson's letter signifies something other than it represents, and this happens through a sort of magic that creates relational links independent of both the author's intent and the interpretive activity of a reader. The "sloped fine hand" of the script generates meaning but it does so by breaking free of the gravitational fields of both writer and reader. As it rests upon the open textbook between Quentin's hands, a "rectangle of paper folded across the middle and now open, three quarters open, whose bulk had raised half itself by the leverage of the old crease" (217), it seems to have "learned half the secret of levitation" (238). Unlike the "flat slabs" in the Sutpen graveyard that "cracked across the middle by their own weight" and "vanishing" (188) into the ground can only signify absence, the "fragile Pandora's box of scrawled paper" (258) raises itself in "weightless and paradoxical levitation" (217) and fills the room "with violent and unratiocinative djinns and demons" (258).

Like the familiar ghosts that haunt Hawthorne's "well-known apartment," these figures are "invested with a quality of strangeness and remoteness (*SL*, 36). They can hardly be thought of as representations since that which they stand in the place of enjoyed only a shadowy existence. Bon, we recall, is present to Miss Rosa, who "never saw him," only as "a picture, an image" (74) which is not the copy of an original but which is suggested to her by "the name, Charles Bon" (75). Hence the picture which has no "skull behind it" is "almost anonymous" needing for a ground only a *"vague inference of some walking flesh and blood desired by someone else even if only in some shadow-realm of make-believe"* (147). And when the *"shadow with a name"* (146) vanishes, the victim of a *"shot heard only by its echo"* (153), it leaves behind only negative traces, a *"print that was his save for* [an] *obliterating rake"* (148), the *"invisible imprint of his absent thighs"* on a *"nooky seat"* (148), the lack of an *"imprint of a body on a mattress"* (152), and a letter without salutation or signature.

Such are the figures that are levitated into the "tomblike room" (336) with a "quality stale and static and moribund beyond any mere vivid and living cold" (345). While Quentin and Shreve sit talking and staring at one another, "their quiet regular breathing vaporizing faintly and steadily in the . . . tomblike

air" (299), listening to the chimes mark the passing hours, moving only to fill a pipe or to put on a bathrobe, and resisting the
temptation to retreat to "bed and warmth" (345) these shades perform "their acts of simple passion and simple violence, impervi-
ous to time" (101). And as the two young men discuss, create,
and at last exist in these shades, they and their room, although
parodoxically still vividly and insistently the same, are transformed into the realm of romance. As they come to identify
more and more with the lives of the shades they are creating, as
their "physical misery" is "transmogrified into the spirits' travail
of the two young men . . . fifty years ago" (345), they transcend
the individual differences that separate them, transcend "degrees
of latitude and temperature" (258), begin to breathe together,
"not individuals now yet something both more or less than
twins" (294), to talk as one, joined in a "happy marriage of speaking and hearing" (316), and finally, to move together with the
shades they have created—"the two of them (the four of them)"
(335) from the room in Massachusetts to the one in New Orle-
ans, to the library at Sutpen's Hundred.

Not two of them in a New England college sitting-room but
one in a Mississippi library sixty years ago, with holly and
mistletoe in vases on the mantel or thrust behind, crowning
and garlanding with the season and time the pictures on the
walls, and a sprig or so decorating the photograph, the
group—mother and two children—on the desk, behind which
the father sat when the son entered; and they—Quentin and
Shreve—thinking how after the father spoke . . . Henry would
recall later how he had seen through the window beyond his
father's head the sister and the lover in the garden, pacing
slowly . . . to disappear slowly beyond some bush or shrub
starred with white bloom—jasmine, spiraea, honeysuckle perhaps myriad scentless unpickable Cherokee roses—names,
blooms which Shreve possibly had never heard and never seen
although the air had blown over him first which had become
tempered to nourish them. It would not matter here in Cambridge that the time had been winter in that garden too, and

hence no bloom nor leaf even if there had been someone to walk there and be seen there since, judged by subsequent events, it had been night in the garden also. But that did not matter because it had been so long ago. It did not matter to them (Quentin and Shreve) anyway, who could without moving, as free now of flesh as the father who decreed and forbade, the son who denied and repudiated, the lover who acquiesced, the beloved who was not bereaved, and with no tedious transition from hearth and garden to saddle, who could be already clattering over the frozen ruts of that December night . . . not two of them there and then either but four of them riding the two horses through the iron darkness. (294–95)

This admirable passage suggests the nature and status of Faulknerian romance. Joined in the "happy marriage of speaking and hearing," Shreve and Quentin break out of their "tomblike room," free now from the confining and defining bodily flesh and are "translated . . . into a world like a fairy tale" (318) where they are not restricted by the boundaries of family and self, time and space. Here lovers walk in a garden alive with flowers in December, their movements governed by "that rhythm" which the "heart marks" (294), and Quentin and Shreve, at once creating and inhabiting it, as free from the demands of verisimilitude as the text is from the restrictions of punctuation, move effortlessly "with no tedious transition from hearth and garden to saddle." This is a magical world created by a sort of alchemical process that rarifies, refines, etherealizes, sublimes away the weight of material existence. Through the magic of "speaking and hearing" physical space becomes verbal space as "vaporized breaths" take the forms of "shadows . . . of shades," those most attentuated of all things. And although this is a realm woven from that "meager and fragile thread," language, it is a surprisingly vital one, characterized by coursing blood, "the immortal brief recent intransient blood" (295), and energized by acts of "simple passion and simple violence" (101).

In this sense the passage can stand as a synecdoche for the

novel. Its action issues from confining spaces, "dim hot airless rooms" (7) and cold tomblike ones and its voices from the mouths of seated, almost immobile, figures—Miss Rosa "bolt upright in the straight hard chair," her legs "straight and rigid" (7), Mr. Compson, seated, his feet on the veranda railing, "letter in his hand" (89), and Quentin seated "facing the table, his hands lying on either side of the open text book on which the letter rested" (217). Into this constrained, restricted world, its limits set by the narrator's insistent, hammering repetition of details of place, time, setting, posture "abrupt" (8) the djinns and demons, "notpeople" talking to one another in "notlanguage" (9) bringing with them movement, alternating gallops and halts, whose rhythms are controlled not by the tic-tocs of time but by the "heart and blood of youth" (294).

Nevertheless this world is the product of an enchantment, the result of Shreve and Quentin's being drawn into a deeply imaginative but antinatural frame of mind, a process that is initiated not by the phantoms that fascinate them, not by the supernatural as such, but by a letter announcing a death. And the inevitable disenchantment occurs when Quentin and Shreve stop talking and like Miss Rosa after the death of Henry Sutpen, "[go] to bed because it was all finished now" (376) to await the "little death" (275), as an "iron and impregnable dark" descends with the empty sounds of Poe's Raven: "Nevermore Nevermore Nevermore" (373). And this moment of disenchantment is the moment of the return of Mr. Compson's letter.

then he could not tell if it was the actual window or the window's pale rectangle upon his eyelids, though after a moment it began to emerge. It began to take shape in its same curious, light, gravity-defying attitude—the once-folded sheet of paper out of the wisteria Mississippi summer, the cigar smell, the random blowing of the fireflies. . . . It was becoming quite distinct; he would be able to decipher the words soon, in a moment; even almost now, now, now.

. . . .

Now he (Quentin) could read it, could finish it—the sloped

whimsical ironic hand out of Mississippi attenuated, into the iron snow. (377)

As Quentin lies "still and rigid on his back with the cold New England night on his face . . . his eyes wide upon the window" (373), the "rectangle of the window" slowly becomes the "rectangle of paper" (217) that undeciphered had produced the supernatural effects of the previous hours. Now, paradoxically, surrounded by darkness he is able to read it, and once it is deciphered it loses its gravity-defying power to elevate and spiritualize. All that remains in the Pandora's box now is the delusive "hope" (377) of an afterlife expressed in Mr. Compson's characteristically ironic tone. The "sloped whimsical ironic hand out of Mississippi" that earlier had been for Quentin the hand that held Bon's letter now becomes pure script and the magical process of attenuation an empty language game as "ironic hand" is attenuated into "iron snow," a linkage that the O.E.D. describes as the result of either "ignorant or humorous perversion."

With the end of the story comes a draining of the creative source. The pressures of the here and now, the weight of an "iron and impregnable dark" (360) become too heavy to resist. The imagination can no longer find the power to conjure up the living shadows whose presence from the beginning has provided the force to resist the threat of annihilation. In the end the present cannot be sustained by a past that is fading away and the imagination cannot maintain its life-sustaining fire when the action through which it lives comes to a stop. In the end that piece of scrawled paper that had generated the ghostly presences provides them with a final resting place: "*The weather was beautiful though cold and they had to use picks to break the earth for the grave yet in one of the deeper clods I saw a redworm doubtless alive when the clod was thrown up though by afternoon it was frozen again*" (377).

Absalom, Absalom!, perhaps more than any of Faulkner's other works, reveals the ghostly dimensions of narrative, the way in which stories give the past an afterlife by opening graves and raising ghosts while at the same time they presuppose and record the fact of death. Faulkner is fond of insisting that he writes in order to say "No to death," but, as his admirable foreword to *The Faulkner Reader* suggests, he is clearly aware of the problematic status of that "No." The words "Kilroy was here" scribbled on the "wall of the final and irrevocable oblivion" seem as much the signs of a radical absence as a form of resurrection. What remains on this side of the wall is the "isolation of cold impersonal print," black marks on the page that stand as the sign of the absence of the author who is only a "dead and fading name." And yet if they presuppose a death, they also exert a supernatural or ghostly effect; words resurrect and energize not the author but a demon who engenders the "deathless excitement in hearts and glands whose owners and custodians are generations from even the air [the author] breathed and anguished in."[30] From this perspective the novel is a Pandora's box containing demons and ghosts ready to be brought back from the grave by anyone who chances to open its covers and read.

SIX

The Romance of the Word: John Barth's LETTERS

Your webfoot amphibious marsh-nurtured writer will likely by mere reflex regard many conventional boundaries and distinctions as arbitrary, fluid, negotiable: form versus content, realism versus irrealism, fact versus fiction, life versus art. His favorite mark of punctuation will be the semicolon.

> –John Barth, "Some Reasons Why I Tell the Stories I Tell the Way I Tell Them Rather Than Some Other Sort of Stories Some Other Way"

Any cell–man, animal, fish, fowl, or insect–given the chance and under the right conditions, brought into contact with any other cell, however foreign, will fuse with it. Cytoplasm will flow easily from one to the other, the nuclei will combine, and it will become, for a time anyway, a single cell with two complete, alien genomes, ready to dance, ready to multiply. It is a Chimera, a Griffon, a Sphinx, a Ganesha, a Peruvian god, a Ch'i-lin, an omen of good fortune, a wish for the world.

> –Lewis Thomas, *The Lives of a Cell*

John Barth's fictive world is one of fluid borders and boundaries. Like those of Hawthorne and Faulkner, it is a realm where one moves easily from the real to the magical and mythical, from dreams of waking to waking dreams. And also like theirs it is a world that derives its originating impulse from a strong sense of place. Barth remarks that "when a writer like Mark Twain, or Hawthorne, or Faulkner—and I hope myself—finds part of his or her imaginative energy in a place, it's likely to be because that place, consciously or intuitively, is a kind of metaphor for the author's real concerns. And these concerns are likely to be just what Aristotle tells us literature should be about: human life, its happiness and its misery.... One way you get at those, as Faulkner does, and I. B. Singer does, and Mark Twain did, and the rest, is through your intimate knowledge of a particular region."[1] And in another place he goes on to add that "if between twins as they get older less and less goes without saying, in a good marriage between a man and a woman or a writer and his place, so much more every season goes without saying that should I grow as old and wise as Sophocles I'll never get it all said."[2]

The ambitious and brilliant LETTERS is Barth's attempt to say what he sees as he looks at his place as a practicing novelist in the 1970s in the United States, having returned at midlife and midcareer to his origins in tidewater Maryland. And what he sees as he surveys the "spreading field, the human scene" (PL, 7), is a marvelous panorama that includes the writer's own history, that of his country, and that of the novel as a genre. For, like Hawthorne and Faulkner, Barth's starting point as a novelist is with inherited materials: the twice-told tale, the old-time legend, old world conventions; and the magic of his art is that of re-energizing and giving new life to time-worn materials. "At heart I am an arranger," he writes, "whose chiefest literary pleasure is to take a received melody—an old narrative poem, a classical myth, a shopworn literary convention, a shard of my experience . . . and, improvising like a jazzman within its constraints, reorchestrate it to present purpose."[3] LETTERS is his attempt to "reorchestrate some early conventions of the Novel," in particular the *"epistolary novel,* already worked to death by the end of the eighteenth century." As a "Doctor of Letters," the Author of LETTERS writes that "I take it as among my functions to administer artificial resuscitation to the apparently dead" (*L,* 654). And the phenomenon of the "Death-of-the-Novel" and the "End-of-Letters" (438) is a dominant theme in LETTERS. Both the Author and his characters nostalgically lament the "fallen state of Literature" (58) and the passing of the "heroic period of the genre" (52) that has "fallen into obscure pretension on the one hand and cynical commercialism on the other" (84). With *"its popular base usurped, fiction has become a pleasure for special tastes, like poetry, archery, churchgoing"* (33).

To be a novelist in 1969 is [the Author writes] a bit like being in the passenger-railroad business in the age of the jumbo jet: our dilapidated rolling stock creaks over the weed-grown right-of-ways, carrying four winos, six Viet Nam draftees, three black welfare families, two nuns, and one incorrigible railroad buff, ever less conveniently, between the crumbling Art Deco cathedrals where once paused the gleaming Twentieth Century Limited. Like that railroad buff, we deplore the shallow "attractions" of the media that have supplanted us, even while we endeavor, necessarily and to our cost, to accommodate to that ruinous competition by reducing even further our amenities: fewer runs, fewer stops, fewer passengers, higher fares. Yet we grind on, tears and cinders in our eyes, hoping against hope that history will turn our way again. (191)

The Author, however, possesses a magical power that will revive the past, bring the dead letter to life, redeem the character of the writtten character. In the same way that "heat + pressure + time turn dead leaves into diamonds," he will employ a "metaphorical physics to turn stones into stars" (652), an "alchemy" (429) to transform "paralyzing self-consciousness [into] enabling self-awareness" (348). Faced with the fragmented ruins that disenchant Hawthorne and the stony silence that paralyzes Melville he turns to a "tender physics" that can change "petrifaction" into "estellation" (348). That turn, however, is not made without struggles and doubts. LETTERS follows (and records) a period marked by false starts and self-questionings that echo those suffered by Barth's American precursors. Before he can construct the spacious structure of LETTERS he must free himself from the dark corridors of the funhouse and the mire of marshy tides, places where, as Tony Tanner has said, one is unable to "disentangle dreaming from doing."[4] From within these mazes the LETTERS project seems a *"vast morass of plans, notes, false starts, in which I grew mired with every attempt to extricate myself"* (C, 202). Suffering from "Writer's Block" (202), the Author loses "track of who I am; my name's just a jumble of letters; so's the whole body of literature: strings of letters and empty spaces, like a code I've lost the key to" (10–11). Like Melville and Hawthorne at crucial stages of their careers, Barth seems momentarily to lose the sense of the value of fictions and any conviction that they may be significantly related to his experience of reality.[5] He is tormented by visions of stories that fail, by a sense that his own work is drifting back to him devoid of meaning, and is haunted by a corrosive doubt concerning identity and its relation to language.

I think I'm dead. I think I'm spooked. I'm full of voices, all mine, none me; I can't keep straight who's speaking, as I used to. It's not my wish to be obscure or difficult; I'd hoped at least to entertain, if not inspire. But put it that one has had visions of an order complex unto madness: Now and again, like mazy marshways glimpsed from Pegasus at top-flight, the design is clear. . . . Between, one's swamped; the craft goes on, but its way seems arbitrary, seems insane. (C, 147)

It is partially in an attempt to identify the "voices" who tell his "tale" and to gain a perspective on his life and craft that the Author of LETTERS, like the Genie in "Dunyazadiad," decides to "learn where to go by discovering where I am by reviewing where I've been—where we've all been" (*C*, 10). Hence the novel springs from the marsh, the "swamp primordial" (*L*, 8), "source of life" (526), its foundations resting "ineluctably on the loam of the Eastern Shore" (178) of Maryland. Ironically, however, the creative energy that the "marsh-nurtured writer"[6] discovers when he returns to his fertile sources, an energy that restores his "imaginative potency" (*C*, 202), is *"an altogether impersonal principle of literary aesthetics.... the Principle of Metaphoric Means, by which I intend the investiture by the writer of as many of the elements and aspects of his fiction as possible with emblematic as well as dramatic value: not only the 'form' of the story, the narrative viewpoint, the tone, and such, but, where manageable, the particular genre, the mode and medium, the very process of narration— even the fact of the artifact itself"* (203). It is this Principle that frees the Author from the mire of the plans, notes, false starts of a "complicated project, a novel called Letters" (202) and allows a "transcension of paralyzing self-consciousness to productive self-awareness" (*L*, 652). And the nature of the relationship between a formal principle and the spellbinding power of story, between wonder and enlightenment, between the magic in the web of narrative and the complexity of its weave is a primary concern of LETTERS. Like James, Barth begins with a "kind of plan or form"[7] that precedes the story itself, but he is able to avoid the Jamesian sense that the "ado" of the plot somehow violates and trivializes the purity of the form. For Barth the artist need not forsake the "world for language, language for the processes of narration, and those processes for the abstract possibilities of form." He may instead be *"enabled to love the narrative through the form, the language through the narrative, even the world through the language"* (650). Hence the complex form of LETTERS, a novel that consists of seven stories told in letters and arranged so that they gradually entwine in such a way that the exposition, complication, and climax of each is implicated in and echoes that of all the others. "There are, in fact in LETTERS," according to Barth, "seven more or less parallel narratives that you can imagine going across the time of the novel like the bars of music in a concert score, and they do intertwine as do the bars of music on a concert score. But a reader who happened, for example, to like Lady Amherst, my middle-aged British gentlewoman in reduced circumstances, and who didn't want to interrupt her story, should just go through and read all her letters. It'll make sense that way, too. This is a novel that could make sense either in parallel form or serial form."[8]

The pattern for the dramatic action is itself echoed by the elaborate design of the novel which consists of eighty-eight letters each of which is assigned a letter of the alphabet so that when arranged on a calendar for the seven months of the action according to the dates of their composition, they spell out the subtitle as well as form the title, LETTERS. The seven correspondents of Barth's seventh book consists of characters from his six previous books plus one invented for this work and each contributes "not only the letters that comprise the story but elements of its theme and form." The book, therefore, will "echo its predecessors in [Barth's] bibliography, while at the same time extending that bibliography and living its independent life" (*L*, 431). That is to say it will move forward by going backward, a movement that is echoed by the plot which "like waves of a rising tide . . . will surge forward, recede, surge farther forward, recede less far, et cetera to its climax and dénouement" (49).

As an epistolary novel written in the late 1970s, LETTERS itself suggests an attempt to move forward by going backward, or as Barth puts it, "to go back and look at the origins of the novel in the English language tradition . . . and see whether I could reorchestrate some of the old conventions to contemporary purposes."[9] This strategy is consistent with his analysis of the direction of postmodernist fiction in his suggestive essay, "The Literature of Replenishment." For Barth the contemporary novelist need not repudiate or imitate either his twentieth-century modernist parents or his nineteenth-century premodernist grandparents. He is free to "rise above the quarrel between realism and irrealism, formalism and 'contentism,' pure and committed literature, coterie fiction and junk fiction." "My most recent novel, LETTERS," he writes, "is postmodernist by my own definition, not however, without traces or taints of the modernist mode, even of the premodernist mode." And indeed LETTERS is an attempt to synthesize "straightforwardness and artifice, realism and magic and myth, political passion and nonpolitical artistry, characterization and caricature, humor and terror,"[10] an attempt to bridge the gap between the novel as a work of art and the novel as a conveyor of real human passions, between storytelling understood formalistically and the story in its moving immediacy: "alphabetics + calendrics + serial scansion through seven several correspondents = a form that spells itself while spelling out more and (one hopes) spellbinding along the way, as language is always also but seldom simply about itself" (*L, 767*). It is a book about real-life kinds of characters who are also written characters, at once "actual people" (97) and "hommes de lettres" (526) who come together in promiscuous yokings that scatter both children and meanings and hatch schemes and plots that produce both stories and anagrams, and its abstract or formal elements echo and figure the emotional rhythms that the stories generate in the reader in such a way that the act of reading becomes a process of interpreting the relation between the literal and figurative, the dramatic and emblematic value of the stories. Hence the "similarity between conventional dramatic structure—its exposition, rising action, climax, and dénouement—and the rhythm of sexual intercourse from foreplay through coitus to orgasm and release" as well as the "popularity of love (and combat, the darker side of the same rupee) as a theme for narrative, the lovers' embrace as its culmination, and post-coital lassitude as its natural ground" (*C, 24–25*). Moreover, the "relation between the teller and the told [is] by nature erotic," (25), with the "teller's role . . . regardless of his actual gender . . . masculine, the listener's or reader's feminine, and the tale . . . .the medium of their intercourse" (25–26). This is not to suggest, however, that the reader's role is a passive or inferior one; a "good reader of cunning tales work[s] in her way as busily as their author" (26). Narrative, therefore, is a "love relation, not a rape: its success depends[s] upon the reader's consent and cooperation, which she [can] withhold or at any time withdraw; also upon her own combination of experience and talent for the enterprise, and the author's ability to arouse, sustain and satisfy her interest" (26) And like all love relations, that between reader and author is "potentially fertile for both partners. . . . The reader is likely to find herself pregnant with new images," and the "storyteller may find himself pregnant too" (26).

This play of images, a process of reception and interpretation, is initiated in LETTERS by the Author's account of his "three concentric dreams of waking" (*L*, 46), for these dreams, in spite of their arbitrary boundaries and "marshy equivocations" (636), are dreams of origins and as such offer the reader several versions of the Author's "self" as well as a sort of "history" of the text. But unlike the concentric circles of a tree trunk that move out from a central point, these seem at first to suggest a "concentricity of pretensions, at best a succession of improvisations and self-ignorances" (187). For these dreams, like the marshland that is their setting, confuse and blur conventional distinctions. Fictive and historical events, persons, and places; actual and invented worlds; real and imagined selves seem to flow together as the Author attempts a narrative that will be the story of his story.

The narrative begins with an account of the relation between the self and its signs, echoing in the process Ambrose Mensch's "ambivalent reflections on the phenomenon of proper names: 'I and my sign . . . neither one nor quite two'" (166); for in the three dreams of waking there are multiple I's and a variety of signs that tend to blend together without ever completely merging and to make it difficult to say which is the first or second, the origin or the image. The dreams, of course, exist in the form of a letter (the eighth of the eighty-eight that constitute the novel and the only one addressed by the Author to "Whom it may concern") and as a written, textual object it immediately raises the question of who is writing and to whom. Moreover, as words, or a "recorded" (47) dream, the letter suggests a double interpretive problem, the first deriving from the Author's decoding of his dream images and the other from the relation between the words of the dreamer and an analytic interpreter. As Lady Amherst will "later" remind the Author, "to put things into words works changes, not only upon the events narrated, but upon their narrator" (80). To write, in short, is to change the world and the self, for life and its signs are "symbiotic" (341). The dreams, then, offer a tangled genealogy of self that is explained by the Author in terms of the development of his writing career, projects finished and unfinished, but their "content" is hardly as "clear" (47) for the reader as for the Author since it depends upon the form of the relation of this eighth letter to the eighty others that form its context.

For the Author, the recurring dream seems to offer a way of affirming meaning and establishing his authority, but for the reader "concerned" with its relation to letters and to LETTERS the "dream must be reread" (484), and this process has the effect of suggesting that the Author can never be unequivocably himself and hence cannot have an unquestioned authority over his own life and work. However, this discovery does not allow the "concerned" reader—call him/her critic—to speak authoritatively about the text, to find a central I and unequivocal meaning in its labyrinth of echoing voices. For words here disclose other words that jostle and echo each other in a way that suggests the presence of a private code or cipher that must be solved before the reader can engage in a meaningful dialogue with the text.

"I woke half tranced, understanding where I was but not at once who, or why I was there, or for how long I'd slept" (46), the Author begins and thereby suggests that the "I" for him, as for Ambrose in *Lost in the Funhouse*, is a mere mark or "hieroglyph and gibber" (*LIF,* 34) without context or content. However, these are slowly supplied as the sun and his watch signify that "it was yet midsummer midafternoon, a few hours into Cancer" and other "sign[s] of life"—"two turkey buzzards . . .

a stand of loblolly pines . . . the hum of millions upon millions of insects . . . bees above all" (*L,* 46) identify the place as the marsh. Self-awareness begins with a half unconscious movement to kill a mosquito (represented in the Author's account by its scientific sign, *Aedes sollicitans*), but with it comes a set of confusing memories.

I recognized that before consulting my wristwatch I'd felt for a pocketwatch—a silver Breguet with "barleycorn" engine-turning on the case, steel moon hands, and a white enameled face with the seconds dial offset at VII, the maker's name engraved in secret cursive under XII, and my father's monogram, HB, similarly scribed before the appropriate Roman Numeral IV—a watch which I did not possess, had never possessed, which could not with that monogram be my father's, which did not so far as I know exist! Reached for it (in the watch pocket of the vest I didn't wear, didn't own) with more reflexive a motion than then turned my left wrist. (46)

This passage is remarkable in a number of ways. It focuses on the relation between a self and its signs, in this case a gesture and an object, but in a way that disturbs the connection. The spontaneous, unconscious gesture of reaching for his father's watch seems to confirm his identity and place by providing him with an origin against which he can define and fix himself. And yet that familiar object, which appears to him with surprising specificity, apparently belongs to the world of dreams. Although he is now more fully awake, he feels "one foot in distant time or dreams." And his confusion is matched by that of the reader who comes to the passage for the first time. For on first reading we can say only that it is the verbal representation of a dream image whose content is not clear. And the reader's uncertainty grows as the dream of waking continues to trouble the Author's sense of selfhood.

I knew "myself," come briefly down under Mason and Dixon's to visit certain cattailed, blue-crabbed, oystered haunts of—aye, there was the rub: I had been going to say "my youth," but what that term referred to, like dim stars and ghost crabs, I could not resolve when I looked straight at it. And when I looked away . . . from my mind's eye-corner I could just perceive, not one, but several "youths," all leading— but by different paths, in different ages!—to this point of high ground between two creeklets where I lay, stiff as if I'd slept for twenty decades or centuries instead of minutes. There was the neutral, sleep-wrapped, most familiar youth, neither happy nor unhappy, begun in Gemini 1930, raised up in sunny ignorance through the Great Depression, Second War, and small town Southern public schools. I knew *that* chap, all right . . . his was the history most contiguous with the hour I'd waked to.

But beside it, like a still-sleeping leg that its wakened twin can recognize, was another history, a prior youth, to whom that pocketwatch and vest and a brave biography belonged. They shared one name's initial: bee-beta-beth, the Kabbalist's letter of Creation, whence derived, like life itself from the marsh primordial, both the alphabet and the universe it described by its recombinations. . . .

Then what was this third, faint-bumbling B, most shadowy of all, but obscured more by mythic leagues of time than by self-effacement or disguise? And not *retreated* to the midday marsh, but fallen into it as though from heaven. (46–47)

As the details of the dream accumulate a certain design or pattern begins to emerge. The self who wakes "half tranced" in the haunts of his youth is a disturbingly multiple one, for present to the eye of his memory are three quite different youths who share only the common experience of falling asleep in the marsh and a common initial. And yet neither figure seems to exist independently of the other two. Each seems somehow to indicate or refer to the others and to be in that sense a sign, hence something other than itself. But if there is a "family Pattern" (481) suggested by the relationship between the "several 'youths,'" the details of its design are not immediately obvious even though the Author fully awake in his study in Buffalo,

New York, maintains that both the origins and the "content" of his dream are "clear" (47). It derives, he believes, from his desire to write a *Marylandiad* with a hero who "would live the first half of his life in the first three dozen years of the republic . . . and the second half in its 'last' . . . with a 128-year nap between" (47), a project that he put aside for LETTERS. The images of his dream, in short, echo and to some extent anticipate the details of his waking world, for when the dream recurs five years later, he finds himself "back in the Old Line state," having "put by Buffalo for Baltimore" (49) and other works for LETTERS. The pattern of his life and work, then, echoes the pattern of his dream: "Having decided in 1968 that the 'Author' character in LETTERS would be offered an honorary doctorate of letters from a Maryland university, I receive in 1969 just such an invitation in the mail. And presuming in 1969 to imagine . . . a 'hero' . . . who falls from mythic irreality into the present-day Maryland marshes—I find myself back in the Old Line state" (48–49).

The "I" in these passages, of course, refers at once to at least two "characters," the "Author" in LETTERS and the author of LETTERS who seem somehow to be different forms of the same self since both are signified by the written character "I." ("He's certainly an authorial chap like me," Barth admits in an interview.[11]) However, neither Author nor author will be found outside of LETTERS, standing unambiguously as its explanatory origin, for the self cannot be reduced to one signification. Each of the selves that the "youths" of the Author's dream becomes will be created by the work itself. The "neutral, sleep-wrapped, most familiar youth" (46), "would-be writer" (80), and mediocre drummer who becomes "John Barth, Esq., Author" (3) is born out of the exchange of letters between the Author and his characters, an exchange that takes the form of a fictional history of the works of John Barth, a "story" (338) of his stories. And as that story is told in LETTERS by letters, we follow the movements of "John Barth" from Cambridge to Johns Hopkins, to Pennsylvania, to Buffalo, to Baltimore and watch as a "local lad" (83) makes good and becomes a Doctor of Letters.

As the Author admits, this is a story of a life "colorless in its modest success" (653), and its hero is a shadowy and passive figure at best. He is represented as the "unnamed other laborer on Mensch's castle" (188) in Ambrose Mensch's autobiographical fragment, *The Amateur;*[12] as a curious college student and would-be writer in Todd Andrews's account of a New Year's Eve party at the Cambridge Yacht Club in 1954, a party that the Author is unable to "recall" (191) in 1969, and as a fellow author and "esteemed collaborator" (408) in a letter by A. B. Cook that is "dictat[ed] . . . by telephone, from notes, into [his] secretary's machine" and "transcribe[d] by her" (408) and sent to the Author, a relationship that the Author vigorously denies. And he appears, too, as the author of eighteen unsigned letters and as the addressee of thirty-one others written to him by fictional characters who believe themselves to be factual. His "presence," in short, is "duly reported" (345) but his "factual existence" remains "more than usually inferential" (533). At times he appears as a "thundering silence" (348), at others as an "epistolary echo" (533) or as a "Near But Distant Neighbor" (440) who is represented by Lady Amherst's description of a "modest cottage" on Lake Chautauqua with "no one at home" (352).

But if the life of the Author's "most familiar youth" is sparsely and colorlessly rendered, the story of the "prior youth to whom the pocketwatch and vest . . . belonged" (47) is told in exciting and flamboyant detail. And this, too, is a story of letters told in letters, a story of A.B.C. IV told in the form of four letters from the hero to his unborn child and five posthumous letters to his widow. And as is the case with all the stories in LET-TERS, it begins and ends in "marshy equivocation" (636) and is marked by genealogical tangles and dreamy confusions. From the time that Henry Burlingame III is found as a baby floating in a canoe on the Chesapeake, his name "*label'd* in red ochre on his chest" (24) the Cook/Burlingame line is troubled by questions of paternity and identity. And these genealogical confusions are echoed in the Author's "Three concentric dreams of waking" that involve him in the tangles of that "family . . . thicket" (130). The pocket watch for which he instinctively reaches in his "half tranced" (47) state, we learn from later letters, is that of Henry Burlingame IV, "father" of A. B. Cook IV, who is, of course, as one of the characters in LETTERS, also engendered by the Author. Indeed, the tangles of the dream become increasingly complex as the reader comes to view the letters that constitute the novel in a comparative fashion. LETTERS is the Author's creation, his "delivered child" (431) and he is "in a sense," to use Todd Andrews's word, the "engenderer" (97) of all its characters. However, this metaphor of physical engenderment that implies that what the artist makes is his child or offspring is partially subverted by the Author's dreamlike sense that the characters he has created have in some way fathered him, since they have become a part of his self-history. When A. B. Cook VI writes to the Author in response to an "invitation to participate in a work in progress" (430), he describes the family watch in words that echo equivocably those that represent it in the "three concentric dreams of waking."

He [Ebenezer Burling] also encloses, by way of proof of his identity, a pocketwatch which he claims was similarly and belatedly given him by his own father: a silver Breguet with "barleycorn" engine-turning on the case, steel moon hands, and a white enameled face with the seconds dial offset at the VII, the maker's name engraved in secret cursive under the XII, and the monogram similarly scribed before the appropriate numeral IV. I have this watch before me as I speak. (413)

In Cook's account, the watch is offered as evidence that "Ebenezer Burling," writing to his twin children in 1827 is actually A. B. Cook IV, their father, who had been reported killed by an errant Congreve rocket just before dawn on September 14, 1814, during the British bombardment of Fort McHenry in Baltimore

Harbor, and the watch reappears in a letter written to the Author by Lady Amherst, where she describes it as being found just before dawn on September 14, 1969, after an explosion "below the ramparts on the West Branch side" (687) of Fort McHenry leaves behind the "shattered remains of an adult male body, clothed in early-19th-Century costume and bearing a miraculously undamaged 18th-Century pocketwatch, still ticking" (688). There is, Lady Amhert maintains, "no reason to doubt that it was [A. B. Cook VI who] went to smithereens where his ancestor did, but less equivocably" (688), and yet there later appears in the text a letter from A. B. Cook VI, addressed to his son and dated 17 September, 1969, in which he describes his own equivocal dream of waking.

I shall only say that I died at Fort McHenry. That this morning, three days later, I woke, as it were, half-tranced on a point of dry ground betwen two creeklets, in the steaming shade of loblolly pines, realizing where I was but not, at once, why I was there. As in a dream I reached for my watchpocket, to fetch forth and wind my ancestors' watch . . . and, as if vouchsafed a vision, I understood that I must not nor need not reappear publicly in any guise. (751)

Henry Burlingame VII, Cook's "son," of course, in a postscript to the Author will maintain that "this letter, like its author, is a fraud" (752) and go on to add, again equivocably, that the "man who died at Fort McHenry was not my father" (754). And the textual tangle is further snarled when we recall A. B. Cook VI's earlier description of the experience of his ancestor, A. B. Cook IV.

"On a point of dry ground between two creeklets, in the shade of a stand of loblolly pines," he rests; he dozes; he dreams . . .
   Of what? We are not told; only that he woke "half tranced, understanding where [he] was but not, at once, why [he] was there" . . . that he was—odd feeling for a Cook, A Burling-

ame, but I myself am no stranger to it—"a different person" from the one who had drowsed off. He fetches forth and winds the pocketwatch sent to him so long ago in France by "H.B. IV"—and suddenly the meaning of his unrecorded dream comes clear, as surprising as it is ambiguous. He must *find his father*, and bring that father to Castines Hundred, to his grandchildren! (483)

This passage illustrates nicely the pattern of displacement that decenters the "brave biography" of A. B. Cook IV as well as those of his ancestors and descendants in the Cook/Burlingame line. The passage is taken from A. B. Cook VI's "digest of [his] decipherment of the first of Andrew Cook IV's 'posthumous' letters: three removes from an original . . . whose author's own wife would not accept as bona fide" (480), and it echoes ambiguously other texts scattered throughout LETTERS. Although the family letters ostensibly are written to represent, explain, and protect parental authority so that the child "(guided by these letters, which must be your scripture if aught should take us from you)" (323) may be freed from the "dismal pattern" (280) of rebellion that dominates the history of the Cook/Burlingame line, they in fact have just the opposite effect. Any sense of an originating authority is undermined by the activities of translating, transcribing, quoting, and editing that occur as they pass from hand to hand, so that they become finally merely words on a page, but, it is important to add, "words that . . . make the wordless happen" (332), for they form a wonderful story with plots and counter-plots, a story of "bravura, intrigue and derring do, sophistication and disguise" (47).

Still the story does not reveal the figure of "John Barth" any less equivocally than does the account of the "most familiar" youth. His presence is suggested by a series of echoes as the crucial details of his dreams of origins reappear as constitutive elements of the Cook/Burlingame history. But as the passages cited above suggest, neither the motif of the dream of waking nor the image of the family watch functions as a key that will unlock the meaning of the Author's dreams of selfhood. To the retrospective eye of the reader, the "original" appearance of the textual elements is equivocated as they become part of a design, that makes them signs that refer to later episodes, and hence to something other than themselves. The result is a situation "richer in associations than in meanings" (385). One obvious implication of the Author's "three concentric dreams of waking" is that his identity is both nourished and troubled by the character that he has created, a character with whom he shares at least "one name's initial: bee-beta-beth, the Kabbalist's letter of Creation, whence derived, like life itself from the marsh primordial, both the alphabet and the universe it described by its recombinations" (47). That character, moreover, is represented in the text by a series of equivocal family letters that are in the possession of his descendant, A. B. Cook VI, who, like his ancestor A. B. Cook IV and the Author, is a "fictitious" dreamer who "imagines himself to be factual." What the dreams point to, in other words, is not some "Pirondelloish or Gide-like debate between Author and Characters" a conceit "as regressive, at least quaint, at this hour of the world, as naive literary realism" (191), but rather to the fact that all of the characters are "hommes de lettres" (526), products of a "novelsworth of letters" (24), and that the illusion of their "factual existence" (533) depends upon the power of words to "make the wordless happen" (332).

Hence, the third "most shadowy" version of the Author's youth appears in the punning form of a "faint-bumbling B," suggesting perhaps that "John Barth" has "come to believe that virtually everyone with his initial" (143) is some version of himself. Certainly the swarming "bees" of the marsh "going about their business" (46) are a "reduplicated image, punning on ['Barth's'] initial" (113) and Burlingame's as well as those of Jerome Bonaparte Bray and Bellerophon, both of whom are suggested by that "blind, lame, vatic figure afloat on the tepid tide" reminding us too, perhaps, of the Bruguet, Buffalo, Baltimore and bomb burst" (47), in short, hinting that the common center of the three dreams is the letter B., the "instrument of creation, the mother of letters and of the world" (328). Not surprisingly, the Author's relation to this shadowy self is an especially interesting one. Barth has said that he hopes that Bray, whom he labels one of the "more fantastic characters," will "elicit a certain amount of sympathy by the novel's close," and there is no doubt that the connection between the Author and this character "who might be a large insect of some kind" is a particularly provocative and problematic one.[13]

If the character of A. B. Cook IV entangles the Author's personal history with that of his country and knots the act of writing to the practice of "the making of history as if it were an avant-garde species of narrative" (73), the "blind, lame, vatic figure" (47) ensnares "Barth's" life with that of the "wandering heroes of myth" (531) and fiction-making with the "writing out for public sale a kind of myths called *novels*" (C, 248). Jerome Bray first appears in "Bellerophoniad" where he drives a "mechanical Pegasus named V. W. Beetle" and lives at Lilydale, "an entire polis of seers and sibyls" (248), and he maintains his mythic status in LETTERS. His grandfather, son of a Tuscaroran Chief, claims to have "conceived" Bray's father "upon a wild Appoloosa mare" (L, 423) and the child is found by H. C. Burlingame VI, "an orphan of the storm . . . rescued from his bulrush basket and raised up in the marsh as though he were [his own] despite his bad foot" (425).

Barth writes in *Chimera* that "*myths . . . are . . . poetic distillations of our ordinary psychic experience and therefore point always to daily reality*" (199) and "Bellerophoniad" and "Persiad" are reorchestrations of classical myths in terms of the themes and conventions for the traditional novel and the forms and structures of modernist fiction. In LETTERS this process of transformation becomes a metaphor for one of the Author's central concerns. The fact that he finds himself transported from Buffalo "back in the Old Line State" after imagining "a 'hero' . . . who falls from mythic irreality into the present-day Maryland marshes" and "put[ting] by LETTERS in pursuit of a new chimera called *Chimera*" (L, 49) suggests a process that we might call (paraphrasing

Barth in "The Literature of Exhaustion") the contamination of reality by myth. As Herbert Schneidau has noted, "one primary attribute of mythology is its communicability and tendency to spread. . . . Myths seem to pass between certain kinds of cultures even through the most evanescent contact, almost as if they were infectious."[14] It is this aspect of myth that leads A. B. Cook IV to maintain that the "future" of the Indian "lay not in history but, as it were, in myth" (320), that "as Lord Amherst infected the Indians with smallpox, Pontiac infected white Americans with Myth, at least as contagious & insusceptible to cure," an infection that results in the "gradual 'reddening' of the whites" (127).

The Indian survives in the present time action of LETTERS in the hybrid figure of Jerome Bonaparte Bray, who possesses a complex genealogy that suggests the mixed forms of life in mythology. Claiming kinship with the Bonapartes, the Iroquois Nation, as well as with the animal and insect worlds, Bray seems to the other characters to be "real" but "mad as a hatter" (368), a "horny maniac," a "lecherous . . . lunatic" (540), the most "hairraisingly creepish male animal upon this planet" (766). And indeed the text leaves open the possibility that he is responsible for most of the violent acts that mark the ending of the novel: the possible rapes of five women; the drone attack on Bloodsworth Island; and the destruction of the *Baratarian* and its crew, among others. However, since all of the events in LETTERS are textual rather than performative ones the usual relation between the text and the circumstances or context that it represents is missing, and this absence leaves all issues of origins, authority and authorship open to question and makes it difficult to say unequivocally what exactly is being textually represented at any particular point. In spite of his assertions to the contrary, Bray too is "an homme de lettres" (36) and his history and story are implicated in those of the "swarm of hommes de lettres" (526) that constitute the novel. The result is that questions concerning the origins and meaning of events and selves are "idle ontologies" (107) that may lead to "illumination" but

never to "solutions" (768). One example will illustrate the point.
In the final section of the novel Todd Andrews, writing to his
"fictitious forebear" (692) concerning his last cruise on the skipjack, *Osborn Jones,* describes an experience of August 28, his
"Last Night Out" (728), which occurs in the "magic Sawmill
Cove: high-banked, entirely wooded, houseless, snug, primeval
. . . a place to make one miss the world" (728).

In the early hours my sleep was broken by a shocking noise:
from somewhere alongshore, very nearby, as feral a snarling as
I've ever heard, and the frantic squeals of victims. A fox or
farm dog it must have been, savaging on a brood of young
something-or-others. For endless minutes it went on, blood-
chilling. Insatiable predator! Prey that shrieked and splashed
but for some reason could not escape, their number diminishing one by pathetic one! I rushed on deck with the 7 x 50's,
shouted out into the pitch-darkness (the moon had set), but
could see and do nothing. The last little victim screamed and
died. Baby herons? Frogs? Their killer's roaring lowered to an
even growl, one final terrible snarling *coup de grace,* then almost a purr. There was a rustling up into the woods, followed
by awful silence. Long moments later a crow croaked; a cicada
answered; a fish jumped; the night wood business resumed.
   I stood trembling in my sweat. Nature bloody in fang and
claw! Under me, over me, 'round about me, everything killing
everything! I had dined that evening on crabs boiled alive and
picked from their exoskeletons; as I ate I'd heard the day's
news: Judge Boyle denies Kennedy request to cross-examine
Kopechne inquest witnesses; last of the first 25,000 U.S. troops
withdrawn from Viet Nam; U.S.S.R. acknowledges danger of
war with China. And Drew would become a terrorist, only
accidentally killing others. And you, sir, killed yourself, the
only lesson you ever taught me. Horrific nature; horrific
world; out, out! (728-29)

No other section in LETTERS deals so movingly with "human
life, its happiness and misery," than does Andrews's account of
his final cruise, and this passage, in particular, renders with a

Shakespearean intensity the horrifying grimness of reality, a reality that resists Todd's attempt to understand it and leaves him at the last "mystified, chagrined, and pooped" (692) and with the suspicion that he may be the victim of an "elaborate conspiracy" (727), a victim of friend and enemy alike. For him there will be no "winding up of business," no "illuminating of mysteries" (730) before ending his life. And yet the pathos of Todd's representation of his failed life is disturbed by the anti-representational mode of Jerome Bray's final lettter which echoes and questions the illusion of reality that characterizes Todd's account.

Dear Granama,
   O see kin, "G.III's" bottled dumps–oily shite!–which he squalidly hauled from his toilet's last gleanings. 5 broads stripped and, bride-starred, screwed their pearly ass right on our ram-part! You watched? Heard our growls and their screamings? Now Bea Golden ("G's" heir)'s Honey-Dusted 4-square: grave food for her bright hatch of maggots next year! Our females are all seeded; our enemies are not alive; so, dear Granama, take *me* to the hum of your hive! (755)

This passage, of course, reminds us of the "squeals," "screams," and "growl" that disturb Todd's sleep on 28 August and invokes a number of the events that threaten and mystify him but in a way that textualizes them and robs them of their horrifying immediacy. The comic rhymes, the outrageous parody of the National Anthem function as antirepresentational elements that disturb our illusion that the characters of the novel are actual, authentic people, engaged in real life problems, each with his or her own needs and desires. Read in the context of Bray's letter, Todd's words lose their reality effect and become merely written signs that echo others that displace them. Todd, we recall, like Bray, insists that "I'm not a *homme de lettres:* my dealings are with the actual lives of actual people" (97); he "rapes" Jeannine a.k.a. Bea Golden "a tergo, puppy-dog style"

(707) recalling both Bray's fascination with bees and Honey dust as well as his search for women to "take delivery in the rear" (426); and Todd's Freudian identification of himself and Jane Mack with the man and woman in the 1921 "advertisement for Arrow shirts" (463)–"It is after all an *Arrow* shirt, and she is its willing target" (464)–suggests Bray and his venemous "barb" (426). Todd's words, in short, disclose Bray's words as well as real life events as the play of repetition overcomes the magic of representation.

However this disturbing infectiousness is in keeping with Bray's American Indian and mythological antecedents since he does possess "abilities, capacities, as extraordinary" (746) and unusual as those ascribed to his ancestors. For example, Levi-Strauss points to the fact that marriage between animals and humans was commonly accepted by the American Indian.

We know what the animals do, what are the needs of the beaver, the bear, the salmon, and other creatures, because long ago men married them and acquired this knowledge from their animal wives. Today the priests say we lie, but we know better. The white man has been only a short time in this country and knows very little about the animals; we have lived here thousands of years and were taught long ago by the animals themselves. The white man writes everything down in a book so that it will not be forgotten; but our ancestors married the animals, learned all their ways, and passed on the knowledge from one generation to another.[15]

Schneidau, who cites this passage, goes on to note that "by mythological expectations the unions of humans with animals might produce human beings who can transform themselves into many shapes. [One of Bray's remarkable abilities.] Metamorphasis emphasizes not the monstrosity of hybrids but the kinship that underlies all forms of life" (94). This characteristic of myth makes it an appropriate metaphor for one of the Author's concerns in his "three concentric dreams of waking," namely, the form of his relation to a mythic self, figured in LETTERS in the

enigmatic character of Bray who shares not one but two names'
initials with "John Barth." This is not a heroic self, but a self
that is a parody of the hero, an "imperfect mimicry" (*L*, 638) of
the mythic figure Bellerophon, "who believes he can achieve
mythic herohood by perfectly imitating the Heroic Pattern and
who learns that by doing so what one becomes is a perfect
imitation of a mythic hero" (637). This "blind, lame, vatic
figure" (47) undermines through parody the success stories of
the other two youths, but the author nevertheless implies that it
too stands, perhaps obliquely, for an aspect of himself.

Bray represents the presence of "mythic irreality" (49) in the
realistic world of LETTERS, and insectlike he infects that world
with his trance-inducing drug, Honey Dust, which with its
seven magical ingredients, including the "freeze dried feces of G.
III" (758), is as "spellbinding" (767) as the Author's seven-part narrative. The mode of Bray's relation to the Author, in other
words, is that of mimicry. The titles in his bibliography mimic
those in "Barth's," and he accuses the Author of plagiarism, an
accusation that the Author responds to in the following way:

Like those book reviewers who choose to mimic (and attempt
to surpass) the author under review, you have seen fit to address me in the manner of my novel, as though you were one
of its characters nursing a grievance against your author.

Such mimicries and allegations are best left unacknowledged: *Claw a churl by the breech,* an Elizabethan proverb
warns, *and get a handful of shite.* (351)

This passage describes nicely the form of the relationship between the Author and the characters in LETTERS. Although, as
Lady Amherst puts it, the Author is "not held in universal admiration" (373)–A. B. Cook VI offers "to arrange [his] assassina-
tion for Joe Morgan" (373) and he is the object of Bray's
threatening vehemence, he refuses (with one exception) to acknowledge any personal relation to the characters who help to
represent him even though they all seek direct access to him. He

insists that their "connection be not only strictly verbal, but epistolary" (52). The one exception is Ambrose Mensch, his one-time "alter ego" (653) with whom he was "close in our growings up and literary apprenticeship" (653). But his connection is an "old and long since distanced" (653) one, and it like the others is "symbolic but not merely symbolic" (551), for in a "sense" the "dialogue" is a "monologue" since "capital-A Authors are ultimately, ineluctably, and forever talking to ourselves. If our correspondence is after all a fiction, we like, we *need* that fiction: it makes our job less lonely" (655). The distinction that this passage makes between Author and character provides a way of understanding the relation between Jerome Bray and "John Barth." As I have suggested, the figure of "John Barth, Author" in LETTERS is an indication that John Barth himself, the author of LETTERS, insofar as the reader can know him in his writing, is the tendency always to dream himself as an imaginary someone else who is, at the same time, an expression of himself.[16] This relationship is figured in the tendency of his fiction to be "mildly prophetic" (48) so that "what has been fiction becomes idle fact, invention history," the "fabulous irreal" a part of the "realistic tradition" (52). From Jerome Bray's side of the "funhouse mirror" (52) of fictive language "John Barth" seems to have plagiarized from Bray's "writings" which were never the *"fictions they represented themselves as being, but ciphered replies to . . . parental communications"* (34), and from the Author's side, Bray seems to mimic or parody "John Barth's" imaginative creations. This relationship suggests at once the formal play and "spellbinding" seriousness that characterizes the world of LETTERS, a place of waking dreams and dreams of waking.

However, these dreams are in the form of letters to "concerned readers" and as such call attention to the fact of writing and the act of reading, and in so doing they disturb the conventional boundaries between the status of the events and characters within the novel and the "reality" that they are supposed to represent. The result is a "sense of mediated immediacy that provokes interpretation"[17] by fixing attention on the nature of language itself and putting into question its referential functions. This does not mean, however, that the relation between writer and reader will be controlled by a set of "tired Modernist tricks" (199), for Barth "works hard to keep his work interesting and literate." He recognizes that "most people read novels for entertainment and delight . . . and most novels are read only once." Nevertheless, if serious fiction like serious music is "ravishing the first time through," the reader will become "enthused and curious and will return to the piece again and again."[18]

Hence the Author of LETTERS initially conceives of the novel as "an open (love) letter to Whom It May Concern, from Yours Truly" (53), and, in its final form, its main plot concerns a torrid love affair that combines "good-humored prurience," "gentle salaciousness" (65) with an equally entertaining emblematic import. The story of Lady Amherst's and Ambrose Mensch's affair, with its "novelistic symmetry" (668) echoes another "perverse attraction" (66), that of the Author for "Reality, a mistress too long ignored," who must now "settle scores with her errant lover" (52). Indeed, the Amherst/Mensch story is the major vehicle for the communication of the emotional and intellectual rhythms the novel excites in the reader, for it at once dramatizes and emblematizes the primary concerns of LETTERS.

As I noted earlier, the Author enjoys a special relationship with Mensch, each having served as the other's "alter ego" and "aesthetic conscience; eventually even as the other's fiction" (653). Mensch, formalist and author of "keyless codes . . . chain letter narratives with missing links . . . edible anecdotes" (39), at once the Author's "comrade and contrary" (165), supplies the *"bare bone sketch"* (165) that becomes the Ambrose sequence in *Lost in the Funhouse,* the "ground plan," "notes," and "alphabetized instructions" for *Chimera,* as well as the design for LETTERS; and the Author, in turn, helps to build Mensch's castle and later takes his aborted autobiographical novel, *The Amateur, or, A Cure for Cancer,* gives it new life, and brings it to completion in LETTERS. Indeed, the story of the Menschhaus, of the broken seawall, the cracked castle, the Mensch "firm . . . and infirmity" (152) is yet another version of the story of LETTERS.

The Amateur, "an early effort, abortive, on the part of 'Arthur Morton King'" (149), Mensch's "fanciful nom de plume" (240), to "come to terms with conventional narrative and himself" (149), recapitulates and dramatizes the problem of *"personal literature"* (188) and the postmodern writer. Ambrose adopts his "corny nom de plume" because, not being sure of who exactly he is, he is unable "to write straightforwardly under his own name" (551). Tormented by the "possibly fancied ambiguity of his siring" (240)—he takes his pen name from his mother, Andrea King Mensch, a descendant of the King family "whose ancestors a century and a half ago conspired on behalf of their friend Jerome Bonapart to spirit Napoleon from St. Helena to Maryland" (240)—and paralyzed by the blank message he receives in a bottle as an eleven-year-old child, he spends his life *"laboring to fill in the blanks,"* seeking *"a way to get the story told and rejoin [his] family"* (188).

However, the story that he attempts to tell is one of a world that is "winding down" (186), a story of a "broken seawall," a "cracked castle," and "sinking tower" (151), one with characters beset by "wasting diseases" (208), its *femme fatale* [Ambrose's mother] now potbellied, shrunken, half deaf, gone in the teeth—a sweetless hive of swarming cells" (241). For the Mensch family "Cancer is the reigning sign; petrifaction the prevailing state" (528). Like *Pierre* and *Absalom, Absalom!, The Amateur* is the account of the collapse of a family; and, like Thomas Sutpen, Thomas Mensch, the "unmoved mover" of the family, is a man about whose "fathering . . . nothing certain is known" (157). It is he who builds the "retaining seawall . . . which like an individual work of art he signed and dated at each end in wet concrete" (158) and establishes the Mensch Memorial Monument Company. But with his death the creative energy of the Mensch family begins to dissipate. Significantly it is not this original author of the family line who builds the cracked castle or who provides the authority for the narrative account of its fall. For this story is another one that questions the relation between family lines and narrative lines. Like *Tristram Shandy*, *The Amateur* is *ab ovo* (153), but the egg from which it is hatched is an intentional rather than a natural object, a marvelous Easter egg with a magical interior that is given to Ambrose's Aunt Rosa by her husband. Like Faulkner's Rosa Coldfield, Rosa Mensch goes to "her grave unfructified" (153), but from her Easter egg with its "magical interior" (170) is hatched the vision that produces the story of Menschhaus. For this egg, with its "wondrous innards" (154), its "emerald landscape," with a "Lorelei, begauzed and pensive," its "grey-green castle turrets . . . velveted with lichen" (170) is an image for the realm of romance, and it generates in Ambrose a Hawthornian desire to "dream strange things and make them look like truth" (*SL*, 31). As he watches the "play of shadows on the ceiling" of his bedroom, "where the streetlamp shown through the catalpa leaves" (170), he invents mysterious origins for his brother Peter, whom he imagines has been fathered by Colonel Morton "upon a European baroness" (169) who will not "forget the issue of her star-crossed passion" but eventually "claim Peter for her own" and take him back to be "master of the castle" (170). And even the more prosaic Peter also has his life shaped by the "miracle inside" (174) the egg: inspired by the vision of his "Grandpa's castle in the egg" (174), he uses his inheritance to buy a section of Erdman's Cornlot and to build a stone house complete with tower for the family to inhabit.

But Peter's efforts only serve to reveal the distance between imagination and perception. The Cornlot is an ironic echo of Camelot (as is Bray's Comalot), and the house, built on the soft "loam of the Eastern Shore" (178), is held together with mortar made from "one part lime to three sand" (188), its construction contaminated by Ambrose's guilt over his affair with his brother's fiancée, the partially completed house having been their "trysting place" (186). And "as the stone house [rises] up about them" (387) on the "shifting sand" (178) Aunt Rosa's "cancer spread[s] like an ugly rumor" (182) and Magda articulates her "cosmic and impersonal" pessimism, a "tidewater Tragic View" (183) that holds that the Choptank itself was a passing feature of the landscape; the very peninsula . . . ephemeral" (185).

From this point of view, then, the "family totem" (245), that "celebrated Easter egg," appears to be "mere family junk or joking relic" (246). Only for "Damaged Angela" (244) does the "vanished country of the Easter egg" (156) retain its power. For Ambrose and Peter its magical autonomous world is abandoned when, "certain the family must fail at last, Ambrose caused the entire tower [of the house] to be converted into a camera obscura" in order to attract "travelers en route to Ocean City" (155). In the place of the "green and rivered landscape of the egg" (164) is one composed of "red brick hospital, weathered oyster-dredger . . . dowdy maples and cypress clapboards of East Dorset" (156), a "view better mediated . . . than viewed directly" (440), for the "dark chamber and luminous plate make the commonplace enchanting. What would scarcely merit notice if beheld firsthand . . . [is] magically composed and represented . . . and [is] intensely interesting" (155-56). However, no matter how fascinating such projections of the "familiar details of . . . life" (85) may be, they cannot halt the fall of the "ill-founded house" (188) or the decay of the "cancerous" (588) family. The "list of the tower" binds the "mechanism" of the camera obscura until it is finally "out of commission" (246), "fixed for keeps upon the county hospital, the broken seawall, the river of incongruous pleasure boats" (559), a reminder of the family "firm" and "infirmity" (152) as Magda, Ambrose, and Lady Amherst "hold hands in reciprocal succour" (559), stare at these frozen images, and await the diagnosis of Peter Mensch's disease while the "damaged daughter" (242) consoles herself by gazing at the "vanished country" through the "blank window" (156) of Aunt Rosa's egg.

At issue here, of course, is an artistic as well as a family disaster, a question of the "Death-of-the-Novel" and the "End-of-Letters" (438) as well as a poignant portrayal of death in the novel and the end of a family. The Easter egg and the camera obscura are emblems of the two forms of representation that have sustained the novel: the first an expression of the desire to modify reality, or as Barth puts it in an early interview, "reinvent the world,"[19] and the other a commitment to "make the commonplace enchanting" (155) by "holding a great mirror up to life," thereby allowing us to "recognize our world and ourselves" (472). And, of course, the "sinking tower" (152) in which Ambrose and his daughter live is an emblem of the traditional home of the artist, symbol of solitariness and loneliness, but also a refuge and beacon, and the sign especially of the alienated modernist who is closed off from normal relations with family and society but who is gifted with powers of perception that make possible the highest form of artistic expression.

Ambrose, however, who lives as a hermit in his "sinking tower, . . . measures the stars with a homemade astrolabe, inventing new constellations, . . . examines bemused beneath a microscope his swarming semen, giving names to (and odds on) individual spermatozoa in their blind and general race" (61), has lost touch with his muse and is "too distracted to compose" (40). As an aborted attempt on the part of "Arthur Morton King to come to terms with conventional narrative and himself" (149) Ambrose's incomplete story emblematizes the dilemma of the contemporary novelist. He reviews his "work-then-in-progress" and his "30 year old life" (149), corks the work in an empty jeroboam, throws it into the Choptank river, takes 30 librium capsules, and goes home to die. But his suicide fails, the jeroboam returns with the tide two days later, to be kept for nine years, uncorked only to provide the Author in 1961 with the "Bee-Swarming, Water-Message, and Funhouse anecdotes" (150). However, the librium capsules do liberate him from the "library of [his] literary predecessors," from "Realism" and all the "traditional contaminants of fiction" (151–52), and it takes nine years for him to become reenamored with the novel, a development that is marked by the beginning of his affair with Lady Amherst. Her "symbolic potential" (61) as well as her person attracts him, for he associates her with the "muse of Austen, Dickens, Fielding, Richardson and the rest" (41), sees her as "Literature Incarnate" (40) *"La Belle Lettre sans Merci,*" whose "old egg" he hopes to impregnate with one of his "sluggish swim-mers" (238).

It is significant, then, that as he prepares to visit his lover "to mark the advent of [his] 40th year," he decides "to try again to launch [his] old chronicle on the tide" (152) by sending it to her to read; and, inspired by her to a "rage for paternity" (347), he conceives a "longish fiction, novella-size at least" (347), based on the classical myth of Perseus, Andromeda, and Medusa, a myth that he reads as a drama of the perils of self-consciousness.

Ambrose's Perseus, middle-aged and ill married, his mythic ex-ploits and heroic innocence behind him, once again 'calls his enemy to his aid' (Ovid's happy phrase, for Perseus's use of the Gorgon's head to petrify his adversaries), attempts to reenact his youthful triumphs, comes a cropper, but with the help of a restored and resurrected Medusa—whose true gaze, seen clearly, may confer immortality instead of death—transcends his vain objective and becomes, with her, a constellation in the sky, endlessly reenacting their romance. (348)

As this description of the Perseus project by Lady Amherst sug-gests, she is delighted by Ambrose's decision to "speak once again to the passions instead of playing his avant-garde games" (348). She is especially taken with the conceit that "by some magic physics of the heart" Perseus and Medusa "will become not stones, but stars, rehearsing endlessly the narrative of their affair," for she sees in it "an emblem of [her] trials thus far, and a future hope" (436).

But for Ambrose, finally, Lady Amherst's person is more im-portant than her "symbolic potential"; hence he sends to the Au-thor the "ground plans" (652) for his Perseus story, leaving to him the task of writing the story while Ambrose devotes his full attention to his lover and family as he attempts to become a "Member" of the "Human Race" (758) and in the process a char-acter in that "most happily contaminated literary genre: the Novel" (151). The form and meaning of this contamination are suggested by the ways the Perseus/Medusa myth informs the Mensch/Lady Amherst story. *"Perseus's conception in Argos upon the virgin Danaë in the brass contraceptive tower, by Zeus in the form of a shower of gold"* (648) is comically echoed and domesticated when Ambrose and Germaine, aroused by the reading of *Clarrisa*'s table of contents, copulate "on a pair of clean 50-lb sacks of Medusa" (440) cement at the top of Schott's Tower of Truth, and Ambrose's reworking of the classical material is suggested when, during their honeymoon evening aboard the *Constellation,* they each have a "vision" (683) as they climax together.

Ambrose's marriage, significantly, is marked by his farewell to Arthur Morton King, his *nom de plume,* who "sprang" "genie-like" (758) from a bottle on May 12, 1940. As he celebrates the beginning of the second cycle of his life, he appears *"in propria persona"* (759) having in effect rejected "Dear (dead) Art" (758) for life with Lady Amherst, his final letter to "Art" being also a proposal of marriage to her. Now no longer the "filler in of blanks" (758) addressed to a "Cruel Yours Truly" who *confirms his dearest hope—that there are Signs—and his deepest fear—that they are not for him"* (168), the "Once & Future Ambrose Mensch" becomes the one "Whom It Ceases to Concern" (646), finally free to author a letter to "Whom it may concern (in particular the Author)" (765) and to sign himself "Yours truly, Ambrose Mensch" (765).

This is a letter that at once echoes and extends the Author's account of his "three concentric dreams of waking," for it brings together origins and ends by providing the design for LETTERS in *"a postscript to the Author"* (765). It is fitting, of course, that Mensch, the "former formalist" (769) and now the Author's "altered ego" (655) should introduce the theme and problem of closure, for he is the only character in LETTERS whose "historic-ity" (191) the Author accepts unequivocally, freely acknowledging that he (the Author) helped to build the Menschhaus and that Mensch supplied the outlines for the Ambrose sketches in *Lost in the Funhouse.* Here, apparently, is the one "connection" in the novel that may not be "strictly verbal" and "epistolary" (52), although it is certainly literary, as the Author makes clear, when, in writing to Lady Amherst, he describes Mensch as "our mutual friend" (52). And just as John Rokesmith in Dickens's novel represents an attempt on the part of John Harmon to deal with the pressures of reality by transforming his real identity into a role, by becoming an imaginative version of himself, so Arthur Morton King suggests a similar response on the part of Ambrose Mensch when he is confronted by the challenge of the bottled message. And "John Barth," Author of LETTERS, acknowledges a parallel situation by confirming his "long since distanced connection" (653) to Ambrose and his modernist pre-occupations. Because "overmuch presence appears to be the story teller's problem" (*LIF*, 101) the Author transforms his "real" situation into a fictive one and in the process frees himself to change his "notes toward a new novel" (*L*, 51) into a book that "neither merely repudiates nor merely imitates either his twentieth-century modernist parents or his nineteenth-century premodernist grandparents,"[20] Robbe-Grillet or Dickens. And once having effaced himself by transforming his real identity into a role, the Author, "like Echo in the myth" disappears and gives back to Mensch his "own words in another voice" (194).

This, then, is the logic behind the conceit that Mensch supplies the Author with the sketches for the Ambrose sections in *Lost in the Funhouse*, with the plans and directions for the writing of *Chimera* and the design for LETTERS, as well as the explanation for the fact that the arrival of "*Water message #2*" (765) brings LETTERS to its conclusion. This second message, although different from the first, is no less ambiguous, for this one consists "wholly of body, without return address, date, salutation, close or signature" (765): "Bottled message: TOWER OF TRUTH 0700 9/26/69, plus some dark, grainy odd-odored solid, like freeze-dried coffee spoilt by moisture" (766). That this letter, like the one of May 12, 1940, takes the form of a note found in a bottle suggests that both Ambrose's story and LETTERS is governed by a law of "reenactment" (39); but since this bottled message consists simply but ambiguously of the signs of a time and place and is contaminated by an odd foreign material, it echoes but does not repeat the earlier one. It is in short a "*suggestion* . . . rather then a replication" (233) of the original. Moreoever its contents and Ambrose's alphabetized reply, like the letter that Judith Sutpen brings to Mrs. Compson, initiate a series of "echoes and connections" (652) that keep us even at the end of the novel still *in medias res.*

Ambrose's final communication, then, is no "bombshell letter" (766) that will provide an explosive release like that of an orgasm or sudden revelation. Unlike the simultaneous visions that Ambrose and Lady Amherst experience on their honeymoon which remain, like Dante's at the end of the *Vita Nuova,* unspoken and generate a "Vast Serenity" (685) and "new serene detachment" (691), the bottled message initiates a flood of words that recycles most of the novel's puzzles: the problem of connexity, the "puzzles of Barataria and *Baratarian*" (768); the question of paternity, of who has been seeded and by whom; the issues of authority and authorship, of who is responsible for the "Break-in at M.M. Co." (766), for the planting of "Water Message #2" (766), and for "Cook VI's Francis Scott Key Letter" (767); and, finally, the problem of ending, what will happen to the Tower of Truth at "dawn's early light 9/28/69" (767).

The mysterious message is enclosed in a "magnum of Mumm's Cordon Rouge" (765), a wine that Todd Andrews enjoys with Jane Mack and Baron Castine aboard the *Baratarian* on Saturday, August 23 while they joke about the location of "Harrison Mack's freeze-dried feces" (714) and discuss the dangers of being "hijacked" in the bay "or on the Intracoastal Waterway, by narcotics smugglers" (716). Subsequently, on September 26 Todd reports that the *Baratarian* is found on 9/19 "derelict & half scuttled, with specimens of Harrison's freeze-dried droppings aboard, and charts of the Mexican Caribbean" (734); and Lady Amherst writes on 9/20 of the discovery the previous day of a "*literal* slick of diesel oil in the Atlantic off Ship Shoal Inlet . . . in the midst of which the Coast Guard finds at last the

derelict *Baratarian*. . . . Nothing material aboard except . . . a letter from the late Andrew Burlingame Cook VI to his son, dated
17 September 1969 . . . the contents whereof the U.S.C.G. is
withholding pending the location of Mr. Cook's next of kin"
(691). However, a copy of this letter is sent to the Author by
H. B. VII on September 15 with a postscript that asserts his absolute authority.

The man who died at Fort McHenry was not my father.
I know who my mother is; have long, if not always,
known. And *she* knows who my true father is, as I know
(what A. B. Cook little suspected) who and where my twin
children, and their mother, are.
· ·
About "Comrade Bray" and "Comrade Mack," not to men-
tion Mr. Todd Andrews, I am unconcerned. I know who they
are, what they "stand for," what they intend, and what will
come to pass: at Barataria Lodge tomorrow; on the campus at
Marshyhope State University a week from Friday.
The "Second Revolution" shall be accomplished on
schedule. . . . The tyrannosaurus blunders on, his slow mind
not yet having registered that he is dead. We shall be standing
clear of his death throes, patient and watchful, our work
done. (754)

Such claims of authorial distance, detachment, and omnisci-
ence are put into question by other letters that serve to question
stable family structures, clear, unambiguous meanings, and a
predictable future. For example the "slick of oil" that marks the
site of the derelict is also a sign for Jerome Bray who leaves the
"lap" of Merope Bernstein's leotard "soiled as if by axle grease"
(534) and who, in his letter of 9/23/69 to his Granama, refers to
the "ex-yacht *Baratarian* a/k/a/ *Surprize,* ha, ha, whose crew and
cargo (Honey-Dust Ingredient #7) not the U.S.N. and U.S.C.G. together will ever find" (755–56). Ambrose, however, will attribute
authorizing authority and control to "Brice and/or Bruce,"

the twinlike, effeminate "curly blond thugs" (549), formerly regents to Reg prince but now apparently acting on their own.

Brice and/or Bruce it was who fetched me that blow that day; the same who—surely—planted Water Message #2 for my discovery yesterday; and they have intimated that Bray may make his "final appearance" at the Tower of Truth dedication ceremonies this Friday: the Ascension sequence, in which, I begin to think, I too must play a role. (766)

"Water Message #2," then raises once again the problem of reading, for it demonstrates the way in which words by surviving their authors and reappearing in and reshaping the meanings of the words of others initiate a ghostly, echoing effect that prevents the reader from experiencing the sense of harmony that normally accompanies closure. Instead we are presented with a series of "hints" that carry us in search of answers back to other letters. "Look it up," Ambrose says, "that's what print's for" (387); but when we follow his advice we find not the answer we had expected but another text whose meaning is, in the words of Geoffrey Hartman, "teasingly evasive."[21]

Ambrose will go on to suggest that all the novel's puzzles may be "diversions," that the "real treasure (and our story's resolution) may be the key itself: illumination, not solution, of the Scheme of Things" (768). And this key, of course, is a letter, more specifically, a Bottled Message, that by its very nature prevents the writing of THE END. As John Irwin observes of Poe's "Ms Found in a Bottle," the fact that the manuscript is cast into the sea at the last moment makes it impossible that the narrative contain a record of that final moment. "The very mechanics of written narration—the necessity to interrupt the text before the moment of ultimate discovery in order to dispatch it before the destruction of the narrator—excludes the written narrative from any access to the absolute."[22] And the organization of LETTERS works to exaggerate the mechanics to which Irwin refers.

Ambrose's "Bottled Message #2" discovered on 9/29/69, refers ambiguously to a place, time, and events that the reader already has experienced since Barth does not arrange the individual letters chronologically. The eightieth letter, in the form of a "Draft codicil to the last will and testament of Todd Andrews" (733), dated "Friday, September 26, 1969," is written in the "Observation Belfrey" (734) of the Tower of Truth and records a series of ominous events that seem to threaten the "demolition of the structure wherein [he] draft[s] it and of [himself]" (734). But the account ends just moments before Todd presumably makes a "thick paper airplane" of the documents and "sail[s] it" (737) out of the window of the tower.[23]

Now Barth has indicated that he "gave considerable thought and attention to the ending of *Letters* [sic]—even, I should say especially, in the very early stages of planning." "Rightly or wrongly, I felt it critical that the reader remain in doubt, for example, about whether that tower Todd Andrews is last seen holed up in blows up or not. I wasn't going to blow it up; I wasn't going to be the one to push the detonator at that point."[24] Instead of "lowering some god down on wires,"[25] Barth offers the reader Ambrose's response to a second "Bottled Message" in the form of a letter of "*Envoi*" (768), some concluding remarks in alphabetical order, the "first such letter from yours truly, to whom these presents may concern, restoppered in your faithful craft along with whatever that brown stuff is: past cape and cove, black can, red nun, out of river, out of bay, into the ocean of story" (768), with a carbon copy to the "Author" (767). Like Andrew's draft codicil to his will and Bray's letter to the future, this document suggests that the denouement of LETTERS will not be the representation of an event that unties the narrative knots or initiates an explosive release but an emblem of the novel itself, "that most happily contaminated literary genre" (151), a "Bottled Message," containing letters about LETTERS and some freeze-dried feces.

And Ambrose's emblematic *Envoi,* with the design for the novel included as a postscript, is echoed by another by the

Author as he brings LETTERS but not letters to an end. This second of two communications to the reader, like the first, calls attention to the problem of time as it relates to the acts of reading and writing.

> But every letter has two times, that of its writing and that of its reading, which may be so separated . . . that very little of what obtained when the writer wrote will still when the reader reads. And to the units of epistolary fictions yet a third time is added: the actual date of composition, which will not likely correspond to the letterhead date, a function more of plot or form than of history.
> . . . .
> The plan of LETTERS calls for a second letter to the Reader at the end of the manuscript, by when what I've "now" recorded will seem almost as remote as "March 2, 1969." By the time LETTERS is in print, ditto for what shall be recorded in that final letter. And—to come to the last of a letter's times— by the time *your* eyes, Reader, review those epistolary fictive a's to z's, the "United States of America" may be setting about its Tri or Quadricentennial . . . or be a mere memory. . . .
> (44–45)

This emphasis on the temporal dimension of fiction is, of course, appropriate in a novel whose "ground theme" is "reenactment" (656), an attempt on the Author's part to "learn where to go by reviewing where I've been" (C, 10). He begins by calling attention to the different times that form the experience of the reader of a novel. There is first, of course, the time of reading, those moments that pass as the reader moves from word to word, from sentence to sentence, from the beginning to the end of the novel, caught up in the fictive events but, like Isabel Archer during her midnight vigil or Quentin and Shreve in their cold Harvard dormitory room, still vaguely aware of passing time and events in the "real" world. Next, as the Author suggests, there is too an awareness of the time when the writer wrote the words "now" being read, and of the fact that the words bear some relation to the writer's own life and time and to the way that he transforms his experience into a fiction. Finally, there are the times of the characters, each of whom has his or her special relation to temporality, and, in the case of LETTERS, this relationship is complicated by the fact that most of the characters are "resurrection[s]" of those from the Author's "previous fictions, or their proxies," who extend the fictions into the "historical present" (341) as well as contribute the "elements of [the] themes and form" (431) to the new one.

The entire process described above is emblematized in the novel by Lady Amherst, who reads "through ["Barth's"] published *oeuvre* . . . a book a month" (556) beginning in March with *The Floating Opera*. Each of the books echoes in a disturbing way her memories of her past as well as the circumstances of her present situation, including her relationship with the Author. She is "introduced . . . by Ambrose Mensch to the alleged original of . . . Todd Andrews" and experiences a "familiar uneasiness about the fictive life of real people and the factual life of 'fictional characters'" (58); she knows "several of [the] characters" from *The End of the Road*, and the Author's representation of Jacob Horner "puts [her] disquietingly in mind of certain traits of [her] friend A.M." (61); The *Sot-Weed Factor* overwhelms her with "'coincidences' of history and [the author's] fiction with the facts of [her] life" (198); the "Giles Boy novel" (348) echoes her own preoccupation with the authenticity of "Andrew Cook IV's four letter family history" (348) that she is preparing for the press; and, finally, her lover Ambrose is "in" the "*Lost in the Funhouse* stories" (347), an especially disturbing fact, for it is at this point that she herself feels "lost" (435) as a result of Ambrose's infidelity. Nevertheless she reports that she "enjoyed the stories— in particular, of course, the 'Ambrose' ones. Your Ambrose, needless to say, is not my Ambrose—but then, mine isn't either" (438). Moreover the fact that she is reading the stories leads her lover to undertake a review of the "origins of *printed* fiction, especially the early conventions of the novel" (438) and that resolve leads directly to the mating season sequence in the phallic

Tower of Truth. This "project of engenderment" (442), we are reminded, takes place on July 14, the "180th anniversary of Bastille Day (and 152nd of Mme de Stael's death)" (438) and provides Ambrose with a "particular spur to his myth in progress (442), and he returns to it during a week marked by the launching of *Apollo 11* and the preparation for Dorchester County's "nine-day tercentenary celebration" (442).

At work here is a process that Paul de Man calls the "discontinuous and polyrhythmic nature of temporality,"[26] one that is revealed by the act of reading with its structure of recollection and anticipation which expresses the way the present moves toward a future that will in some form include a reassimilation of the past. But this movement seems threatened in LETTERS by the fact that by July Lady Amherst "has now gone quite through [Barth's] published *oeuvre*." "What am I to read in August? In September?" (556), she asks, a question that is reemphasized by her lover when he reminds the Author that "my good Dame History—has caught up with your production and needs a quickie to tide her over while you do that long one" (652). Toward that end Ambrose sends to him the "ground plan for that Perseus-Medusa story I told you of, together with more notes on golden ratio, Fibonacci series, logarithmic spirals than any sane writer will be interested in," as well as "alphabetized instructions" for the writing of *Chimera* and the "theme" for LETTERS, leaving to the Author to "work out a metaphoric physics to turn stones into stars . . . dead notes into living fiction" (652).

The story that results, of course, is the one that Lady Amherst regards as "Ambrose's and mine" (435), and she sees in it "the emblem of my trials thus far, and a future hope" (436). That is to say she finds in art a way of understanding her own past life and a way of moving away from it to the future that it will help generate. And the Author following the instructions of his alter ego, acting as "both protagonist and author, so to speak . . . overtake[s] with understanding [his] present paragraph as it were by examining [his] paged past, and thus pointed, proceed[s] serene to the future's sentence" (C, 80–81). Or to put the point another way, the act of recycling characters from the Author's previous fictions into LETTERS is emblematic both of the process of writing, of the act of giving life to the dead letter and demonstrating that the "stories of our lives are negentropic" (768), and the process of reading, an activity characterized by a movement from our sense that the people represented by the written words are real human beings beset with real life problems to an awareness of the complexities of the verbal surface, of the play of the written characters.

Hence the novel concludes with two letters: the first is an "alphabetized wedding toast" from the Author to his central characters – Germaine Pitt, his "heroine" and "creation" (53), and Ambrose Mensch, "old fellow toiler up the slopes of Parnassus" (655) and "alter ego" (653) – a "greeting" (677) that is duly acknowledged by Lady Amherst before she lapses forever into silence; the final one is an *Envoi* to the reader that at once extends far beyond the time of the action of LETTERS to the times of its writing and reading and at the same time, as the second of two such documents, looks back to the novel's beginnings. This "second letter to the Reader" (45), dated "Sunday, September 14, 1969," but actually written on "Tuesday, July 4, 1978," both echoes and differs from the first that was "March 2, 1969," but started in October 1973 (44) and completed in January 1974 (45). The first announces that "LETTERS *is 'now' begun*" (42) while the second tells us that "LETTERS *is 'now' ended*" (771), but both documents insist on the presence of the reader and by doing so suggest the Author's mortality and his separation from the text. "Perhaps," the Author writes at the end of the first letter, "you're yet to have been conceived, and by the 'now' your eyes read *now*, every person now alive upon the earth will be no longer, most certainly not excepting Yours truly" (45). However, this Author is the one who "participates as a character" in LETTERS and as such "isn't the real author at all," for the real one "lives and works in a dimension quite other than that of his creatures (but reminiscent of theirs – he has made them in his image)."[27] Hence in the final letter there is "An end to I" (169) as the writing self—call him John Barth—shifts to the "third-person viewpoint" (166) to record the final details of the work of writing.

In the interim between outline and longhand draft, as again between longhand draft and first typescript, first typescript and final draft, final draft and galley proofs, he goes forward with Horace's "labor of the file": rewriting, editing, dismantling the scaffolding, clearing out the rubbish, planting azaleas about the foundations, testing the wiring and plumbing, hanging doors and windows and pictures, waxing floors, polishing mirrors and windowpanes—and glancing from time to time, even gazing, from an upper storey, down the road, where he makes out in the hazy distance what appear to be familiar loblolly pines, a certain point of dry ground between two creeklets, a steaming tidewater noon, someone waking half tranced, knowing where he is but not at first who, or why he's there. He yawns and shivers, blinks and looks about. He reaches to check and wind his pocketwatch. (771)

This passage, written "a decade since [the Author] first conceived an old time epistolary novel by seven fictitious drolls etc." (771) and nine years after the time of the action that LET-TERS represents, is marked both by the question of its relation to the letters that precede it as well as by its implied reference to the present and future. The allusion to Horace recalls his advice to authors in the *Ars Poetica* to "put your parchment in the closet and keep it back til the ninth year"[28] and hence suggests not only the nine-year period that separates the time of action from the time of writing in LETTERS but also echoes Ambrose Mensch's relation to *The Amateur*, which he keeps corked in a "jeroboam of Piper-Heidsieck" (149) for nine years before trying "to launch it on the tide" (152). However the allusion also reminds us of an important difference between *The Amateur* and LETTERS for Horace commends Homer for beginning his story *in medias res* rather than *ab ovo*, and, as the echoes here of the Author's "three concentric dreams of waking" suggest, he follows Homer's example rather than that of his alter ego. Moreover, by emphasizing the craft and work required to produce the universe of the novel, the passage moves the writer and reader outside the fictive cosmos leaving them free both to admire its harmony and to feel its relation to that other universe in which they dwell. The novel ends with a description of "real life" events that at once echo those within LETTERS and anticipate those that will form the basis for Barth's next novel, *Sabbatical: A Romance.*

Sloop *Brillig* found abandoned in Chesapeake Bay off mouth of Patuxent River, all sails set, C.I.A. documents in attaché case aboard. Body of owner, former C.I.A. agent, recovered from Bay one week later . . . bullet hole in head . . . Nature of documents not disclosed. Time now to lay the cornerstone, run Old Glory up the pole, let off the fireworks, open doors to the public. (772)

Rising above the flood of events that mark the "now" for both writer and reader is the open house of story, a place that promises both wonder and illumination; for the world seen from its "upper storey" is a marvelous one, the product of a magic that combines the spell of the camera obscura with that of Aunt Rosa's Easter egg. Because it is made of letters, "epistolary fictive a's-to-z's" (45), it inscribes quotation marks around its perspective and events, thereby creating a world where it is possible to "say the unseeable, declare the impossible" (393), a place where "words . . . make the wordless happen" (332).

Conclusion   When we speak metaphorically
of echoes between texts, we
imply a correspondence between a precursor and, in acoustical actu-
ality, a verbal source. What is interesting and peculiar about this is
that whereas in nature, the anterior source has a stronger presence
and authenticity, the figurative echoes of allusion arise from the later,
present text. But it has many sorts of priority over what has been re-
called in it. In one way, the relation between echo and source is like
the curious dialectic of "true" meanings of words: the etymon and
the present common usage each can claim a different kind of authority. (The dialectic might be called the field of combat between synchrony and diachrony. That field is the domain of poetry as well.)

—John Hollander, The Figure of Echo

The essays of interpretation that constitute this book are offered as a contribution to the exploration of the theoretical problem of literary form. It now remains for me to point to some of the ways that my series of readings may be drawn together by suggesting a sequential coherence as well as a certain exemplarity. As I suggest in the preface, each of my examples has been chosen with the others in mind in order to establish an echoic relation among them. For the ghostly domain of echo is not only a field of combat betweeen synchrony and diachrony but also one between writing and reading. Considered as a metaphor of allusion, echo inextricably tangles together the acts of reading and writing, for it depends on the reader to achieve its effects. Any reading itself echoes a prior act of writing, and it, in turn, echoes other acts of reading and writing. Seen diachronically this process produces a negative theory of literary repetition, one that associates it with the fragmentation of an original utterance and its progressive diminution and decay. Scott's "Essay on Romance," with its controlling assumption that the "fashion of all things passes away" (177), suggests just such a process. For him romance carries within it "fragments of shadowings of true history" which "remain hidden under the mass of accumulated fable" (180), as the original utterance of the founding patriarch is passed from "mouth to mouth, and from age to age" (177). And as the mass of fable accumulates, adding to the artificial and magical force of the form, the more seductive it becomes, stimulating the reader's sympathetic faculties and threatening him with a loss of boundaries and generating a fear of absorption.[1]

I have argued that the American tradition in fiction differs from the British by making the experience of reading explicit in a way that disturbs and blurs the distinction between creative and interpretive acts and raises the question of its own relationship to history and tradition. By figuring themselves as readers, the writers that I discuss seek to maintain their priority and authority by absorbing and interpreting the fragments that have been broken off from a prior and more complete utterance.

They sense that for readers the question of chronological priority is a matter of perspective since the text in hand always echoes, repeats, and displaces others.[2] Hence all texts seem linked together in a conceptual space (in Melville's words, "federated in the fancy; and so regarded as a miscellaneous and Pantheistic whole" [*P,* 284]) where each can claim equal originality.

It is in this sense that Emerson can maintain that "there is creative reading as well as creative writing."[3] And indeed, as Joseph Riddel has pointed out, it is Emerson who poses most clearly the American problem of reading. In his remarkable essay "Quotation and Originality," Emerson seeks to make quotation "genetic rather than mimetic, or prospective rather than retrospective. Quotation becomes a kind of originality to the degree that it adds or supplements, translates and transforms. Quotation is hermeneutical, and in a sense, it is preoriginal because it breaks the law of genealogical succession by its additions."[4] For Emerson, then, as for Hollander, questions of originality and priority may be seen as the result of a momentary perspective and hence the question of chronological priority must always be posed within the context of the creative activity of a reader. But to do so is to disturb the familial analogy that uses the father-son relation to explain the genesis of story and to ground the authority of literary representation. Hence the American novelist's preoccupation with genealogical crisis and problems of fictional form. For readers, questions of originating texts, relations between models and copies, are matters of perspective and perspectives change, making it possible for the child to be the father of the man. But for writers, the form-making act depends on something which sustains and validates it, and this diachronic impulse points to an incompatibility between the acts of reading and writing and makes the problem of form an essential theme.

My readings, by focusing on this particular problem, tell a certain story about the American novel, of how it poses the problems of reading and writing within the context of the author's search for an authority lost as the result of a genealogical crisis provoked by the ghostly figure of a reader.[5] My story begins with Hawthorne seen as the "father" of American romance and with his search in the eternal city at the end of his career for a magic that will reenergize his creative authority and resurrect the corpse of his Gentle Reader. But he, as an American writer, a "foreigner," must remain outside the aesthetic economy of exchange that in Rome regulates the relations between history and romance, object and image, and voice and writing. Miriam's model, the spectral figure of representation that has no origin, haunts the writer as well as his characters so that present utterances become fragments, broken off from a prior, more complete one, which resist his efforts to incorporate them into a new and complete narrative. Creative reading can be an active form of hearing that leads to writing, but the "vague whisperings" (*MF,* 92) that the author overhears in the Borghese Grove suggest a process of decay and diminution that precludes that possibility. Hollander observes that any song "would only echo hollowly to the unhearing skull in a grave,"[6] and it is precisely a sense of hollowness and fragmentation that torments the author in *The Marble Faun.* With the death of the Gentle Reader goes the writer's ability to tranform the corpse of the past into a new life. Without the translating and transforming activities of a reader the worn fragments and ghostly shadows with which the writer begins remain just that. Instead of echoes of origination, living language answering language, the writer is surrounded by "Subterranean Reminiscences," diminishing echoes reverberating from the hollowness of the Roman catacombs. For Hawthorne, Rome's "magic" is the "destruction of all other magic" (*MF,* 336) because by insisting on the priority of the past it exposes the fatal charm of the natural magic of representation and makes death the companion of the author.

The relation between echo and the voices of the dead is one that Melville's negative way had led him to discover in Hawthorne eight years before the publication of *The Marble Faun.* But for Melville that discovery does not result in a nostalgic sense of loss or in a view of narrative as "fragile handiwork" (*MF*, 455). His emphasis on an active, interpretive reading, one sensitive to nuance, echo, and allusion leads to his discovery of the unsettling effect that past writing has on present writing. The result is that the writer's creative authority is replaced by an authority of reference that maintains itself by way of "barren, bootless allusions."[7] The writer's present is inhabited by fragments of representations, relics from memory, words, sentences, passages from books, overheard stories, epitaphs and inscriptions, all of which stand between him and the world and preclude the possibility of an original relationship to it. Presence becomes, in Geoffrey Hartman's words, "a ghostly *effet de realité* produced by words . . . "[8] and perception a form of repretion. Hence the tangle of genealogical and representational metaphors that characterize *Pierre* and *The Confidence Man*.

The original man, of course, is one having the quality of that which proceeds from himself, being without imitation or dependence on others. He is new, underived and hence capable of original ideas and action. But original also pertains to origin, to the first and earliest, the primary, primitive, innate, hence that from which everything else is derived. These are, of course, issues of genealogy, but the notion of originality also raises problems of representation: it suggests a thing or person in relation to something else that is a copy, imitation, or representation of it, or an object or a person by a picture or an image; or a writing or a literary work in relation to another that is a translation of it or that reproduces its statements. Melville is aware of all of these aspects. Even at the origin there is no originality. Adam at the beginning already lives with the burden of an absent father whose words and acts he is doomed to repeat in a diminished key. To speak or to write is to repeat and to repeat is to expose oneself to the arts of "some malignant sorceress" ("The Encantadas," 194), to give in to the charm of language. For Melville the result of this spell is a world where ambiguity prevails, where the acts of reading and writing are contaminated by imposture and belatedness, and where the disenchanted, like Marianna, sit "never reading, seldom speaking, yet ever wakeful" (13), doomed to a life of "weariness and wakefulness together" (P, 14).

Melville's "anxiety about language," which is an "anxiety of language, within language itself,"[9] is the expression of a crisis of signification produced by the act of reading and the deceptions and mirages that it generates by imposing a structure on the self and world that makes perception itself a form of representation. Now as Fred See has brilliantly argued, James's realism may be seen as an attempt to restore to language and literature the "solidity of specification," and this restoration involves the suppression of a "tradition of metaphysical allusion" that situates itself between the writer and world and prevents an original relation between the two.[10] The strategy of interpretive appropriation that for James marks both the acts of reading and writing is one manifestation of this repressive urge. James's mastery of his own strong American precursor in his study of Hawthorne is achieved by reading Hawthorne in terms of the earlier writer's childishness and provincialism. And a similar strategy is apparent in the preface to the *Portrait* where James celebrates his triumph over Shakespeare, Eliot, Scott, and Stevenson by Miltonically attempting a "task" as yet "unattempted" by other novelists. These gestures of appropriation are designed to avoid the sequence and displacements of time and to reassert the authority of present writing, or to use Hollander's formulation, to chart a diachronic line in order to establish a synchronic model.

The prefaces tell a story of growth and development, but it is a story told from the perspective of the mature writer, a perspective that seeks to combine the acts of reading and writing. The authoritative re-reader of the prefaces is also a revisor and corrector, that is to say, a writer, and the story that he tells is a story of story, a "thrilling tale" of writing. This is an account of the construction of the text, one that figures and transfigures its plot or fable and moves it to a purely aesthetic level. Of central importance is what the story represents to the mature "critical sense" now "inevitably" and "thoroughly" awakened by "time."[11]

For the critical reading will result in the revelation of the innocence of the earlier text and that revelation will engender
further writing. That is to say that the time of memory, the
time of reading, and the time of writing are joined, the "vivacity
of incident" transformed into the "economy of picture" (*PL*, 14),
and the individual texts that dot the line of the writer's career
unite in a conceptual space to give that career the authoritative
aspect of an intelligible destiny.

But the authority of writing is nomadic because it is occasional, tied to a particular moment and a specific place,[12] and
directed toward an other. So while James authoritatively appro-
priates and quiets the ghostly voices that haunt Hawthorne and
Melville, he does not escape the domain of echo. As Hollander
observes, in acoustical reality a "certain amount of echoing over-
hang is necessary . . . in order to avoid a sense of sonic death, or
an absorbent ambiance that gobbles up all morsels of speech or
song we produce, returning none and thus ruining our full perception of what we ourselves utter."[13] And just as voice and
echo may be indistinguishable in reality so in a text a meaning
is a form of repetition whether one repeats one's precursors or
oneself. The modes of self-echo that mark James's prefaces and
the texts they introduce initiate a force of figuration that disturbs the authoritative model of the writer as reader, for they acknowledge that a text is constituted by an act of reading as
much as by an act of writing in the same way that an identity is
partially constituted by the "impress" (*PL*, 8) of an other. The re-
bounds of echo here call attention to the printed book and to
the intensifying alienation that it generates by suggesting a
world that is irreducibly double, one where the acts of reading
and writing cannot be spatially or temporally confined. Once
the printed text enters the public world of subscribing, lending,
borrowing, and purchasing, the author and his authority exist
only in the form of ghostly echoes within the text itself. Hence
the realist impulse that seeks to establish the authority of
present writing by aggressively appropriating the past ends up
by replacing the older conventions governing the relation of

writer and reader with those of a marketplace economy.

Faulkner and his modernist contemporaries share James's sense that the acts of reading and writing have been contaminated by the massive pressures of economic and social forces. Faulkner's fascination with the "rag-tag and bob-ends of old tales and talking" (*AA*, 303) points to his desire to revitalize the older conventions of the storyteller and the storytelling situation but to do so in a way that avoids the bankrupt fiction of an authorial presence that generates and sustains the authority of the text as well as the notion of a reader who either submits to or challenges that authority. Faulkner's complicated narrative hermeneutic—What really did happen? Who is related to whom? Who knows the entire story? What motivates the characters to tell it? Can individual impressions be added together to produce a single solution to the narrative puzzle?—tends at once to deny the presence of any such authority and to generate further writing. Here the enabling energy of the text is not as in Hawthorne, Melville, and James either the shaping authority of an author or the interpretive activity of a reader but a peculiar process of textualization whereby fragments of raw material, a scrap of paper, a bit of gossip, stand in a relationship of textual generation one to another. This self-generation of the text takes the form of reverse echoes as fragments engender utterances that emerge in the form of a new detail, a different perspective on the story, another speaker who becomes for a moment the center of narrative interest before being displaced by still another echoing voice.[14]

This power of the story to reproduce itself, like ripples spreading across a pool, is best understood in terms of the strange energy possessed by the remnants of an attenuated past which are able to reproduce in the minds of those who encounter them the experiences of long-dead and perhaps imaginary protagonists. And this activity within the story echoes that of the act of reading it. The black marks on the page, like "letters without salutation or signature" (*AA*, 100) are orphaned remnants of the past that at once record the fact of death and induce the mind of the reader to replicate the "deathless excitement"[15] that motivated the author. This emphasis on the ghostly effect of writing suggests at once the desire to conjure back the imagined unity of an older literary institution that had joined writer and reader and a recognition that any such attempt is a form of memorializing, of providing a final resting place for the past in the cold black marks on the page.

For John Barth, however, the writer need not regard himself as "irrevocably cut off from the nineteenth century and its predecessors by the accomplishment of [his] artistic parents and grandparents in the twentieth."[16] As a "postmodern" writer, he feels free "to come to new terms with both realism and antirealism" (129), and that freedom is expressed in his insistence that the seemingly dead letter still sustains life. As a "bona fide honorary Doctor of Letters," he "makes it a part of his business to administer artificial respiration to the apparently dead, whether the patient is the classical myths or certain exhausted conventions of the novel."[17] And primary among these conventions is the representational fiction of the storytelling situation organized around the notions of a capital A Author and his trusted Reader.

Unlike Faulkner, Barth insists that "I always worry about my readers' interests and feelings—moreso, I think, as I get older and perhaps wiser. Probably if I were a little more attuned to the lines of thought of our modernist masters, I would take a more disdainful, more Olympian attitude. . . . But I find myself lately putting some respectful distances between those masters and myself, and one of those distances involves myself and my readers."[18] And another obviously includes his sense of the Author, creator of the text, as one who is "authorised to authorship" (*L*, 759) and who associates the act of writing with that of physical engenderment.

Barth's use of these obsolete metaphors, however, is not the result of "innocence or conservative inclination," a desire to pretend that the "phenomenon of modernism and all that gave rise to it in the history of Western art hadn't happened."[19]

Rather it is the expression of his belief that a writer "creates his own precursors."[20] Barth believes that a writer who is "too fixated upon his/her distinguished predecessors" resembles a "disoriented navigator . . . who mistakes the stars he steers by for his destination."[21] He shares with "authors of antiquity" a sense that "originality" is a "matter of rearrangement,"[22] and cites approvingly Horace's advice: *"safer shall the bard his pen employ / With yore, to dramatize the Tale of Troy, / Than venturing trackless regions to explore, / Delineate characters untouched before."*[23] In Barth's world the voices and inscriptions from the past do not have the sepulchral quality of those in Faulkner's. For Barth the bodiless nymph "edits, heightens, mutes, turns others' words to her own ends" (*LIF,* 100). In LETTERS echoes are both "heartfelt" (261) and "fleshly" (547) and suggest that the relation of past and present, like that of art and life, is "an ongoing collaboration or reverberation" (233). That is to say that the novel is governed by a "notion of echoes and reenactments significant in themselves without necessary reference to their originals" (356). Indeed, according to Barth, its "ground-theme" is "reenactment versus mere repetition,"[24] a process made possible by an enabling principle of contamination. The source and its echo contaminate one another through a process of reciprocal turning or troping so that each casts the other in a new light and makes it emblematic, with the result that the artist's form becomes a metaphor for his concerns.

Hence for Barth, the Novel, "that most happily contaminated literary genre" (*L,* 151), is characterized by its ability to absorb and thrive "upon all sorts of extrinsic input." As the "turkey-buzzard of art,"[25] it can live on anything: an exhausted convention, a discredited sub-genre, a familiar political or philosophical idea, a quotation or allusion, characters from the author's earlier work, a historical fact or event, the works of one's great precursors. And once absorbed the contaminant is no longer its "innocent existential self"[26] but a vital, functioning part of a new organism. Like the books of chivalry for Cervantes, inherited materials become for Barth enabling contaminants that at once make him aware of the artificial or magical force of all human constructions and free him to transcend that potentially paralyzing perception and to go on with the accomplishment of his work. Hence his career provides my story of American romance with a happy ending and at the same time carries it back to its theoretical beginnings in Ortega's notion of the absorption that marks the novel as a genre. This, I believe, is an appropriate conclusion for Barth is a writer whose "spiritual fathers . . . are mainly European"[27] but one who finds his imaginative energy in his situation as an American.

NOTES

Preface

1. Fredric Jameson, *The Political Unconscious* (Ithaca: Cornell University Press, 1981), 107. As Nina Baym recently has shown, the critical focus on a specifically American genre is an expression of the persistent desire of scholars and critics to identify the national characteristics of our literature. Indeed, according to Baym, the idea of romance as a specifically American genre is a critical invention designed to mediate "between a conviction that literature and the works comprising it are valuable in themselves . . . and a simultaneous rejection of merely formalist, aesthetic, or affective modes of assessment and analysis" ("Concepts of Romance in Hawthorne's America," *NCF* 38 [March 1984]: 426). Baym's revisionary essay seeks to put into question the historical validity of the concept that has played such a major role in constructing the accepted canon of American literature by showing that the "term romance" was "used so broadly and so inconsistently" (430) in Hawthorne's America that any attempt to fix its meaning is a creative rather than a descriptive activity. Indeed, she insists that Hawthorne himself was seen by his contemporaries "neither as the romance writer he claimed to be, nor as the essentially representative writer he has come to be" (443). The implications of Baym's argument here are more fully expressed in her earlier compelling essay, "Melodramas of Beset Manhood: How Theories of American Fiction Exclude Women Authors," *AQ* 33 (Summer 1981): 123–39. While my readings do not address Baym's arguments directly, they do, I believe, suggest that the exclusions she describes may be less the result of particular critical theories than of a set of problems inherent in the relation between genealogy and genericity.

Evan Carton's recent study raises once again Baym's skepticism regarding the usefulness of romance as a critical concept (*The Rhetoric of American Romance: Dialectic and Identity in Emerson, Dickinson, Poe, and Hawthorne* [Baltimore: Johns Hopkins University Press, 1985]). He proposes a "revisionary approach to American romance" (265) because he believes that its worth as a critical concept has been devalued by its "formalistic application to a species of extended prose narrative" (1). After citing Baym's observation that the category American romance as previously applied has little "historical authority or explanatory force" (266) he sets out to "vitalize" the term by "reconceiving it as a specific and urgent kind of rhetorical performance" (1) that transgresses formal generic boundaries and "interconnects the diverse literary productions of the American Renaissance" (21): Emerson's essays, Poe's stories, Dickinson's lyrics, and Hawthorne's novels. Uniting these four genres is a set of common structures and strategies that the four writers share. And by naming the common features in texts by Emerson, Poe, Dickinson, and Hawthorne, Carton, presumably, will undermine the formalistic understanding of romance and open up the canon by connecting a number of diverse literary works.

2. Jacques Derrida, "The Law of Genre," in *On Narrative,* ed. W. J. T. Mitchell (Chicago: University of Chicago Press, 1981), 61.

3. José Ortega y Gasset, *Meditations on Quixote,* trans. Evelyn Rugg and Diego Marin (New York: W. W. Norton, 1961), 113.

4. See J. Hillis Miller's helpful discussion of the concept of form in *The Linguistic Moment: From Wordsworth to Stevens* (Princeton: Princeton University Press, 1985), 60–63.

5. William C. Spengemann, review of Michael Davitt Bell's *Development of American Romance, NCF* 36 (September 1981): 204.

6. See Northrop Frye, *The Secular Scripture: A Study of the Structure of Romance* (Cambridge: Harvard University Press), 28–31.

7. A. C. Hamilton, "Elizabethan Romance: The Example of Prose Fiction," *ELH* 49 (1982): 297, 298–99.

8. Joseph N. Riddel, "The 'Crypt' of Edgar Poe," *Boundary 2* 7 (Spring 1979): 124.

9. See the chapter "The Novel as Beginning Intention" in Edward Said, *Beginnings: Intention and Method* (New York: Basic Books, 1975; Baltimore: Johns Hopkins University Press, 1978), 81–188 and *The World the Text and the Critic* (Cambridge: Harvard University Press, 1983), 16–24.

ONE *The Thematics of a Form:* Waverley *and American Romance*

1. José Ortega y Gasset, *Meditations on Quixote,* trans. Evelyn Rugg and Diego Marin (New York: W. W. Norton, 1961), 139.

2. See Walter L. Reed's fascinating discussion of this process in *An Exemplary History of the Novel: The Quixotic Versus the Picaresque* (Chicago: University of Chicago Press, 1981), 19–42.

3. Frank Kermode, *The Art of Telling: Essays on Fiction* (Cambridge: Harvard University Press, 1983), 125.

4. The fact that *Don Quixote* is written against the chivalric romances no doubt partially accounts for the distinction made in the eighteenth century between romance and novel. Sir Walter Scott defines romance as a "fictitious narrative in prose or verse; the interest of which turns upon marvelous and uncommon incidents" and novel as a "fictitious narrative, differing from the Romance, because the events are accommodated to the ordinary train of human events, and the modern state of society" ("Essay on Romance" in *Essays on Chivalry, Romance and the Drama* [1834; reprint, Freeport: Books for Libraries Press, 1972], 129). But as Scott often observes, all novels carry elements of romance within them with the result that the "word *romance*" is widely used as "synonymous with fictitious composition" (Ioan Williams, ed., *Sir Walter Scott on Novelists and Fiction* [London: Routledge & Kegan Paul, 1968], 314).

5. Note, for example, the following passage written in 1754:

The error I mean is putting romances into the hands of young ladies; which being a sort of writing that abounds in characters no where to be found, can, at best, be but a useless employment, even supposing the readers of them to have neither relish nor understanding for superior concerns. But as this is by no means the case, and as the happiness of mankind is deeply interested in the sentiments and conduct of the ladies, why do we contribute to the filling their heads with fancies, which render them incapable either of enjoying or communicating that happiness? Why do we suffer those hearts, which ought to be appropriated to the various affections of social life, to be alienated by the mere creatures of the imagination? In short, why do we suffer those who were born for the purpose of living in society with men endued with passions and frailties like their own, to be bred up in daily expectation of living *out* of it with such men as never existed . . . ? I know several unmarried ladies, who in all probability had been long ago good wives and good mothers, if their imaginations had not been early perverted with the chimerical ideas of romantic love . . . by the hopes of that ideal happiness, which is no where to be found but in romance.

Richard Berenger, *The World*, July 4, 1754, in Ioan Williams, ed., *Novel and Romance, 1700–1800: A Documentary Record* (New York: Barnes & Noble, 1970), 214–15.

6. From a review of *Emmeline, The Orphan of the Castle, Analytical Review,* July 1, 1788, in ibid. 355.

7. "The pain of suspense, and the irresistible desire of satisfying the curiosity, when once raised, will account for our eagerness to go quite through an adventure, though we suffer actual pain during the whole course of it," J. and A. L. Aiken wrote in 1773. "We rather chuse," they continued, "to suffer the smart pang of a violent emotion than the uneasy craving of an unsatisfied desire. . . . This is the impulse which renders the poorest and most insipid narrative interesting when we once get fairly into it. . . . When children, therefore, listen with pale and mute attention to the frightful stories of apparitions, we are not, perhaps, to imagine that they are in a state of enjoyment, any more than the poor bird which is dropping into the mouth of the rattlesnake— they are chained by the ears and fascinated by curiosity" (Three essays from "Miscellaneous Pieces in Prose and Verse, 1773," in Williams, *Novel and Romance,* 284).

Worth noting here is the central role that curiosity and suspense have for Roland Barthes. He attempts in *S/Z* to disrupt the "flowing discourse of narration, the naturalness of ordinary language" (13) by manhandling and interrupting (15) the text of Balzac's story is an effort to undermine the operations of suspense, "artifices more spectacular than persuasive" (16), by situating his reading "behind the transparency of suspense" which is "placed on the text by the first avid and ignorant reader" (165). *S/Z,* trans. Richard Miller (New York: Hill & Wang, 1974).

8. Pierre Daniel Huet, *The History of Romances,* trans. Stephen Lewis (1715) in Williams, *Novel and Romance,* 43.

9. This is an idea that has persisted in the criticism of fiction. One thinks of Wayne Booth's attacks on Joyce's ambiguity and Stephen Heath's defense of the politics of the nouveau roman, but more revealing, perhaps, is Wolfgang Iser's assertation that "if reading were to consist of nothing but an uninterrupted building up of illusions, it would be a suspect, if not downright dangerous, process: instead of bringing

us into contact with reality, it would wean us away from realities. Of course, there is an element of 'escapism' in all literature, resulting from this very creation of illusion, but there are some texts which offer nothing but a harmonious world, purified of all contradictions and deliberately excluding anything that might disturb the illusion once established, and these are the texts that we generally do not like to classify as literary. Women's magazines and the brasher forms of detective story might be cited as examples" ("The Reading Process: A Phenomenological Approach," *NLH* 3 [1972]: 289).

10. Daniel Defoe, *Moll Flanders,* ed. J. Paul Hunter (New York: Thomas Y. Crowell, 1970), 4.

11. Kermode, *The Art of Telling,* 124.

12. Ibid., 73.

13. The remarkable influence of Scott on subsequent novelists is well documented. George Levine writes that Scott "transformed the history of narrative in Western Europe" (*The Realistic Imagination: English Fiction from Frankenstein to Lady Chatterley* [Chicago: University of Chicago Press, 1981], 81–82), and Perry Miller describes his influence in America as follows: "A generation had grown up breathing the atmosphere of Romance as naturally as they breathed the air of America. And there can be little doubt that the intermingling of the literary form with the consciousness of the nation was wrought in the early decades of the century, not by an American, but by the Wizard of the North, 'the Author of *Waverley*'" (*Nature's Nation* [Cambridge: Harvard University Press, 1967], 243).

14. Henry Fielding, *Tom Jones,* ed. Sheridan Baker (New York: W. W. Norton, 1973), 706. I am indebted to Homer O. Brown for pointing me to Scott's use of Fielding's metaphor.

15. Scott, in Williams, *Sir Walter Scott,* 260.

16. Ibid., 299.

17. Ibid., 230.

18. Ibid., 235.

19. Ibid., 231.

20. Alexander Welsh, *The Hero of the Waverley Novels* (New Haven: Yale University Press, 1963), 82–92.

21. Compare Barthes' assertion that "narrative is determined not by a desire to narrate but by a desire to exchange: it is a medium of exchange, an agent, a currency, a gold standard" (*S/Z,* 90).

22. Compare Barthes' description of the way we are led to read a classic text:

a rhythm is established, casual, unconcerned with the integrity of the text; our very avidity for knowledge impels us to skim or to skip certain passages (anticipated as "boring") in order to get more quickly to the warmer parts of the anecdote . . . we boldy skip (no one is watching) descriptions, explanations, analyses, conversations; doing so, we resemble a spectator in a nightclub who climbs onto the stage and speeds up the dancer's striptease, tearing off her clothing, *but in the same order,* that is: on the one hand respecting and on the other hastening the episodes of the ritual (like a priest *gulping down* his Mass). (*The Pleasure of the Text,* trans. Richard Miller [New York: Hill & Wang, 1975], 10–11)

23. Scott, in Williams, *Sir Walter Scott,* 90.

24. Ibid., 117.

25. I am indebted here to Homer O. Brown for his discussion of the issues involved in the 1745 Rebellion and their relation to the problems of narrative authority in *Tom Jones.* See his "Tom Jones: The Bastard of History," *Boundary 2* 7 (Winter 1979): 205–11. I have also profited from the reading in manuscript of "In the Relation of Fathers: Plot and Counterplot in the Jacobite Novels of Walter Scott," a chapter from Brown's forthcoming book on the eighteenth-century novel.

26. I am indebted here to Tony Tanner for his discussion of heraldry in *Adultery in the Novel: Contract and Transgression* (Baltimore: Johns Hopkins University Press, 1979), 134.

27. The relation between questions of genealogy, inherited authority, and narrative authority is a concern of contemporary criticism. Edward Said writes that the "generic plot situation of the novel is to repeat through variation the family scene by which human beings engender human duration in their action" (*The World, the Text, the Critic* [Cambridge: Harvard University Press, 1983], 117). See also his *Beginnings: Intention and Method* (New York: Basic Books, 1975; Baltimore: Johns Hopkins University Press, 1978), 81–188. Peter Brooks, echoing Said, argues that "paternity is a dominant issue within the great tradition of the nineteenth-century novel . . . a principal embodiment of its concern with authority, legitimacy, the conflict of generations, and the transmission of wisdom" (*Reading for Plot: Design and Intention in Narrative* [New York: Alfred A. Knopf, 1984], 63). See also Homer Brown's

discussion of the implications of the genealogical pattern in his essay "Tom Jones."

28. George Levine argues that the painting makes possible a comfortable relationship between past and present by transforming the past into an image (*The Realistic Imagination,* 105). In my discussion of the painting I am indebted to Levine for his reading.

29. Scott, "Essay on Romance," 134. Until indicated otherwise parenthetical in-text page citations refer to this essay.

30. See Said, *Beginnings,* 84.

31. Scott, in Williams, *Sir Walter Scott,* 226. Compare his observation that the

worst evil to be apprehended from the perusal of novels is, that the habit is like to generate an indisposition to real history, and useful literature; and that the best which can be hoped is, that they may sometimes instruct the youthful mind by real pictures of life, and sometimes awaken their better feelings and sympathies. . . . Beyond this they are a mere elegance, a luxury contrived for the amusement of polished life . . . and are read much more for amusement, than with the least hope of deriving instruction from them. (54)

32. Ibid., 274.

33. Ibid., 89.

34. Ibid., 317.

35. Ibid., 117.

36. Levine, *The Realistic Imagination,* 94. Levine argues that Scott establishes the precedent for the realistic fiction that follows him by setting fact against dream.

37. Geoffrey H. Hartman, *Criticism in the Wilderness: The Study of Literature Today* (New Haven: Yale University Press, 1980), 51.

38. See Michael Davitt Bell's discussion of the problems of being a romancer in nineteenth-century America in his *Development of American Romance: The Sacrifice of Relation* (Chicago: University of Chicago Press, 1980), 3–36.

39. Washington Irving, "Abbotsford," in *The Crayon Miscellany,* ed. Dahlia Kirby Terrell (Boston: Twayne Publishers, 1979), 159–60. I am indebted to Stephen Bann for calling my attention to this passage in his *Clothing of Clio: A Study of the Representation of History in Nineteenth-Century Britain and France* (Cambridge: Cambridge University Press, 1984), 106.

40. Levine, *The Realistic Imagination,* 87.

41. Laurence Sterne, *Tristram Shandy*, ed. James Aiken Work (New York: Odyssey Press, 1940), 109.

42. Charles Feidelson, *Symbolism and American Literature* (Chicago: University of Chicago Press, 1953), 10.

43. John J. Enck, "John Barth: An Interview," *Wisconsin Studies in Contemporary Literature* 6 (1965): 5–6.

44. Kermode, *The Art of Telling*, 73.

45. Enck, "John Barth: An Interview," 8.

46. John Barth, "The Literature of Exhaustion," *The Atlantic* 245 (August 1967): 33.

47. John Barth, *The Sot-Weed Factor* (New York: Grosset & Dunlap, 1964), 625.

48. Enck, "John Barth: An Interview," 7.

49. Barth, "Literature of Exhaustion," 30.

50. John Barth, "Muse Spare Me," in *The Friday Book: Essays and Other Nonfiction* (New York: G. P. Putnam's Sons, 1984), 57, 58, 59.

51. John Barth, "Tales within Tales," in *The Friday Book*, 236.

52. Scott, "Essay on Romance," 134.

T W O   *The Limits of Romance: A Reading of* The Marble Faun

1. John Bunyan, *The Pilgrim's Progress*, ed. Roger Sharrock (New York: Penguin Books, 1965), 358, 355.

2. For a useful discussion of the problem of representation in "The Custom House" and *The Scarlet Letter* see Evan Carton, *The Rhetoric of American Romance: Dialectic and Identity in Emerson, Dickinson, Poe, and Hawthorne* (Baltimore: Johns Hopkins University Press, 1985), 191–216.

3. Hawthorne did not decide on a final title until the book was in press, but several of the ones that he considered raise the problem of the relation between art and life. See Claude M. Simpson's "Introduction" to the Ohio State edition of *The Marble Faun*, pp. xxv–xxvii.

4. I am indebted here to Geoffrey H. Hartman for his brilliant discussion of the ghostly effects of representation in *Saving the Text: Literature/Derrida/Philosophy* (Baltimore: Johns Hopkins University Press, 1981), 118–57.

5. For two related discussions of Miriam's model see Jonathan Auerbach, "Executing the Model: Painting, Sculpture, and Romance-Writing

in Hawthorne's *The Marble Faun*," *ELH* 47 (1980): 103-20 and Carton, *The Rhetoric of American Romance*, 258-64.

6. I am indebted here to Jean Starobinski for his discussion of ruins in *The Invention of Liberty, 1700-1789*,trans. Bernard C. Swift (Geneva: Skira, 1964), 180.

7. Edgar A. Dryden, *Nathaniel Hawthorne: The Poetics of Enchantment* (Ithaca: Cornell University Press, 1977), 111-42.

8. See Thomas Woodson's "Historical Commentary" in *The French and Italian Notebooks*, 903-35.

9. In *The French and Italian Notebooks* Hawthorne writes: "My wife and I went yesterday to the Pantheon, which stands in the central intricacy and nastiness of Roman lanes" (60).

THREE   *The Entangled Text:* Pierre *and the Romance of Reading*

1. For a full discussion of earlier readings of the relation between "The Piazza" and "The Old Manse" see William Dillingham, *Melville's Short Fiction, 1853-1856* (Athens: University of Georgia Press, 1977), 319-40.

2. I am indebted here to Harold Bloom for his definition of trope in *A Map of Misreading* (New York: Oxford University Press, 1975), 93.

3. William Makepeace Thackeray, *Rebecca and Rowena*, in *The Works of Thackeray*, 20 vols. (London: Macmillan, 1911), 3:95.

4. William Wordsworth, "Essays upon Epitaphs," in *Wordsworth's Literary Criticism*, ed. W. J. B. Owen (London: Routledge & Kegan Paul, 1974), 123.

5. I am indebted here to Roland Barthes, *S/Z*, trans. Richard Miller (New York: Hill & Wang, 1974), 20-21, 73-74.

6. I am following here John T. Irwin's discussion of the difference between the Judaic and Christian concepts of genealogy in *Doubling and Incest/Repetition and Revenge: A Speculative Reading of Faulkner* (Baltimore: Johns Hopkins University Press, 1975), 130-32.

7. I am indebted here to Edward Said for his discussion of the problem in *Beginnings: Intention and Method* (New York: Basic Books, 1975; Baltimore: Johns Hopkins Univesity Press, 1978), 263-64.

8. Paul de Man, *Blindness and Insight: Essays in the Rhetoric of Contemporary Criticism* (New York: Oxford University Press, 1971), 123-27.

9. H. Bruce Franklin focuses on this process in his admirable analy-

sis of *Pierre.* See his *Wake of the Gods: Melville's Mythology* (Stanford: Stanford University Press, 1963), 99–125.

10. I am indebted here to Earl R. Wasserman for his discussion of the pyramid in *Shelley: A Critical Reading* (Baltimore: Johns Hopkins University Press, 1971), 493.

11. See Eugenio Donato's discussion of this theme in "Mnemonics of History: Notes for a Contextual Reading of Foscolo's *Dei Sepolcri*," *Yale Italian Studies* 1 (1977): 1–23. My discussion of abandoned tombs in *Pierre* is heavily dependent on Donato's valuable analysis.

12. For an account of Melville's knowledge of the Memnon myth see Dorothea Metletsky Finkelstein, *Melville's Orienda* (New York: Octagon Books, 1971), 136–40.

13. Wordsworth, "Essays upon Epitaphs," 123.

14. Geoffrey H. Hartman, "Wordsworth, Inscriptions, and Romantic Nature Poetry," in *Beyond Formalism: Literary Essays, 1958–1970* (New Haven: Yale University Press, 1970), 206–30.

15. The phrase is Jean Starobinski's and is taken from his admirable discussion of ruins in *The Invention of Liberty, 1700–1789*, trans. Bernard C. Swift (Geneva: Skira, 1964), 180.

16. Edgar A. Dryden, *Melville's Thematics of Form: The Great Art of Telling the Truth* (Baltimore: Johns Hopkins University Press, 1968; 1981), 117–41.

17. Hegel's remarks on the pyramid are worth quoting at length:

Here we have before us a double architecture, one above ground, the other subterranean: labyrinths under the soil, magnificent vast excavations, passages half a mile long, chambers adorned with hieroglyphics, everything worked out with the maximum of care; then above ground there are built in addition to those amazing constructions amongst which the Pyramids are to be counted the chief. On the purpose and meaning of the Pyramids all sorts of hypotheses have been tried for centuries, yet it now seems beyond doubt that they are enclosures for the graves of kings or of sacred animals. . . . In this way the Pyramids put before our eyes the simple prototype of symbolical art itself; they are prodigious crystals which conceal in themselves an inner meaning and, as external shapes produced by art, they so envelope that meaning that it is obvious that they are there for this inner meaning separated from pure nature and only in relation to this meaning. But this realm of death and the invisible, which here constitutes the meaning, possesses only one side, and that a formal one, of the true content of art, namely that of being removed from immediate existence. . . . (*The Aesthetics,* trans. T. M. Knox [London: Clarendon Press, 1975], 1:356).

18. Pierre, as he reads Isabel's note, is subject to "two antagonistic agencies within him. . . . One bade him finish the selfish destruction of the note; for in some dark way the reading of it would irretrievably entangle his fate. The other bade him dismiss all misgivings . . . Read, Pierre, though by reading thou may'st entangle thyself, yet may'st thou thereby disentangle others" (*P,* 63).

FOUR *The Image in the Mirror: James's* Portrait *and the Economy of Romance*

1. John Carlos Rowe, *The Theoretical Dimensions of Henry James* (Madison: University of Wisconsin Press, 1984), 32. My discussion of the James/Hawthorne relationship owes much to Rowe's suggestive reading.

2. Richard Chase, *The American Novel and Its Tradition* (New York: Doubleday & Co., 1957; Baltimore: Johns Hopkins University Press, 1980), 125.

3. Henry James, *Hawthorne* (New York: Doubleday & Co., n.d.), 95.

4. Ibid., 96–97.

5. Ibid., 96.

6. Henry James, preface to *The American,* in *The Art of the Novel,* ed. R. P. Blackmur (New York: Charles Scribner's Sons, 1937), 30, 24.

7. Henry James, preface to *Roderick Hudson,* in Blackmur, *The Art of the Novel,* 4.

8. Henry James, preface to *The Golden Bowl,* in Blackmur, *The Art of the Novel,* 344.

9. Ibid., 345.

10. James, preface to *The American,* 26, 25, 34.

11. Ibid., 25–26.

12. Thomas Gray, "Ode on a Distant Prospect of Eton College," ll. 52, 56 in *The New Oxford Book of English Verse: 1250–1950,* ed. Helen Gardner (New York and Oxford: Oxford University Press, 1972), 439.

13. James, preface to *The American,* 31. Subsequent quotations from this preface in this paragraph are cited in the text.

14. James, preface to *The Ambassadors*, in Blackmur, *The Art of the Novel*, 313.

15. James, preface to *Roderick Hudson*, 4.

16. James, preface to *The Golden Bowl*, 338–39.

17. Henry James, preface to *The Spoils of Poynton*, in Blackmur, *The Art of the Novel*, 120.

18. Chase, *The American Novel*, 119.

19. George Simmel, *The Philosophy of Money*, trans. Bottomore and David Frisby (London, Henley, and Boston: Routledge & Kegan Paul, 1978), 212–17.

20. Henry James, "Honore de Balzac," in *Notes on Novelists, with Some Other Notes* (New York: Charles Scribner's Sons, 1914; New York: Biblo & Tannen, 1969), 117, 118.

21. Henry James, "The Future of the Novel," in *Henry James: Selected Literary Criticism*, ed. Morris Shapira (London: Heinemann, 1963), 185.

22. See Simmel, *The Philosophy of Money*, 237–38.

23. Ibid., 212–16.

24. I am indebted here to Marc Shell for his useful discussion of Plato and money in *The Economy of Literature* (Baltimore: Johns Hopkins University Press, 1978), 36–62.

25. Tony Tanner, "The Fearful Self": Henry James's *The Portrait of a Lady*," in *Henry James: Modern Judgements*, ed. Tony Tanner (London: Macmillan, 1969), 143.

26. Henry James, "The Lesson of Balzac," in *The Question of Our Speech* (Boston: Riverside Press, 1905), 93.

27. Henry James, "The Art of Fiction," in Shapira, *Henry James*, 50.

28. Henry James, "Alphonse Daudet," in *Partial Portraits* (1888; Ann Arbor: University of Michigan Press, 1970), 228.

29. James, "The Art of Fiction," 50–51.

30. Ibid., 54.

31. Henry James, preface to *The Princess Casamassima*, in Blackmur, *The Art of the Novel*, 65.

32. James, "The Art of Fiction," 54.

33. James, "The Lesson of Balzac," 71.

34. Ibid., 92.

35. James, "Emile Zola," in *Notes on Novelists*, 60.

36. Percy Lubbock, ed., *The Letters of Henry James*, 2 vols. (New York: Charles Scribner's Sons, 1920), 2: 181–82.

37. James, "The Art of Fiction," 57.

38. James, preface to *The Princess Casamassima,* 64–65.

39. For a different but suggestive reading of James's view of representation see Laurence Holland, *The Expense of Vision: Essays on the Craft of Henry James* (Princeton: Princeton University Press, 1964), 120–38. Holland's reading of *The Portrait* emphasizes the analogy between writing and representational painting.

40. I am indebted here to Geoffrey H. Hartman for his discussion of this problem in "Christopher Smart's 'Magnificat': Toward a Theory of Representation," in *The Fate of Reading and Other Essays* (Chicago: University of Chicago Press, 1975), 74–75.

41. Holland, "The Expense of Vision," 121–22.

42. James, *Hawthorne,* 57.

43. James, preface to *The Princess Casamassima,* 64.

44. Lubbock, *Letters,* 1: 142.

45. James, preface to *The Spoils of Poynton,* 120.

46. James, "The Future of the Novel," 181.

47. James, "The Art of Fiction," 53.

48. James, preface to *The Awkward Age,* in Blackmur, *The Art of the Novel,* 106.

49. Lubbock, *Letters,* 1:325.

50. James, "London Notes," in *Notes on Novelists,* 436.

51. James, "The Future of the Novel," 182.

52. James, "Alphonse Daudet," 227–28.

53. James, preface to *The Princess Casamassima,* 65.

54. James, "The Future of the Novel," 181, 183.

55. James, preface to *The Ambassadors,* 317.

56. James, "The Lesson of Balzac," 102.

57. James, "Alphonse Daudet," 227.

58. James, "The Future of the Novel," 188.

FIVE *Faulkner and the Sepulcher of Romance:*
The Voices of Absalom, Absalom!

1. William Faulkner, "Classroom Statements at the University of Mississippi," in *Lion in the Garden: Interviews with William Faulkner, 1926–1962,* ed. James B. Meriwether and Michael Millgate (New York: Random House, 1968), 55.

2. Meriwether and Millgate, *Lion in the Garden,* 181, 243, 125, 239.

3. William Faulkner, *Faulkner in the University: Class Conferences at the University of Virginia, 1957–58*, ed. Frederick L. Gwynn and Joseph L. Blotner (Charlottesville: University of Virginia Press, 1959), 24.

4. Meriwether and Millgate, *Lion in the Garden*, 238.

5. Ibid., 284.

6. Malcolm Cowley, *The Faulkner-Cowley File: Letters and Memories, 1944–1962* (New York: Viking Press, 1966), 126.

7. David Minter, *William Faulkner: His Life and Work* (Baltimore: Johns Hopkins University Press, 1980) 102–3.

8. Ibid. Minter's admirable study is particularly good in suggesting subtle connections between Faulkner's life and work. See especially the chapter, "The Faces of Fame," 220–51.

9. See J. Hillis Miller's suggestive discussion of this process in "The Problematic of Ending in Narrative," *Nineteenth-Century Fiction*, 33 (June 1978): 3–7.

10. Joseph Blotner, ed., *Selected Letters of William Faulkner* (New York: Random House, 1977), 78–79.

11. Faulkner, *Faulkner in the University*, 275.

12. See Meriwether and Millgate, *Lion in the Garden*, 73, 103, 177–78, 253; Faulkner, *Faulkner in the University*, 61, 286; and William Faulkner, "foreword" in *The Faulkner Reader* (New York: Random House, 1961), viii–ix. Also see Robert W. Hambin "'Saying No to Death': Toward William Faulkner's Theory of Fiction," in *"A Cosmos of My Own": Faulkner and Yoknapatawpha 1980*, ed. Doreen Fowler and Ann J. Abadie (Jackson: University Press of Mississippi, 1981), 3–35.

13. Meriwether and Millgate, *Lion in the Garden*, 70–71.

14. William Faulkner, letter to Harrison Smith, cited by Joseph Blotner, *Faulkner: A Biography*, 2 vols. (New York: Random House, 1974), 1:854.

15. I am indebted here to John T. Irwin, *Doubling and Incest/ Repetition and Revenge: A Speculative Reading of Faulkner* (Baltimore: Johns Hopkins University Press, 1975), 93.

16. I am indebted here to John T. Irwin, "The Dead Father in Faulkner," in *The Fictional Father: Lacanian Readings of the Text*, ed. Robert Con Davis (Amherst: University of Massachusetts Press, 1981), 162–64, and to Andre Bleikasten, "Fathers in Faulkner," in ibid., 117–19.

17. Faulkner, *Faulkner in the University*, 80–81.

18. For some interesting comments on the meaning of the myth of Narcissus in Faulkner see Irwin, *Doubling and Incest*, 33, 35, 36, 41, 163,

167, 168. Irwin's focus is primarily on the figure of Narcissus himself. He has little to say concerning the role of Echo. Useful discussions of the myth of Echo include those of Angus Fletcher in *The Transcendental Masque: An Essay on Milton's Comus* (Ithaca: Cornell University Press, 1971), 198ff.; Geoffrey H. Hartman in *The Fate of Reading and Other Essays* (Chicago: University of Chicago Press, 1975), 290–93, and "Words, Wish, Worth: Wordsworth," in Harold Bloom et al., *Deconstruction and Criticism* (New York: Seabury Press, 1979),177–216; John Brinkman, "Narcissus in the Text," *Georgia Review* 30 (1976): 293–327; John Hollander, *The Figure of Echo: A Mode of Allusion in Milton and After* (Berkeley and Los Angeles: University of California Press, 1981); and Jefferson Humphries, "Haunted Words, or Deconstruction Echoed," *Diacritics* (Summer 1983): 29–38.

19. Geoffrey H. Hartman, *Saving the Text: Literature/Derrida/Philosophy* (Baltimore: Johns Hopkins University Press, 1981), 151.

20. This is an aspect of the novel that is also discussed by Arthur F. Kinney in *Faulkner's Narrative Poetics: Style as Vision* (Amherst: University of Massachusetts Press, 1978), 194–215.

21. These words are from J. Hillis Miller's admirable essay on *Wuthering Heights* in *Fiction and Repetition: Seven English Novels* (Cambridge: Harvard University Press, 1982), 71. My understanding of *Absalom, Absalom!* has benefited immeasurably from Miller's suggestive essay. Faulkner's novel seems remarkably similar to Bronte's.

22. William Wordsworth, "Essays upon Epitaphs," in *Wordsworth's Literary Criticism*, ed. W. J. B. Owen (London: Routledge & Kegan Paul, 1974), 122.

23. Homer Obed Brown, "The Errant Letter and the Whispering Gallery," *Genre* 10 (Winter 1977): 579. See also my discussion of gossip in "Hawthorne's Castle in the Air: Form and Theme in *The House of the Seven Gables*," *ELH* 38 (June 1971): 314–17.

24. For a different but parallel discussion of these letters see David Krause, "Reading Shreve's Letters and Faulkner's *Absalom, Absalom!*" *Studies in American Fiction* 11 (Autumn 1983): 153–69 and "Reading Bon's Letter and Faulkner's *Absalom, Absalom!*" *PMLA* 99 (March 1984): 225–41.

25. Brown, "The Errant Letter," 590.

26. A similar passage occurs on page 275: "His remark was not intended for flippancy nor even derogation. It was born (if from any source) of that incorrigible unsentimental sentimentality of the young

which takes the form of hard crass levity—to which, by the way, Quentin paid no attention whatever, resuming as if he had never been interrupted, his face still lowered, still brooding apparently on the open letter upon the open book between his hands."

27. For a brilliant discussion of this aspect of writing see Hartman, *Saving the Text*, 118–57.

28. Irwin, *Doubling and Incest*, 114.

29. "Attenuate" is used in a similar way in *Pylon*, the novel Faulkner wrote while he was having difficulties with the *Absalom, Absalom!* manuscript. "As soon as he closed them [his eyes] he would find himself, out of some attenuation of weariness, sleeplessness, confusing both the living and the dead without concern now, with profound conviction of the complete unimportance of either or of the confusion itself, trying with that mindless and unflagging optimism to explain to someone that she did not understand now without bothering to decide or care whether or not and why or not he was asleep" (*Pylon* [New York: Random House, 1935], 261–62).

30. Faulkner, *The Faulkner Reader*, viii, ix.

SIX *The Romance of the Word: John Barth's Letters*

1. Ellen Coughlin, "John Barth Takes Inventory," *Books and Art* 1 (October 1979): 6.

2. John Barth, "Some Reasons Why I Tell the Stories the Way I Tell Them Rather Than Some Other Sort of Stories Some Other Way," *New York Times Book Review*, May 9, 1982, 33.

3. Barth, "Some Reasons Why," 30.

4. Tony Tanner, *City of Words: American Fiction, 1950–1970* (New York: G. P. Putnam's Sons, 1979), 255. Tanner's reading of Barth is an especially suggestive one.

5. See Tanner, *City of Words*, 253.

6. Barth, "Some Reasons Why," 29.

7. Coughlin, "John Barth," 4.

8. Ibid., 5.

9. Ibid., 4.

10. "The Literature of Replenishment," *The Atlantic* 245 (January 1980): 70, 66.

11. Charlie Reilly, "An Interview with John Barth," *Contemporary Literature* 21 (Winter 1981): 4.

12. In this letter, dated August 24, 1969, the Author writes to Ambrose concerning the "house I once helped you build" (655), a structure that obviously anticipates and forms a part of the "house" of *Letters*.

13. "An Interview," 18–19.

14. Herbert N. Schneidau, *Sacred Discontent: The Bible and Western Tradition* (Berkeley and Los Angeles: University of California Press, 1977), 51.

15. Ibid., 91–92.

16. I am indebted here to J. Hillis Miller for his discussion of a similar concern in Thackeray. See *Fiction and Repetition* (Cambridge: Harvard University Press, 1982), 74–76.

17. Geoffrey H. Hartman, *Criticism in the Wilderness* (New Haven: Yale University Press, 1980), 266.

18. "An Interview," 8.

19. John J. Enck, "John Barth: An Interview," *Wisconsin Studies in Contemporary Literature* 6 (1965): 8.

20. "The Literature of Replenishment," 70.

21. Geoffrey H. Hartman, *Saving the Text: Literature/Derrida/Philosophy* (Baltimore: Johns Hopkins University Press, 1981), 149.

22. John T. Irwin, *American Hieroglyphics* (New Haven: Yale University Press, 1980), 69.

23. There is evidence, however, in Barth's most recent novel, *The Tidewater Tales* (New York: G. P. Putnam's Sons, 1987), that Todd does not die in 1968 and is alive and well in 1980. Peter Sagamore, sailing with his wife in the Chesapeake, reports that "a dignified elderly gentleman in a three piece summer seersucker sails by, necktie and all, apparently singlehanding a skipjack impeccably converted for cruising" (235).

24. Reilly, "An Interview," 20.

25. Ibid.

26. Paul de Man, *Blindness and Insight: Essays in the Rhetoric of Contemporary Criticism* (New York: Oxford University Press, 1971), 58.

27. John Barth, *The Friday Book: Essays and Other Nonfiction* (New York: G. P. Putnam's Sons, 1984), 23.

28. Horace, *Satires, Epistles, and Ars Poetica*, trans. H. R. Fairclough (Cambridge: Harvard University Press, 1970), 483.

Conclusion

1. Geoffrey H. Hartman, *Criticism in the Wilderness* (New Haven: Yale University Press, 1980), 50.

2. See Jefferson Humphries's useful discussion of this issue in his review of Hollander's study, "Haunted Words, or Deconstruction Echoed," *Diacritics* (Summer 1983): 30–31, 36.

3. Emerson, "The American Scholar," in *The Complete Essays and Other Writings* (New York: Modern Library, n.d.), 51.

4. Joseph Riddel, "The Hermeneutical Self—Notes Toward an American Practice," *Boundary 2* 12/13 (Spring/Fall 1984), 83.

5. My argument here endorses and extends Eric J. Sundquist's description in *Home As Found: Authority and Genealogy in Nineteenth-Century American Literature* (Baltimore: Johns Hopkins University Press, 1979) of the crises of genealogical authority that trouble American writers of the nineteenth century. I am also indebted to Jay Fliegelman's *Prodigals and Pilgrims: The American Revolution against Patriarchal Authority, 1750–1800* (Cambridge: Cambridge University Press, 1982), a study of the rebellion that changed the American understanding of the nature of authority.

6. John Hollander, *The Figure of Echo: A Mode of Allusion in Milton and After* (Berkeley: University of California Press, 1981), 22.

7. Herman Melville, "The Encantadas or Enchanted Isles," in *Piazza Tales*, ed. Egbert S. Oliver (New York: Hendricks House, 1962), 171.

8. Geoffrey H. Hartman, *Saving the Text: Literature/Derrida/Philosophy* (Baltimore: Johns Hopkins University Press, 1981), 121.

9. Jacques Derrida, "Force and Signification," in *Writing and Difference*, trans. Alan Bass (Chicago: University of Chicago Press, 1978), 3.

10. Fred G. See, "Henry James and the Art of Possession," in *American Realism: New Essays*, ed. Eric J. Sundquist (Baltimore: Johns Hopkins University Press, 1982), 133.

11. Henry James, preface to *The American*, in *The Art of the Novel*, ed. R. P. Blackmur (New York: Charles Scribner's Sons, 1937), 25–26.

12. Edward Said, *Beginnings: Intention and Method* (New York: Basic Books, 1985; Baltimore: Johns Hopkins University Press, 1978), 23.

13. John Hollander, *The Figure of Echo: A Mode of Allusion in Milton and After* (Berkeley and Los Angeles: University of California Press, 1981), 53.

14. I am indebted here to Fredric Jameson for his discussion of

Conrad's modernism in *The Political Unconscious* (Ithaca: Cornell University Press, 1981), especially 219–24.

15. William Faulkner, *The Faulkner Reader* (New York: Random House, 1961), xi.

16. John Barth, "The Spirit of Place," in *The Friday Book: Essays and Other Nonfiction* (New York: G. P. Putnam's Sons, 1984), 128–29.

17. John Barth, "My Two Muses," in *The Friday Book,* 159–60.

18. "An Interview with John Barth," *Contemporary Literature* 21 (Winter 1981): 11.

19. Barth, "The Spirit of Place," 128.

20. John Barth, "My Two Uncles," in *The Friday Book,* 157.

21. John Barth, "Getting Oriented," in *The Friday Book,* 138–39.

22. Barth, "My Two Muses," 159.

23. John Barth, "Muse Spare Me," in *The Friday Book,* 58.

24. John Barth, "Algebra and Fire," in *The Friday Book,* 170.

25. John Barth, "The Prose and Poetry of It All, or, Dippy Verses," in *The Friday Book,* 243.

26. Ibid., 247.

27. Ibid., 154.

INDEX

Absalom! Absalom! (Faulkner), 139,
141; gossip in, 154, 155; human
family in, 147; inside/outside, 145;
reading and writing in, 159–60;
significance of words in, 161–62;
visual and vocal forms in, 148, 151,
153, 158, 160, 164. *See also* Genealogical issues; Letters (correspondence) in novels; *and other
individual themes*
Absorption, process of, 2, 4, 110, 112,
221
Action, 64
Aeropagitica (Milton), 120
Allegory, 128
Ambiguity, 215
American, The (James), 112
Aristotle, 123
Ars Poetica (Horace), 209
Art: in Hawthorne, 42, 44–45; life
and art in James, 133–34, 135; vs.
marketplace, 119; personal life
and, 138–39. *See also* Imitation;
Originality
Artificiality, 212, 221; in Hawthorne,
40, 43–44, 45–46
Attenuation, act of, 159–60, 161, 218,
238*n*29
Auerbach, Jonathan, 230*n*15

Austen, Jane, 6–7, 20
Author, role of, x–xi, xii. *See also*
Narrator; Writer/reader relations
Authority issues, 10, 67, 68, 217, 218;
authorship and, 67, 68, 177, 201,
212–14; creative, 87, 118, 215; discredited, 75; of father, 144; of
illusion, 74; novelistic authority,
16–17; in *Pierre*, 77, 81, 83, 103. *See
also Waverley* (Scott); *other individual authors and works*

Barth, John, 25; fluidity in, 170; on
readers and writers, 219–20; on
story-telling, 26–28. See also
LETTERS (Barth); *individual
images and themes*
Barthes, Roland, 226*n*7, 227*n*21,
228*n*22, 231*n*5
Baym, Nina, 223–24*n*1
Bell, Michael Davitt, 229*n*38
Biblical imagery. See *Pierre* (Melville)
Blithedale Romance, The (Haw-
thorne), 32, 35, 58–59
Bloom, Harold, 231*n*2
Booth, Wayne, 226*n*9
Brooks, Peter, 228*n*27
Brown, Homer, 154, 228*nn*25, 27
Bunyan, John, 34

243

Index

Index

Fragmentation, theme of, 54–55, 57, 59, 60

Franklin, H. Bruce, 231n9

French and Italian Notebooks, The (Hawthorne), 41–42, 57, 59

Frye, Northrop, xi

"Future of the Novel, The" (James), 136

Genealogical issues, xii, 10, 38, 213–14; in Barth, 177, 181–82, 183–84, 187, 194–95, 201; in Faulkner, 140, 141–46, 153–54; in Melville, 76, 78–81, 82, 103, 106–7, 215

Genre, idea of, ix–x

Gossip, 154, 155

Gray, Thomas, 19

Hamilton, A. C., xi

Hamlet (Shakespeare), 68–69, 70, 94; "Hamletism," 90, 92, 94

Hartman, Geoffrey, 20, 91, 203, 215, 230n4, 235n40, 238n27

Hawthorne (James), 110, 111

Hawthorne, Nathaniel, 20, 139, 150, 162, 170; Barth and, 171, 172; conventions in, 32–34; influence on James, 110–12; influence on Melville, 62–63, 65–66, 72; on reading and writing, 21–24, 214. See also *Marble Faun, The* (Hawthorne); *individual images and themes*

"Hawthorne and His Mosses" (Melville), 23–24, 62, 69–70

Heath, Stephen, 226n9

Hegel, G. W. F., 95

History, Romance and, 14–15, 29

Holland, Laurence, 127

Hollander, John, 213, 217

Homer, 209

Horace, 209

House of the Seven Gables, The (Hawthorne), 51, 52

Human relations, 45–46

Ideas, 127–28

Identity, concept of, 127, 172, 178, 217

Illusion, 74

Imagination, 64, 74, 195–96

Imitation, 26–28, 35, 62, 81–82, 159; Barth on, 174–75, 191, 192; in Hawthorne, 42, 44

Incest, 78–79, 106, 144, 145

Innocence, 39, 49–50, 55, 56, 112, 113

Interment and inscription, theme of: in Faulkner, 149–51; in Melville, 89–90, 91–92

Interpretation, process of, 2, 4, 22, 34, 56, 212; in Barth, 175, 176, 177; in Faulkner, 140, 154; in Hawthorne, 37, 39–40, 50, 51, 53; in James, 112, 114, 129

Irony, 144, 146, 166

Irving, Washington, 20–21

Irwin, John, 158, 203, 231n6, 236nn15, 16, 18

Iser, Wolfgang, 226n9

Ivanhoe (Scott), 65

James, Henry, 112, 113, 114, 139; attitudes on reading and writing, 24–25; authority of, 216–17; on Hawthorne, 110–11; on writer's relation to art and reader, 115–18. See also *Portrait of a Lady, The* (James); *individual images and themes*

Jameson, Fredric, ix, 240n14

Kermode, Frank, 2, 4

Kinney, Arthur F., 237n20

Krause, David, 237n24

Index

Natural man, 37–39
Nature: man's relationship with, 46,
47, 67, 68, 71, 77–78, 89–90
Nostalgia, 32, 44, 47, 55, 62, 65, 171
Novels, 125, 126; power of, 3–5;
romance and, 2, 3. *See also*
Writer/reader relations; Writing,
process of; *individual authors and
works*

Observation, power of, 112, 113
"Old Manse, The" (*MOM,* Haw-
thorne), 56
Originality, xii, 35, 75, 212, 213; in
Barth, 173, 220–21; in Faulkner,
148, 166; in Melville, 62, 77, 81,
106, 215–16
Ortega y Gasset, José, x, 2, 221
Our Mutual Friend (Dickens), 117, 119

Painting, 81–82. See also *Pierre* (Melville)
Paolo and Francesca, in *Pierre,* 75,
76, 86
Paradise Lost (Milton), 120
Parody, 191, 192
Past, influence of, 87–88, 152–53, 166,
171–72
Paternity, 10. *See also* Genealogical
issues
Perception, 2, 195–96
"Piazza, The" (Melville), 63; artificial
and conventional in, 66–69; disenchantment in, 64, 69, 71–72, 73,
74–75; narrator in, 67–68, 69, 70,
72, 74–75; recall and substitution
in, 64–65
Pierre (Melville), 24, 63, 75, 76, 152,
215; Christ imagery in, 80–81, 82,
83, 94, 95–96; guitar image, 83, 105,
106; handkerchief image, 103–5;
interpretation theme in, 91–92;

loss and absence themes, 89–90;
mountain image, 82, 83, 92, 93,
94–95, 97, 101, 102; movement
from name to thing, 94–95; paintings in, 83–88; writing and reading
in, 96–100, 103–6. *See also* Genealogical issues; Interment and
inscription, theme of; *other individual images and themes*
Pilgrim's Progress, The (Bunyan), 33,
63, 72
Place, sense of, 170, 178
Plato, 123
Portrait of a Lady, The (James):
books as objects in, 131–32, 133;
language and vision, 127–29, 130;
reading metaphor in, 129, 130;
spoken discourse in, 132–33; value
and money in, 116–24. *See also*
Representation, process of; Textuality; Writer/reader relations;
Writing, process of
Prefaces, role of, 3–4, 5, 25; in Hawthorne, 56, 57, 58–59; in James, 112,
114, 115, 119, 120, 124, 125, 133, 217;
in Melville, 63; in Scott, 16–17
Punning, 185–86
Pyramid metaphor, *in Pierre,* 88, 93,
94, 95, 150, 232*n*17

Queen Ho Hall (Strutt), 17

Reading, experience of, xi, xii, 2, 4,
34, 138, 226–27*n*9; in Barth, 192–93,
208; "Gentle Reader," 54, 55, 214;
in Hawthorne, 22–23, 53, 65; James
on, 110–12, 133; kinds of reader, 2–
3, 4–5; in Melville, 62, 76; problems of reading and writing, 19–
21; reader as consumer, 114–15, 134,
135, 136, 218; reader's relation to

About the Author

Edgar A. Dryden is professor of English at the University of Arizona and editor of the *Arizona Quarterly.* He is the author of *Nathaniel Hawthorne: The Poetics of Enchantment* and *Melville's Thematics of Form,* the latter also available from Johns Hopkins.

The Form of American Romance

Designed by Chris L. Smith
Composed by A. W. Bennett, Inc., in Garamond Antiqua text and display.
Printed by BookCrafters on 50-lb Book Text Natural and
bound in GSB #13 and stamped in pewter.